JOE MOSER'S ROUTE AS A NAZI POW

August 1944–April 1945

Weser R.

Elbe R.

Ode.

Berlin

GERMANY

(D) • Zagan

Spremberg

Dresden

(C)

Prague

CZECHOSLOVAKIA

Nuremberg • (E)

(F&G)

Moosburg •

Munich •

AUSTRIA

ITALY

© 2021 Jeffrey L. Ward

KEY

Nazi Concentration-POW Camps

✕ Crash Site

Car Transport

Train Transport

March

o Miles 150
o Kilometers 150

LIGHTNING DOWN

LIGHTNING
DOWN

A WORLD WAR II
STORY OF SURVIVAL

TOM CLAVIN

ST. MARTIN'S PRESS
NEW YORK

First published in the United States by St. Martin's Press, an imprint of St. Martin's Publishing Group

LIGHTNING DOWN. Copyright © 2021 by Tom Clavin. All rights reserved. Printed in the United States of America. For information, address St. Martin's Publishing Group, 120 Broadway, New York, NY 10271.

www.stmartins.com

Endpaper map by Jeffrey L. Ward

The Library of Congress Cataloging-in-Publication Data is available upon request.

ISBN 978-1-250-15126-1 (hardcover)
ISBN 978-1-250-15127-8 (ebook)

Our books may be purchased in bulk for promotional, educational, or business use. Please contact your local bookseller or the Macmillan Corporate and Premium Sales Department at 1-800-221-7945, extension 5442, or by email at MacmillanSpecialMarkets@macmillan.com.

First Edition: 2021

10 9 8 7 6 5 4 3 2 1

To Leslie Reingold

CONTENTS

Prologue   1

ACT I: The Farm Boy   5

ACT II: The Passenger   47

ACT III: The Prisoner   119

ACT IV: The Survivor   203

Epilogue   285

Acknowledgments   297

Bibliography   299

Index   303

LIGHTNING DOWN

Prologue

There were well over two thousand men and women trapped
inside the train chugging toward somewhere in Germany.
For the American pilot Joe Moser, his world had been reduced to
the one railcar where he and other Allied airmen were pressed
together desperately trying to stay alive. It was August 1944 and
the air was very hot and there was not enough of it to go around.

The interior of the railcar stank terribly. The oppressive odor
was the combination of it having previously been used to haul
farm animals and now prisoners jammed together into a filthy,
perspiring, frightened mass of humanity. Every stop and jerking
startup of the train shoved the men into each other all over again,
jarring nerves and threatening the little sense of cooperation remaining among them. Plus, many of them had been stricken with
dysentery.

This last train to have left Paris before it was liberated carried
inmates from the Fresnes prison. None of the suffering men in

the railcars knew where they were going. Another prison, probably, or maybe just to a remote location to be shot. Their only hope of survival was, oddly, that the German guards had not executed them when they had the opportunity.

It had happened two—or was it three, or four?—days earlier. A hammer had been discovered in the car. Even the lowliest German soldier would not be ordered to be inside the repellent cars, so in this particular one the prisoners were free to use the hammer to loosen several floorboards. When there was a hole that could accommodate men slipping through it, seven did, then they lay flat on the tracks. Once the train passed over them, they got up and ran away from the train.

But not far enough before they were spotted by the German guards. The train was stopped and pursuing guards ran down the tracks. As the chase continued, the cattle cars were searched, and the hole in one of them was discovered. The German officers were furious, as though they had been betrayed, their "benevolence" not being reciprocated. The weak and weary occupants were ordered out of the cattle car.

A red-faced Prussian officer began shouting at them. One of the Allied flyers translated: "I have been instructed to tell you that to prevent further escapes, and by way of punishment, men from this carriage are to be shot."

Two machine guns on tripods were trained on them. There was some muttering among the men about charging the guns en masse, overwhelming the guards, and using their weapons against the other German soldiers and officers. But no one moved. The prisoners stood in the broiling summer sun alongside the train. A dozen or so guards lined up opposite them. Joe watched the guards' fingers for the moment when they would begin to squeeze the triggers. Some of the men began to pray while others stared defiantly at the guards.

However, after several excruciating minutes, the men were

told to climb back into the cattle car. Pieces of wood had been nailed over the opening in the floor. The train lumbered forward. For the American, British, Canadian, and other flyers there was relief and gratitude.

But the journey would not end, day after agonizing day. How far could their destination be? And what was it? With every mile, the men became more miserable and apprehensive. Surely, there had to be POW camps that were not so deep into Germany. Finally, their destination was revealed—but it was not the one the downed airmen expected.

The train stopped at a station to unload the several hundred female passengers and the men were allowed to struggle out of the cars. But after less than five minutes of fresh air they were herded back in again. The train entered a forest, and there was anticipation that they were finally about to arrive at the POW camp designated for them, one where there would be contact with Red Cross representatives and, more urgently, they would be given water and food. There was a fresh surge of curiosity and excitement when in the late afternoon the train halted and the cattle-car doors were dragged open.

The bedraggled prisoners stood in the slanted glare of the August sun. Joe's back and legs were stiff and sore, and like the others he was filthy and desperately hungry and thirsty. Many of the men swayed with exhaustion as the German guards conducted yet another head count.

As this was being done, Joe and the others glanced around at the train station. They saw tall fences with barbed wire and within were drab gray buildings and prisoners who appeared to be walking skeletons wearing striped and filthy uniforms. Waiting for them at one entrance was a gauntlet of guards holding the leashes of barking German shepherds that were salivating at the prospect of tearing into human flesh. There was a burning, sweet stench in the air.

Joe and the other pilots were certain immediately that this

facility could not possibly be a POW camp. How could its inmates be so emaciated? What of the Geneva convention? With a burst of shouts and the cracking of batons on heads and backs, the guards forced the perplexed men to march. And as they staggered forward, a sickening understanding dawned on the ones who had heard of the existence of concentration camps.

The Allied flyers had not been sent here to sit out the war but to die. They would learn quickly this was indeed a camp of relentless death—and its name was Buchenwald.

ACT I
THE FARM BOY

—◆—

Oh, Hedy Lamarr is a beautiful gal
And Madeleine Carroll is, too;
But you'll find, if you query, a different theory
Amongst any bomber crew.
For the loveliest thing of which one could sing
(This side of the Heavenly Gates)
Is no blonde or brunette of the Hollywood set,
But an escort of P-38s.

—T/Sgt. Robert H. Bryson (KIA),
Stars and Stripes, 1943

1

The future P-38 Lightning pilot Joseph Frank Moser was born in Ferndale, Washington, on September 13, 1921. Ferndale was at that time a community of 750 people surrounded by farms 16 miles south of the Canadian border, 85 miles north of Seattle, and east of Puget Sound. If a world war had not intervened two decades later, young Joe may well have spent his entire life in the Ferndale area as a farmer, raising corn, onions, asparagus, and dairy cows.

His father, Joseph Melchior Moser, was twenty-seven years old when he emigrated from Switzerland in 1911. Born into a Catholic farming family, he had grown up in a town called Sattel. His misfortune was that he was not a firstborn son. In fact, there were six siblings ahead of him. Because his turn at running the farm would probably never come and with few other jobs available, Joseph Moser chose to leave Sattel and explore the possibilities America offered. He was drawn to the Seattle area because of its

Swiss immigrant population. He settled in Kent, south of Seattle, and found work on a dairy farm.

It took some years, but he eventually found a wife too. Her name was Mary Imhof. She was only fifteen when she met Joseph Moser, who by then was thirty-eight. Mary's father, Frank Imhof, had grown up in the same region in Switzerland as Joseph Moser but had emigrated not to America but to New Zealand. It was not quite to his liking, so he crossed the Pacific and wound up, with a family, in Ferndale. The Imhof farmhouse became well known in the region's Swiss-Catholic communities for hosting dances. When news of it reached Moser's ears, and being still a bachelor, he traveled north to the next dance.

His son described the elder Moser as "a small and lean man with dark hair and a dark moustache who smoked a pipe incessantly, wearing down the teeth he used to clamp down on the pipe, and was fond of homemade whiskey. He also loved to dance." Noticing him at his first dance in Ferndale was young Mary Imhof. Despite the twenty-three-year age difference, the two became immediately smitten with each other. Joseph Moser lost no time in relocating to Ferndale.

The couple must have found other places besides the dance floor to meet because when they married in June 1921, Mary was six months' pregnant. About his parents' situation, Joe Moser reflected, "I've always explained that the reason I am so short is that my mom had only a three-month pregnancy."* He added that "such happenings," even in the small, religious community, "were more frequent than most adults of that time talked openly about."

Joseph Moser rented a farm known as the 101 Ranch that was on the Lummi Indian Reservation. He did not work that land

---

* Even when Joe filled out in the army, he topped out at a less-than-robust five foot six and 155 pounds.

long because Frank Imhof, soon after his grandson, Joseph Jr., was born, decided to move to another house, and he invited the Mosers to move into the Imhof house and take over the farming work there. As soon as he was able, young Joe was out in the field with his father: "I can tell you that I started very early."

Those early experiences included hunting for eggs and milking his pet twin cows. After a rainstorm, Joe would jump in puddles on one side of the Nooksack River, on the path that led to Grandpa Imhof's home. And as soon as he could handle a pitchfork, he was piling up stacks of hay.

Over the years the family expanded to include Louise, Josephine, Frank, and Rosalee, the latter born in 1935. Joe recalled that even in the Depression the Moser family had "an almost idyllic farm life in one of the most beautiful places in the world."

The "almost" refers to a tragedy: One day, the fifteen-month old Josephine carried apples to the water trough used by the horse, and with no one noticing, she managed to climb in. The child drowned.

The family persevered, and there was plenty of work to keep them occupied. A robust Joseph Moser led and supervised it all. "In addition to being short and very strong," Joe remembered about his father, "he was exceptionally quiet and a no-nonsense father. We definitely had to toe the mark when dad was around."

Despite the nation's economic woes, the farm prospered. The family had not only forty-five cows to milk but also "some of the most advanced farming technology in the region," Joe recalled. "We already had the latest and greatest milking machines, powered by a generator." The Mosers also raised calves, chickens, pigs, horses, and other animals, all requiring care every day of the year, good weather and bad. Sundays, though, the family made time to faithfully attend services at the nearest Catholic church, St. Joseph's, in Ferndale.

Family life and hard work had not persuaded Joseph Moser to

give up liquor. He was one of many Swiss farmers around Ferndale who made their own "schnapps," which was really whiskey. "Any get-together was an occasion to break out this powerful stuff, and I did not enjoy seeing what it did to my uncles, cousins and other family members and friends," Joe reported. "Particularly, I hated what it did to my dad." As a result, Joe vowed to abstain from alcohol, and would later find himself one of the very few pilots to refrain from drinking it, even when on leave.

For young Joe, the only break from chores on the farm, aside from Mass on Sunday mornings, came from attending school. In August 1935, he began at Ferndale High School. Soon after completing his freshman year, tragedy again struck the family. The incessant pipe smoker Joseph Moser developed a cough that rapidly grew worse, to the point that he began throwing up blood. By the time that he was diagnosed with pneumonia, it was too late to do anything about it. He died during the summer of 1936, at fifty-three years old.

The responsibility of running the farm now fell on Joe, just turning fifteen, and his mother. Mary Moser had buried a child and husband and was only thirty-one years old with two sons and two daughters—one just a year old—to feed and clothe. She first reduced the number of cows and other animals, then hired a worker to take over many of the chores. This meant the family made less money, but she was determined that Joe continue at Ferndale High.

There, in addition to his academic labors, Joe was drawn to football. This presented two challenges: one, he was then all of five foot two and 120 pounds and likely the least formidable player on the field, and two, to go home every evening after football practice he had to run almost five miles down the country road past Frank Imhof's farm on the Imhof and Slater roads to the Moser farm off the Slater road. Then he had to help with the chores, eat dinner, squeeze in a few hours of sleep, and get up before five A.M. to help with the morning milking before catching the school bus at the end of the one-third-mile-long driveway.

Joe played baseball too but it was football that actually offered the opportunity to excel. By his senior year he had "bulked up" to five foot three and 130 pounds and was the starting halfback on the Ferndale High team. He did not slack on the academics, earning a listing on the honor roll every year, and in his senior year he was elected the student body treasurer.

Somehow, Joe found time for a new interest, one that quickly grabbed ahold of him—airplanes. Whenever he was working out in the field on the family farm and one flew overhead, he had to pause and stare up at the sky. Joe could not explain the fascination. "There was no history of flying in my family and no great tradition of recklessness or risk taking," he reflected. "Just dairy farmers who loved the land, family, dancing, and our own unique way of life."

Joe devoted a few dollars to a subscription for a magazine on airplanes. In one, he saw a photograph of a prototype of a Lockheed P-38 Lightning, a fighter plane the Army Air Corps was developing. It had engines and twin booms and a slender metal fuselage. "Somehow it conveyed both beauty and menace, and I was hooked," Joe recalled. "I fell head over heels in love with the Lockheed P-38 and couldn't stop thinking about it. I knew I had to fly that plane."

However, in the spring of 1940, he might as well have vowed to fly a rocket to the moon. Even with his younger sisters and brother able to take on more of the work on the farm, the family was barely getting by, and running off to become a pilot was a totally farfetched notion. Joe looked into it anyway, and learned of another obstacle—two years of college was necessary to even begin training to become a fighter pilot in the Army Air Corps.

Given that, his nine-year-old brother Frank had as much chance to fly a P-38 as he did. As Joe acknowledged, "My life direction seemed all too inevitable: farm work and more farm work."

Like millions of other Americans, life changed significantly for Joe Moser on December 7, 1941. He was cleaning the barn late that Sunday morning when the news of the attack on Pearl Harbor was broadcast on the radio. One consequence of the United States entering the wars raging in Europe and Asia was an expansion of the Army Air Corps. The production of planes shifted into high gear, and America needed men to fly them. Gone was the college education requirement. It was replaced by a test that had a passing score of 82, plus the remaining requirement of passing the physical exam.

Fortunately, Joe was not then put into the position of choosing between his dream of being a pilot and the family farm. Mary Moser had been thinking that the running of the farm was too much of a burden, and she decided this was the best time to put it up for sale. (Her father, Frank Imhof, had died in 1940.) Before long, it sold, and she found a job in Ferndale. Joe was on his way to war. . . .

But not so fast. The pilot training entrance exam proved to be quite a tough test. Even so, the score of 74 he received was lower than he expected. Yet there was nothing he could do about it. Deeply disappointed, Joe began to consider enlisting in the navy, and perhaps that would offer a chance of becoming a pilot. While Joe pondered this, the window of opportunity closed—his army draft notice arrived: "I felt my fate as a foot soldier was sealed."

Arriving immediately afterward, though, was another notice, this one containing miraculous news. The Army Air Corps informed him that because a grading error had been corrected, his true score was 84, and Joe was invited to reapply for pilot training. He could not get to Seattle fast enough. When Mary Moser bid farewell to her oldest son, like so many other mothers in the new world war, she had to be gripped with fear that she would never see him again.

In May 1942, Joe enlisted. Though undersized, his athlete body easily passed the physical. If he had been an army infantryman, it was possible that a rifle-carrying Joe would have been sent overseas before the end of the year. However, to become a fighter pilot, and especially one qualified to fly a P-38, he had to expect twenty-one months of training.

That was okay, whatever it took. "Oh man, my dreams were coming true," Joe thought. He was ready for the challenge.

2

Joe Moser's first stop as a fledgling Army Air Corps aviator was Santa Ana, California, where he completed a program of physical training and classroom work that seemed like just another three months of high school. He graduated to primary flight training at Sequoia Field in Visalia. Advanced training was given at Minter Field in Bakersfield. After two months of that, Joe left California to undergo additional training at Chandler Field outside Phoenix.

Along the way, perhaps the most discombobulating lesson was conducted in a device called a Link Trainer. Pilots flying in the Pacific Theater or European Theater had to know how to do so in terrible weather conditions or under a cloud-filled sky at night, when little or nothing was visible to the naked eye. That meant flying on instruments alone. The Link Trainer was an enclosed box simulating a cockpit with only the flight instruments visible. Instructions were provided by a voice piped into the device, and Joe, like many trainees, had no idea to whom the voice belonged.

It was at Chandler Field, in the final phase of that training program, that Joe was finally introduced to the P-38. Flying that plane was one dream come true. The other came on October 1, 1943—when he received his wings and was commissioned a second lieutenant in the Army Air Corps. Finally, Joe thought, it was time to go overseas and take the fight to the enemy.

Well, again, not so fast. U.S. commanders in Europe and the Pacific were desperate for pilots because of staggering and unprecedented losses. During the war over 43,000 American aircraft were lost overseas. Two months before Joe earned his wings, in August 1943, 60 B-17s were shot down in a single mission over Europe. In the two theaters of war combined, more than 121,000 airmen were killed, wounded, or captured in less than four years of combat. Depleted American units in England and in the southwest Pacific anxiously awaited shipments of fresh pilots.

However, the military top brass also knew that inexperienced pilots would also be fresh kills if not trained extensively. An equal or greater concern was that pilot loss usually meant the loss of the expensive machines they flew in. Joe Moser and his fellow newly commissioned colleagues were not shipping out just yet. Joe was, at least, allowed to recharge his batteries with ten days of liberty in Los Angeles. Then, on October 14, he reported to the Van Nuys airfield in Hollywood Hills. There he was assigned to the 429th Fighter Squadron, which was part of the 474th Fighter Group.

The squadron had been activated in Southern California in August 1943 specifically as a P-38 fighter unit under the IV Fighter Command. If Joe Moser wanted to see combat in Europe, this was the squadron to be in, since before too long it would be assigned to the Ninth Air Force in England.

It certainly would not lack confidence. A memo about the 429th prepared in fall 1943 by one of its officers regarding its chain of command and operations stated that "it appears as if the future of this squadron is already assured." The memo concluded: "Our history has not been one of outstanding accomplishment because it has been too brief, but we earnestly believe the future will find the 429th unfurling as good a record in combat as any squadron that has already gone across to meet the enemy."

Joe found himself surrounded by Lockheed P-38 Lightnings—those fantasies from high school had become a reality: "I felt fulfilled, that this was right, that my life was on track and I was in the place that destiny had meant for me."

He was fortunate in another way—his commanding officers. The squadron commander was Captain Burl Glass Jr., and Joe's flight leader was Lieutenant Merle Larson.

Glass, only twenty-four years old, had been born in Gray County, Texas, and graduated from West Texas State with a degree in agriculture. He had worked as a park ranger at Carlsbad Caverns National Park before enlisting in the Army Air Corps in 1941. He'd already received almost ten months of training when the attack on Pearl Harbor took place that December. This experience enabled him to rise up the ranks quickly during that first year of the war, being promoted to captain in December 1942.

The comprehensive history report on the 429th Squadron—which sported the nickname the "Retail Gang" because the word "retail" had been its code name in radio transmissions—included a sketch about Captain Glass. It confided that he had "a pleasing smile, a gentle disposition, and countless other admirable characteristics, but he can be firm when the occasion demands. To state it simply, Capt. Glass is a man's man." He also already had some overseas experience, having ferried a P-38 to Casablanca in Morocco.

Merle Larson had the advantage of having combat experience—and, of course, surviving it. The South Dakota native was still in training in the summer of 1942 when the desperate plight of the thin U.S. forces resulted in his unit being hurried overseas. Larson and his fellow pilots went by ship to Scotland, then were trucked to Northern Ireland, where they were stationed on a Royal Air Force field. In December 1942, Larson was transferred to Africa. On the way there, his formation was attacked by German fighters but arrived safely in Oran. Larson spent Christmas Day again in the air, this time as a pilot protecting a convoy in the Mediterranean Sea. After that, on almost all of his missions he was a fighter escort on bomber runs over North Africa.

He did get into the occasional dogfight, and he gave at least as good as he got. But he took little pleasure in it. "There is no glorious feeling in knocking an enemy plane out of the sky," Larson said. "The thrill you would normally expect just isn't there because you're too tense yourself not knowing when you're going to get yours. My biggest thrill was coming in from a mission and seeing the rest of the fellows in my flight come home safely."

Larson spent ten months overseas and met the required numbers of combat. Back in the United States he enjoyed some R&R, but the Army Air Corps was not finished with him. With the 429th, he would become an important figure in Joe Moser's life.

Joe did not think it was possible, but the training at the Van Nuys airfield—which had once been an orchard—was even more intense than what had previously been doled out. But it was a joyful experience for Joe because the training focused exclusively on P-38 Lightnings, their capabilities and design intricacies down to the last bolt. At times, though, that joy was tempered: "The seriousness of the business we were in was brought home with the deaths of two of my roommates from training accidents. We were young, hotshot pilots, and the reason they send 20-year-old

kids to war is because with youth comes a sense of invulnerabil-
ity. But these deaths were like losing brothers."

Such tragedies brought home to young pilots the kinship they
shared. Joe Moser was by far not the only one to go through such
a demanding training regimen and witness losses along the way.
A similar experience was had by Levitt Clinton Beck, a native of
Houston who was twenty-three in 1943. A big difference, though,
between Beck and his fellow flyers was that he wrote about being
a young pilot while he was becoming one. When published, his
book was simply and aptly titled *Fighter Pilot*.

Beck enlisted in the Army Air Corps in March 1942 and, like
Joe Moser, was sent to Santa Ana. When his basic training was
complete, "Our parents came over to see us graduate and our
mothers pinned on our wings. It was a day never to be forgotten
by them or us. As we stood up to take our oath, I don't suppose I
ever felt anything more deeply impressive in my whole life, than
I did, as I repeated those words. I don't suppose the words 'I do,'
would have as much of a hold on me."

He was assigned to Luke Field in Phoenix. After that, it was
off to Drew Field near Tampa, then on to Sarasota. In August
1943, Beck was still training, this time at Randolph Field in Texas.
On November 9, he was promoted to first lieutenant, yet like Joe
Moser he was still waiting to confront the real enemy. Finally,
Beck and his fellow trainees were on a train to New York. He
would cross paths with Joe Moser on the other side of the world,
on the ground as well as in the air.

For the pilots of the 429th Squadron, the end-of-year holidays
held poignancy. As the Retail Gang log and history report—
compiled by the squadron's intelligence officer, Karl Swindt—
stated, "The Christmas season was pressing hard and we all
wanted to make the most of it knowing it would be our last on
home soil for perhaps some time to come. Red Cross women

in Van Nuys went all out to brighten our diggings with deco-
rated trees. Candy-filled stockings and peppermint canes gave a
warmer touch to walls covered with war charts, gun racks and
security posters. Everyone was trying for a few days leave to get
home and see the folks. A few actually made it." Joe, alas, was not
one of them, with Christmas 1943 spent at the Van Nuys base.

However, the first day of the new year, 1944, offered a welcome break from the rigors of training exercises. In the Rose
Bowl that day the University of Washington was taking on the
University of Southern California. Joe had not made it as far as
college, but this was his home team anyway and he managed to
score a ticket. He scored more than the Huskies did, however,
as the Trojans humbled them 29–0. One highlight of the game
for Joe was that one of his fellow pilots flew over the stadium in
Pasadena and dropped a practice bomb onto the field. The perpe-
trator with a mischievous sense of humor was never found.

Training continued at a new base, Lomita Field, near Redondo
Beach, and after that Palmdale in the Mojave Desert. There, pilots assisted in testing a new system of radar being installed at
nearby Edwards Air Base. Joe was one of the pilots assigned to
get his plane in the air fast when approaching "enemy" aircraft
was detected. It was during one of these exercises that he came
closest to crashing.

His P-38 was hurtling down the runway at an increasing
speed but just wouldn't lift into the air. Joe cut the throttles and
slammed the brakes, but he still ran out of runway. He hit the
field beyond it at 90 mph. The plane kept going through a fence
and across a ditch before finally coming to rest. Although uninjured, Joe said, "My legs were shaking so badly that it took 10
minutes for them to settle down to allow me the strength to
crawl out of the plane."

However, still filled with "piss and vinegar," only a week later

Joe came even closer to death. During yet another training mission, and on his own in the sky, he took his P-38 up past 31,000 feet. He was not being foolhardy—he needed to know the edges of his plane's durability in case he found himself in an extreme situation, such as eluding enemy fighters by going higher than they could. Joe leveled off at 31,600 feet and cruised for some time, "enjoying the astounding view." It then occurred to Joe to see how fast a dive he could do from that altitude.

This, he soon learned, *was* foolhardy—taking a plane of at least 20,000 pounds propelled by V-12 engines down into a dive. Soon, he was going at 575 mph . . . 161 mph more than the P-38 was built to withstand. "She started to shake like crazy and I knew I had pushed her too far."

Almost drowning in his own sweat, Joe pulled the throttles and the stick back with every ounce of strength he had. His dangerous problem was made much worse when his windshield and the canopy side glass frosted over. He was not only diving out of control but also doing it blind.

Then there was hope for surviving: "The plane finally stopped shaking, so I knew I was not in immediate danger of the plane falling apart." But "those mountains were high and I had no idea where they were." At ten thousand feet, the windshield began to clear. Thankfully, the first thing Joe saw was not a mountain directly in front of him but clear sky. By this time he was in a shallow dive and was able to level off for a peaceful return to Palmdale.

The 429th lost another one of its trainees, Lieutenant Merle Ogden, on January 17. Approaching the Lomita runway, Ogden's plane began having a mechanical problem exacerbated by his being unable to get his landing gear down. The last moments of the twenty-three-year-old pilot from Iowa were reported by the *Los Angeles Times*: "Heroically guiding his disabled plane away from a crowded high school playground, [Ogden] rode a P-38 to his death as it crashed in a victory garden adjacent to 1925 254th St., Lomita. One wing of the plane crashed into the home of Mrs. J Wilson Jones, wife of a Navy chief warrant officer, just as she and her seven-year-old son raced from the house. Mrs. Jones and her son were in Pearl Harbor when the Japs attacked on December 7th, 1941, and narrowly escaped death there."

At last, the seemingly endless training exercises were finished. "By the last of January '44, we were in pretty good shape," according to the official 429th Fighter Squadron history. "Our records were all up, reports in, Squadron to full strength with qualified personnel, and equipment complete. Captains Glass and Heiser took the gang on an overnight bivouac to round out the program and then we were ready." A formal send-off dinner and dance for the members of the squadron was held at the Redondo Beach Country Club.

On February 15, Joe and the rest of the squadron—279 enlisted men and 37 officers—as ready as they would ever be, boarded a train bound for Boston. The journey overseas to confront the enemy had begun.

3

By the time Joe Moser and the rest of his fellow flyers and their support personnel arrived in Europe, the war in that theater had much changed from when it had commenced in September 1939.

That month had begun with the invasion of Poland, followed by a series of blitzkriegs by Adolf Hitler's armies and air forces that allowed Nazi Germany to sweep westward across Europe to the English Channel and south into Italy and North Africa. The survival of Great Britain was barely on life support, with its capital city, London, under constant attack by the Luftwaffe. The Crown's vaunted navy, which had once ruled the seas, was running low on ships and sailors. Hitler had become confident enough to turn his attention east, and in June 1941 his infantry and tanks smashed into Russia. The Luftwaffe, like the other branches of the German military, appeared unbeatable there too.

But the landscape had shifted significantly by early 1944. The

Allies had kicked German forces out of North Africa. The invasion of Sicily the previous year had touched off a series of beach landings, which led to the Allies pushing steadily north up the boot that was Italy. That country's dictator, Benito Mussolini, had been deposed and was under arrest. The Eastern Front campaign had proved to be a disaster for Hitler, and the Red Army counteroffensive had brought Russian troops to the border of Poland.

This front would ultimately be the bloodiest theater of the war and was the deadliest conflict in human history, with over thirty million killed, most of them Russian civilians. The German armed forces suffered 80 percent of their military deaths in World War II on the Eastern Front, which involved more land combat than all other war theaters combined. One unavoidable result for Germany was a dramatic decrease in manpower, weapons, and equipment available to retain territories it had occupied in Europe.

By early 1944, most of the German efforts were defensive ones. Hitler still controlled France, but it was expected that once Italy was secured the Allies would mount an invasion somewhere along that country's western coastline. The combination of American manufacturing might and the bombing of German plants meant the Allies were flooding Great Britain with planes and equipment faster than the Nazis could counter them. However, to the consternation of the Allied military brass, the Nazi war machine was not breaking down under the strain. Despite the naval blockades and air raids, the still-respected Luftwaffe had more aircraft in 1944 than ever before.

How was this possible? Yes, blockades were having an impact on Germany's access to raw materials, but the country had thus far been able to supplement domestic stocks with ore obtained from its allies as well as plundered from the countries the Nazis occupied. More frustrating for the Allies was Germany's ongoing ability to import raw materials from such officially neutral countries as

Sweden, Portugal, and Turkey—to the tune of 4.5 million tons of iron ore in 1944 alone.

However, a change in airpower was underway. Having more aircraft available did not necessarily mean they were all being used in combat operations. Raw materials and Herculean manufacturing efforts could not supply more veteran pilots to the Luftwaffe. Those killed, captured, and incapacitated were being replaced by less-experienced men or not replaced at all, leaving bombers and fighters on the ground. Fuel shortages were becoming more common too, further infringing on flying operations. Though it was happening slower than the Allied commanders and civilian leaders would have liked, Allied air forces were increasingly taking control of the skies over Europe.

What is now the United States Air Forces Central Command descended from the Ninth Air Force, which was established early in the war. Immediately after the attack on Pearl Harbor, the focus of the Army Air Corps was the defense of the U.S. mainland and bases in the Caribbean, Greenland, Iceland, and the Panama Canal. Then, as planes and pilots began to trickle out of assembly plants and training fields, they were rushed to help defend Australia and the southwest Pacific posts trying to hold out against the Japanese juggernaut. In Europe, the British were standing up to the continuing German attacks, which had been undermined to some extent by the frightful losses in Russia and the efforts to hold on to North Africa.

The Ninth Air Force had become operational in November 1942, when the U.S. Middle East Air Force was redesignated and placed under the command of Major General Lewis H. Brereton. Its air support of the Allied armies in North Africa against the forces of Field Marshal Erwin Rommel were critical to their eventual success. General Brereton was ordered to take the Ninth HQ to England in October 1943 to build a tactical air armada for the anticipated invasion of Europe. By D-Day the following June, it had become the largest air force ever assembled under one command with 250,000 people and 3,500 airplanes in 1,500 bomber, fighter, and other units.

By then, the commanding officer was Elwood Quesada, who at that point in time was one of the brightest and upwardly mobile of generals.* Born in 1904 in Washington, D.C., to a Spanish father and an Irish-American mother, he attended the University of Maryland and Georgetown University before, at twenty, enlisting in the Army Air Corps. He gained notice five years later, in 1929, for earning a Distinguished Flying Cross and being one of the three men who developed the process of air-to-air refueling.

His rise through the ranks accelerated when war broke out: first lieutenant in 1932, captain in 1935, major in 1941, lieutenant colonel and also brigadier general in 1942, and then major general when he took command of the Ninth Air Force in 1944. One area of expertise for Quesada was the concept of close air support for ground forces, which would certainly come into play that year whenever there was an invasion of France.†

One of the units under General Quesada's command was Joe Moser's, and its formal title was the 429th Electronic Combat Squadron. It had been activated the previous August specifically as a P-38 Lightning fighter squadron.

------

* Though he was Elwood James Quesada, his nickname was Pete.

† After the war, Quesada became the first commander of the Tactical Air Command. He was only forty-seven when, as a lieutenant general, he retired from the Army Air Corps. He had married a war widow who was a granddaughter of the newspaper baron Joseph Pulitzer, adopted her two children, had two children with her, and pursued a higher-paying career in business and government. Among his positions were being an executive at the Lockheed Aircraft Corporation, serving on the American Airlines board of directors, and being the head of the Federal Aviation Administration when it debuted in 1959. Two years later, Quesada resigned to become owner of the expansion Washington Senators baseball club.

The ship carrying the 429th Fighter Squadron as well as other American military units had left Boston on Sunday, February 27. Joe, like many of the passengers, was not looking forward to a long voyage on an ocean infested with German submarines. On that cold and cloudy morning, according to Karl Swindt, "A Red Cross unit serving coffee and donuts on the dock did little business. For some, the gangplank looked like scaffold steps leading up to the executioner. The first man seen at the top railing turned out to be our Group Chaplain which didn't help the picture any."

The 158 officers and 1,941 enlisted men spent their first night "at sea" on the ship, which had not yet been cleared for departure. Finally, the next day the *Excelsior*, once a South American banana freighter, was given the green light. It steamed away from Boston and into the bitterly cold north Atlantic.

The *Excelsior* became part of a convoy that zigzagged its way west, prompting more than a few of the passengers to declare, "I'm never going to travel by boat again." For the first couple of days attendance at dinner was not robust, but as the next days passed there were more seats at the table occupied. Some of the conversations were about their eventual destination. A strong hint about what they could expect was provided in a pamphlet published by the War and Navy Departments titled "A Short Guide to Great Britain," handed out on the ship. There was a lot of restless inactivity on the crowded ship, so a highlight of the long voyage was the showing of a movie, *Rose Marie,* featuring Nelson Eddy and Jeannette MacDonald, who had been one of Hollywood's most popular duos in 1936, when the musical was released.

On March 5, Joe and hundreds of others attended church services, which were held in the enlisted men's mess. Those who hoped for a safe trip had their prayers answered at two the following morning, when a German submarine sent a torpedo at the *Excelsior* but missed. Not quite as bad but nasty enough were the rough seas complementing the rough conditions. One of the pilots in the 429th, Don Cerveny, reported, "The stench from unwashed bodies, the seasickness, and men vomiting in their helmets, the rotten meat and potatoes—these things will be in my memory for the rest of my life." Joe had to be having second thoughts about leaving the comforts of his family and Ferndale.

Finally, on March 9, the *Excelsior* dropped anchor twenty-five miles west of Glasgow. The 429th log for that day records, "All are anxious to get the hell off this damn boat." It would be another two days, though, before the two-thousand-plus men filed down the gangplank, free of the *Excelsior* and its banana-boat conditions. They boarded trains that took them from Glasgow to Manchester and then on to Southampton on England's southeast coast. At stops along the way, the train was met by the British NAAFI women offering tea and crumpets.* The 429th's log keeper felt compelled to confide, "We found that the stories we had heard about English girls having piano legs and big feet were true only in a few cases."

Joe and the others discovered that their new home would be the air base at Warmwell. It was three miles inland from the south coast that overlooked the English Channel and almost five miles east and south of Dorchester in the county of Dorset. Despite the war raging in what was often called "Fortress Europe" and the coast of France being only twenty-one miles across the water, Warmwell was in a peaceful part of the English countryside, surrounded by grass-covered rolling hills and populated by small homes with well-tended gardens. The base had been built in 1937, when its

* The Navy, Army, and Air Force Institutes was an organization established by the British government in 1920 when the Expeditionary Force Canteens and the Navy and Army Canteen Board were combined to run the recreational establishments needed by the Armed Forces, and to sell goods to servicemen and their families.

original name was RAF Woodsford. Another quaint aspect was that aircraft took off and landed on a field of closely cropped grass.

But there was no doubt a war was in progress. The Warmwell base was enclosed by barbed wire and surrounded by anti-aircraft batteries that were manned around the clock. There were also buildings on the base yet to be repaired that had been damaged during German raids. For the new arrivals from America, these damaged structures were a relatively mild yet clear introduction to the destructive and deadly power of all-out war.

Otherwise, though, the first impression of the members of the 429th Squadron, especially after the rigors of their travels, was a good one: "The air was fresh and clean and we had a bright blue sky overhead," Joe observed. "British soldiers in the blue uniform of the RAF milled around on their bicycles, looking us over while we stood and looked at them. Everything appeared to be very casual and informal and could have passed for a Sunday morning at the country club."

Later in 1944, Joe Moser would reflect on his first months as a fighter pilot based at Warmwell as "incredible," adding, "There are few pleasures in life greater than sharing terrifying and life-changing moments with the very few people on earth who have survived the same kind of experiences and find the same meaning and thrill in them."

Though a quiet man perhaps more given to introspection than most, Joe cherished more than anything else the company of other young pilots with whom he was united in a common cause. As he also reflected, "I was a quiet farm boy from a Swiss Catholic family. I ended up a fighter pilot because I had the dream of a great many young, adventurous boys of that time."

4

That quiet farm boy's dream was on the verge of becoming a reality. However, to the frustration of the pilots in the 429th, instead of jumping into action there was yet more training, a full six weeks of it. As the days grew longer into mid-spring so too did the hours of training. The American and RAF pilots began to have a grudging respect for each other, and after the initial sizing-up stage was over, they shared drinks and what they had heard about raids now being carried out by B-17 and other bombers into Germany itself.

The officers gathered nightly "in the Tap Room after dinner for ale, stout, and the quaffing of any other available beverages," as Joe recalled. The Yank pilots were introduced to dart throwing, "the prevailing pastime all over the continent." In addition, the British "had a remarkable collection of inspiring songs and the singing would fairly make bottles rattle on taproom shelves." However, "some nights the toasts and drinks were to fallen comrades."

Finally, for the Americans, it was the real thing at last. The 429th Squadron was presented with twenty-six P-38 Lightnings, the J model that required just a bit more training. The Luftwaffe was about to get an even bigger dose of the plane that had already proved itself not only in Europe but also in the Pacific Theater against the Japanese.

Safe to say, the P-38 Lightning was the most distinctive-looking fighter plane deployed by the Army Air Corps. It had twin booms and a central nacelle containing the cockpit and armament. The cockpit was centered on the wing between the two counter-rotating engines, and the tails were connected by a boom that served as the horizontal stabilizer. A big advantage of the plane's engines was that the counter-rotation offset much of the torque, providing pilots with turning and maneuvering abilities that exceeded other fighter planes. It could also out-turn single-engine planes while remaining in control.

The P-38 earned two nicknames, one in each theater of war— the Germans dubbed it *der Gabelschwanz-Teufel* or "fork-tailed devil" and to the Japanese it was *Ni hikoki, ippairotto* or "two planes, one pilot." By any name, the P-38 Lightning haunted the sleep of enemy pilots, ground troops, and sailors.

What also made it so valuable to the Allied cause in both Europe and the southwest Pacific was its versatility. Depending on the most immediate need or how it fit into an overall strategy, the P-38 was a fighter, a dive-bomber, a supporter of ground attacks, a photo-reconnaissance craft, an evacuation plane, and seemingly anything else it was called upon to be. Its range was impressive too—anywhere from 475 to over 1,100 miles depending on altitude and speed. The range could be enhanced by the Lightning being able to carry two 200-gallon fuel tanks fitted between the cockpit and the port-side fuselage and the starboard fuselage. The P-38 was a fearsome attack plane too, with the nose housing four

.50-caliber machine guns as well as a 20-millimeter cannon. The P-38 could also serve as a bomber if need be, and some models were equipped with the Norden bombsight, the same device used by bombardiers on Flying Fortresses.

Such a powerful weapon for the Allies had a rather humble beginning. As Joe Christy and Jeff Ethell describe it in their *P-38 Lightning at War:*

> In February 1937 when the US Army Air Corps asked America's struggling aircraft industry to submit design proposals for a new "interceptor," Lockheed Aircraft Corporation was a small company. Its cash on hand was approximately equal to one month's operating expenses; and its sole product, the twin-engined Electra, aimed at the feeder airline market, could claim a production run of less than 80 machines during the preceding three years. Nevertheless, Lockheed made a bold response to the Air Corps' request, submitting drawings of an airplane so advanced that, if built, it would demand answers to engineering and aerodynamic questions for which no answers yet existed.

The Army Air Corps took a chance and gave the upstart Lockheed Corporation the green light to proceed.* The design team was headed by Clarence Johnson and Hall Hibbard, who concocted the twin booms to accommodate the engines, two turbo-superchargers, and the tail assembly. Another innovation was the armament in the nose, introduced when tests proved the theory that, unlike wing-mounted guns, the Lightning could shoot accurately and hit targets up to a thousand yards away.

---

* Initially, the Roosevelt administration approved a plane that would be a defensive weapon only, because in 1937 that was the only kind that would be funded by a Congress wary of being drawn into overseas conflicts.

After prototypes were tested and tweaked, the first of what was then labeled the YP-38 made its debut flight in September 1940. The encouraging results meant that the plane could go into mass production. This next green light did not come a moment too soon, because the war in Europe was already a year old and Japanese aggression in Asia had begun even earlier. While there was still a firm isolationist sentiment in the United States, there was also a strengthening belief that the United States would play more of a role in an expanding conflict. Still, the country was not at war yet, so "mass production" was not robust. In all of 1941, there were just 196 P-38 fighters produced by the Lockheed Corporation.

As Christy and Ethell point out, the company "did the best it could with what it had when there wasn't enough of anything, from metal to money to manpower, to go around; and did so according to priorities. Meanwhile, the financing of plant expansion programmes in America had to depend upon private money sources until the US Congress enacted the Lend-Lease Bill on 11 March 1941."

At last, in mid-1941, P-38 models began making their way to Army Air Corps units. And, of course, the attack on Pearl Harbor that December dramatically changed the American industrial landscape. The following year, production of the P-38G alone was 150 units per month. By the end of 1943, over 5,300 P-38s had been constructed and deployed.

Thus, in the European Theater early in 1944, when bomber crew members looked out their windows, it was routine to see the Lockheed P-38 Lightning escorting them. However, the plane was part of a team protecting the Flying Fortresses and other bombers as they attacked deeper into Germany.

Another fighter plane they would often find accompanying them was the P-51 Mustang. It was found that with external fuel tanks the plane could actually accompany bombers all the way to Germany and back. But the bad news was the P-51's Allison engine had a single-stage supercharger that caused power to drop off rapidly above fifteen thousand feet, where American Air Corps bombers routinely flew, thus making for an ineffective escort.

It was a man named Ronald Harker who came to the rescue. He was a test pilot for the Rolls-Royce company in England, and he floated the idea of fitting a Merlin 61 engine into the aircraft, one that had been used in the British Spitfire fighter plane. The Merlin 61 had a two-speed, two-stage intercooled supercharger that gave an increase in horsepower from the Allison's 12,900 hp to 16,200 hp. This provided an increase of top speed from 390 to 440 mph and raised the service ceiling to almost 42,000 feet. Initial flights of a new version of the Mustang were conducted at the Rolls-Royce airfield in October 1942. Meanwhile, in the United States, designers were exploring the possibility of combining the P-51 airframe with the Packard version of the Merlin engine.

The first flight of the XP-51B took place in November 1942, but the Army Air Corps was so interested in the possibility that a contract for four hundred aircraft had already been placed that August. The conversion led to production of the P-51B beginning in June 1943 at a plant in Inglewood, California, and P-51s started to become available to the Eighth and Ninth Air Forces in the winter of 1943–44.

A third major player providing escort services was the P-47 Thunderbolt. Its "fathers," in a sense, were two men, Alexander de Seversky and Alexander Kartveli, who, at different times, had fled the Bolsheviks in Russia and immigrated to the United States. The P-47, manufactured by the Republic Corporation and first deployed in 1941, was designed around the powerful Pratt & Whitney R-2899 Double Wasp engine. Its primary armament was eight .50-caliber machine guns. In the fighter-bomber ground-attack role it could carry five-inch rockets or a bomb load of 2,500 pounds. Fully loaded, the P-47 weighed up to eight tons, making it one of the heaviest fighters of the war, which had an impact on its range because it burned fuel faster. The Thunderbolt was most effective as a short- to medium-range escort and as a high-altitude air-to-air combat and ground-attack fighter.

By the time that Joe Moser was finally flying his Lightning over France in the spring of 1944, bomber-escort defenses were layered, using the shorter-range P-38s and P-47s as escorts during the initial stages of the raid and then handing over to the P-51s when it was time for the fighters to turn for home. Joe might have disputed this, but as the months went by the Mustang was so clearly superior that the Army Air Corps began to steadily switch its fighter groups to the Mustang, first swapping arriving P-47 groups to the Ninth Air Force in exchange for those that were using P-51s, then gradually converting its Thunderbolt and Lightning groups. By the end of 1944, fourteen of its fifteen groups flew the Mustang.

There was also a change of strategy being implemented. At the start of 1944, Major General James Doolittle, who had led the daring raid on Tokyo in 1942 and was now the commander of the Eighth Air Force, ordered many fighter pilots to stop flying in formation with the bombers and instead attack the Luftwaffe wherever its planes could be found. The aim was to achieve air supremacy. Mustang groups were sent far ahead of the bombers in a "fighter sweep" in order to intercept German fighters before they could coordinate an attack. Units of the Ninth Air Force, including the 429th, would be carrying out this new strategy too.

Joe's first combat mission took place on April 25. At that time, most of the missions of the P-38 Lightning squadrons were still to escort bombers across the English Channel to targets deep in France and, increasingly, Germany itself. This was not as "adventurous" as being hunter-killer flyers, airborne wolf packs seeking their own targets, such as fighter pilots wearing German uniforms. However, the fighters' presence was absolutely essential. Without the P-38s and P-47 Thunderbolts and P-51 Mustangs, the flotillas of lumbering bombers would be easy prey for the rapacious German fighters.

These enemy planes were formidable foes indeed. The German pilots were well trained, and even those who were not members of or supporters of the Nazi Party were devoted to the war effort or to doing their job or, at least, were dedicated to defending their homeland as Allied air attacks swept eastward over Europe. For close to a decade, the German manufacturing plants had been churning out some of the best fighter planes the world had seen.

The first specifications for what would become the Messerschmitt Bf 109 were issued by the German Ministry of Aviation in 1934. A prototype was flown just two years later, and the 109's first test in combat conditions came in 1937 during the Spanish Civil War—in support of, of course, the Fascist forces. During the next few years the plan would undergo redesigns and adjustments, until finally the Messerschmitt Bf 109G went into mass production—it is believed that a total of thirty-five thousand were built before the German manufacturing plants were either destroyed or shut down. The Bf 109G-14 was the model used by Major Erich Hartmann of the Luftwaffe to record the incredible total of 352 confirmed victories.* The Bf 109 could reach a maximum speed of 387 mph and a ceiling of 38,500 feet. Because its normal range was 450 miles, it was less a bomber escort than a

---

* While this record would be an enviable achievement for any combat pilot, it should be noted that the majority of Major Hartmann's victories came on the Eastern Front, where German fighters were clearly superior to the Soviet Union's fighter planes, which were easy pickings.

defensive fighter over France—and, eventually, the homeland as the Allied air forces brought the war inexorably closer to Berlin.

The Focke-Wulf Fw 190 was as much of a workhorse aircraft as the Messerschmitt 109. It was an escort plane, an attack plane, and a ground-attack plane and was found flying in the North African campaign, on the Eastern and Western Fronts, and finally in defense of Germany itself.

Its introduction in August 1941 was bad news for the British because it proved to be a better fighter than the Spitfire, the workhorse on the other side of the conflict. The situation grew worse for the British into the spring of 1942, before there was a significant impact from America being in the war. Then there was a stroke of luck: In June, Oberleutnant Armin Faber, flying a Focke-Wulf Fw 190, landed on a British airfield in error. Military analysts immediately went to work on the accidentally captured aircraft.

What they gleaned led to Spitfire upgrades. The playing field in the air became more level for the British and, eventually, all the Allies once planes and pilots and support personnel began arriving from the United States. On the German side, the pilot Heinz Bar claimed the most victories flying a Focke-Wulf Fw 190, with 221, which included downing twenty-one heavy bombers.

On his first mission in the last week in April, Joe's P-38 Lightning was one of the sixteen planes in the 429th Squadron—a unit in the 474th Fighter Group that, in turn, was a unit in the IXth Tactical Fighter Wing of the Ninth Air Force. The squadron was led into the air by Captain Burl Glass. There they joined planes from the 428th and 430th Squadrons, all combining for a 474th Fight Group "sweep" into enemy territory to hunt for enemy fighter planes. Their primary destination was Rennes in France, southeast of the Normandy coast. Joe and his comrades were glad to leave training behind, but understandably their "nerves were completely on edge."

The group was no sooner across the English Channel when the cry of "Bandit, three o'clock!" was heard over the radio in all the cockpits. This was almost immediately followed by, "Bandit, 10 o'clock high!" The more experienced officers soon realized that these enemy planes, which continued to be sighted during the two-hour-plus mission, were only the products of fevered imaginations.

Even so, and feeling slightly abashed, Joe was "at last a real live fighter pilot. Confident, but not cocky. But as ready as I could ever be for the life and death challenges ahead."

They would come soon enough.

5

As did his fellow pilots, Joe Moser took pride in protecting the ships that carried the precious cargos of bombs to be dropped above German military installations, factories, and rail hubs. Each bomber downed by the Luftwaffe was a fresh cause of sadness and disappointment as well as the loss of a valuable machine. Each returning airship was one to be patched up, resupplied with bombs, and sent off again to chip away at the German might. From time to time, the escort flyers' efforts were recognized.

On April 30, Joe's commanding officer, Burl Glass, was promoted from captain to major. That was a particularly busy day for the Ninth Air Force—its Bomber Command sent over three hundred B-26s and A-20s to attack German weapons and construction sites and railroad yards in France, while 114 B-17s hit the Lyon/Bron Airdrome, which included a German radar installation. There were over six hundred escort flights flown by P-38, P-47, and P-51 fighters, with five of those planes lost in action.

But they gave more than they got, with eighteen German pilots going down just between 9:20 A.M. and noon, as well as inflicting devastating destruction to the airdrome.

After the 429th Squadron's mission that day, the pilots were assembled and Glass was presented with the twin oak leaves that represented his new rank and congratulations were offered. A corporal who attended the ceremonies recorded in the unit's log, "Everyone was glad to see our lean, straight-forward C.O. make the grade. We all can be certain that with men like Major Glass in this squadron, nothing can stop us."*

Such bravado was understandable . . . but also unrealistic. Every day dozens of pilots took off from Warmwell, and not all of them returned to sing songs that night in the taproom. Every time Joe flew into the sky, he knew there was no guarantee he would come back. But, yes, having capable and even inspiring leaders increased the pilots' chances.

It helped, too, to have the romantic idealism and zeal of youth. Certainly Lieutenant L. C. Beck was an example of that, as reflected in his writing: "Mom, before I came over here, I didn't feel like giving my life for my country, that I just wasn't that patriotic. Well, I am now, and I shall be very proud to die for my country. You can't realize just how I feel perhaps, but you must believe me with all your heart. And you, Dad, you can throw back your shoulders and say, 'My son gave his life fighting for America. He died a brave man and I am proud to say—He was my son!'"

A week after his promotion, Major Glass led two missions in the same day, with Joe participating in both. The first looked to be pretty routine—escort a flock of B-26s on a bombing run over France. However, during it, suddenly about fifteen Focke-Wulf

---

* Ten days later, Merle Larson, the squadron's operations officer, was promoted to captain.

190s came from out of the sun to attack the formation. The P-38s fought them off in a desperate air battle but lost two of their own, Lieutenant Buford Thacker and Lieutenant Milton Merkle. Thacker's fighter was last seen disappearing into a cloud bank with its left engine on fire. No one saw a parachute. The same was true for Merkle after his plane was hit by one of the German fighters. Colonel Clinton Wasem, commanding officer of the 474th, reported that he saw Merkle falling away from his burning plane but "it was impossible to determine whether or not his parachute opened." The Lightnings also doled out some punishment, with an Fw 190 hit and reeling and later listed as a "probable" kill.

The second mission that day was a break from the routine, a fighter sweep over Reims. The pilots' blood was boiling to avenge the loss of their two colleagues, but this time no enemy aircraft was encountered. The P-38s trudged back to base. A day that had begun at dawn did not end until 9:30 that night with little to show for it.

Though just twenty-two and with only a few weeks of combat experience under his belt, Joe already felt close to being a grizzled veteran: "It didn't take too long to change from high-strung combat rookies to experienced, professional fighter pilots. It is true that the thrill of sliding those throttles forward and feeling all fourteen hundred and fifty of those horses contained in the twin Allison 12-cylinder engines pulling me into the deep blue never diminished. But neither did the gut-chilling dread of knowing each time we left the 'comfort' of our cold, drizzly southern English base, it might be our last time."

In *Fork-Tail Devil*, James G. Speight writes that after an initial period of getting used to each other, "Generally, the British welcomed the young Americans, but whenever they went into a pub, some attendee of the evening festivities might be heard to mutter knowingly: "There are only three things wrong with the Yanks: they're overpaid, oversexed, and over here.'"*

One of Joe's more memorable escort missions occurred in mid-May. He and other P-38 pilots were to rendezvous with an array of B-17s that in broad daylight had attacked Berlin. Whatever physical damage the bombers inflicted would be at least equaled by the psychological damage of having Hitler's capital city punished. The fighters would meet the B-17s over the Baltic Sea east of Denmark and protect them on the way back to their base in England. Especially vulnerable were any stragglers—bombers damaged during the raid and having trouble keeping up with the flotilla. Targeting them, of course, was the easiest way for the German pilots to make sure there would be fewer Flying Fortresses hurting their homeland the next day. It was also an easier way to add to their count of kills.

The American fighter pilots flew east far enough to meet up with the returning B-17s. When over western Denmark, 88-mm anti-aircraft batteries on the ground opened up. Bombers and fighters alike were in the midst of deadly flak—the bombers at twenty thousand feet, the escorts five thousand above them. The American planes scattered to lessen the odds of a hit. When the flak was left behind, the planes would regroup.

That was the plan . . . but it did not work that way for Joe. He was not only free of flak but of his squadron too. "This was not good," he thought, "not good." Joe was alone in the sky, and still within reach of foraging German fighters.

He set a course back to his base at Warmwell, "rubber necking all the way" for his mates and to spot the enemy, who "would try

---

* At this time in the war, the monthly pay for a U.S. Army Air Corps pilot was $246.70, of which $6.50 was deducted for insurance. The insurance policy provided a $10,000 payment to the wife or family of a pilot who died while on duty.

at every opportunity, as we did, to attack from out of the sun and from above to maximize their speed as they dived down."

Finally, Joe spotted an American plane. It was a B-17, and as he flew lower and closer, he saw how slow it was flying. Then he noticed two of its engines had been shot out, and there was other damage too. This was the kind of wounded straggler the Germans loved to feast upon. Joe tried to contact it by radio, but when there was no response, he figured the radio was also destroyed. Now, Joe realized, "I had a purpose. Even a single P-38 flying near a crippled bomber was enough to discourage the Luftwaffe from trying to pick off the stricken plane."

Joe flew figure eights as he stayed above the B-17. This maneuver enabled him to keep the Lightning on pace with the damaged bomber, which could only manage 200 mph, and Joe was at 300 mph. It also enabled him to better scan the surrounding sky for enemy aircraft. Joe had to assume that his presence offered hope to the B-17 crew that they just might live through this.

However, while over the English Channel, it became apparent that the bomber was not going to maintain enough altitude to reach land. But the crew was not going to give up easily. Joe watched as ammunition, machine guns, heavier clothing, and almost anything not nailed down or riveted was thrown out the hatches. And then Joe realized he was in some danger himself—of running out of fuel. The figure eights burned gas faster than straightforward flying. If he remained the lone bomber's escort, Joe risked either not reaching land himself or, if he did make the coast of England, having to survive an emergency landing in a field. But he couldn't bear the thought of abandoning the wounded bird. Sometimes, one simply has to hope for the best.

Both planes did reach the far side of the Channel. As they neared London from the north, the B-17 veered right, toward its base. On fumes, Joe passed London by and headed for Warmwell.

There could only have been ounces of fuel left when he touched down. As he clambered out of the cockpit, Joe prayed the Flying Fortress crew had made it home.

It was not until fifty years later that Joe learned that his prayers had been answered. He was attending a midsummer barbecue at St. Joseph's Church in Ferndale when he heard a man talking to others about being the waist gunner on a B-17 during World War II. Joe was to learn that the man's name was Earl Thomas, visiting from nearby Lummi Island.

Thomas was telling his listeners about a particular day in 1944, when his bomber was returning from a long mission over Berlin with two engines shot out. "I thought we were a goner," he said. Thomas continued, as Joe joined the group: "Suddenly I saw this plane up above and behind us. When I noticed it had the twin tails that only belonged to one of our fighters, the P-38, I can't tell you what a welcome sight that was. That guy followed us all the way back to England, doing figure-eights behind us all the time so he could stay tucked in behind us. He saved our lives, I'm sure of it."

Unable to stay silent a moment longer, Joe extended his hand and introduced himself, adding, "I think I was flying that P-38."

He would write in his memoir, "The joy, gratitude and amazement we felt for each other that day was nothing less than if I had landed behind that bird and had discovered that one of my fellow churchmen from right near my own town had been in that plane that I was protecting all the way over Europe."

The actions of the entire 429th Squadron that day in accompanying the bombers over eight hundred miles, and much of that over water, were greeted soon after its return by a commendation from the commander of the Ninth Air Force, General "Pete" Quesada: "It is with pleasure that I extend my personal congratulations to you and your pilots. Your splendid work of escorting bombers deep in enemy territory reflects the highest credit upon yourselves and your command. Your organization displayed a high state of training, discipline and sense of responsibility."

During May, a routine had become well established. When weather permitted, every day was essentially the same for Joe and his mates—be briefed on the mission, prepare themselves, get in their P-38s and take off, and fulfill the mission, whatever the risks and the losses. They sensed the Allied firepower gaining in strength and the balance tipping against the Germans, with perhaps an even greater conflict to come. "During this period of May 1944," the 429th log explains, "we were building up our striking power to its peak and hitting with maximum intensity." By this time, the enemy was being hit from the air somewhere virtually every hour that the weather permitted.

As much as their rudimentary accommodations at Warmwell had become home, complete with the taproom, it was a relief when the Americans got to leave the base from time to time. Three-day passes were issued, with the duration of the getaway increasing the more missions a pilot had survived. With the less restrictive passes, some pilots ventured as far as London. They were able to go by train because, despite the efforts of German bombers, most rail lines in the area were intact. Another popular destination was Bournemouth, a resort town featuring a pavilion where "tea dances" were held, allowing the young Yanks to socialize with Englishwomen from the surrounding area.

The escort missions went longer distances, straining the fuel supplies of the P-38s, as more raids included targets deep in Germany as well as in France. One of the longest was a six-hour mission that took Joe and other pilots to Berlin itself, escorting a fleet of B-17s. Because the flak was so heavy as the flotilla neared the target area, the fighters were ordered to break formation and leave the sky to the Flying Fortresses dropping their payloads. The Luftwaffe's Fw 190s saw this as an opportunity and began an attack.

However, they stalled in their tracks when the P-38s reappeared.
The bombs were dropped, and the B-17s swung around, heading
back to England with their feisty escorts. By this time, most of the
P-38 pilots had come to recognize and perhaps make peace with
the idiosyncrasies of the Lightning. One was having a game plan
for bailing out if necessary . . . if that was possible. The plane's
unique design, especially the twin booms, posed difficulties pilots
did not face in other planes. Of course, when his plane was damaged, a pilot's first priority was to keep the plane in the air and try
to get back to Allied territory rather than risk a crash landing or
being taken prisoner by German ground forces. But if the damage
involved fire or was otherwise so extensive that adequate speed or
altitude could not be maintained, a pilot had to get out and take
his chances with a parachute.

In *Fork-Tailed Devil*, Martin Caidin offers the recollection of
Brigadier General Edward Giller about his experiences as an
Army Air Corps major and P-38 pilot during World War II: "The
consensus was you should bail out at high speed or at very low
speed just above stalling. It was intended that you would crawl
out of the cockpit and slide from the wing and go out under the
boom. At high speed, greater than 350 miles per hour, one would
remove the canopy, roll full forward trim, then suddenly turn
loose of the wheel and give yourself a kick upwards and thereby
go out over the tail boom. Unfortunately, a considerable percent-
age of people accounted for a number of unsuccessful bailouts."

In other words, when the time came, the pilot might have to
improvise. Some flyers got free of the damaged plane; others did
not. During the flight that changed his life, Joe Moser would find
himself somewhere in between.

Through the rest of the month, the Ninth Air Force hurled
everything it had against German strongholds in France and the
homeland, with Joe just one of the hundreds of fighter pilots

being protective escorts. On May 19, 495 B-17s struck Berlin, dropping bombs through heavy cloud cover. Over Germany and the Baltic Sea that day, seventy-one enemy aircraft were downed. Two days later, Operation Chattanooga Choo-Choo began, targeting rail lines in Germany, and ninety-one locomotives were reported destroyed. But the highest fighter losses to date were posted, with twenty-seven P-38s, P-47s, and P-51s knocked from the sky.

On the twenty-fifth, 325 heavy bombers attacked German coastal batteries at Fécamp and St.-Valery as well as marshaling yards and airdromes in France and Belgium. A different record was set on May 28: The Army Air Corps sent 1,341 bombers into the air to obliterate oil and rail targets in Germany, and combined the XIIIth and IXth Fighter Command provided 1,224 escort sorties. There was little rest for all the pilots of the Ninth Air Force as momentum built toward the invasion everyone knew would happen soon.

At the very end of May, Joe received his first personal commendation, the Air Medal, for a full month of being a fighter pilot. He had indeed achieved his dream, the one that began as he stood in a farm field outside Ferndale and saw a plane flying overhead. Lying in bed that night at the Warmwell base, no matter how many new dreams he'd had about the future, Joe could not possibly have imagined the nightmare ahead.

ACT II
THE PASSENGER

———— ◆ ————

We must have our troubles here;
—Our hearts torn by loss,
—Our hands made bloody by war,
—Our future left unknown.

—Lieutenant L. C. Beck Jr.

6

G eneral "Pete" Quesada of the Ninth Air Force remained a strong advocate for tactical air support of ground troops but thus far, however, in France, there were no Allied ground troops to support. On June 6, 1944, that would change, and confirmation that the day was fast approaching was Joe Moser's 429th Squadron doing fewer bomber escorts and more ground attacks.

The squadron's logbook reported that as June began it received orders "to bomb special bridges, marshalling yards and supply dumps in that area of France lying just behind the proposed assault site." To the pilots, this was more to their liking.

Echoing that preference was Joe's recollection: "We were sent on mission after mission to attack railroad yards, other transportation facilities, bridges, truck convoys, trains and just about anything else that looked like it might hinder a successful invasion," he recalled. "We all knew it was coming."

An invasion, the flyers assumed, was the reason why all outgoing mail was stopped from leaving the base. Loose lips not only sank ships, they could help stop an invasion in its tracks. Another indication of something big about to happen was observed by the residents of the Warmwell base: It seemed like every able-bodied soldier that the Allies had was arriving in their section of southern England.

And there were no getaway passes or even rest for the pilots now, with each mission feeling more crucial to the war effort. On June 2, the target was the bridge at Bennecourt that crossed the Seine west of Paris. But the pilots of the 429th Fighter Squadron knew they could damage a lot more than just one bridge. Each P-38 Lightning could drop two thousand-pound, high-explosive bombs—the heaviest they could carry and still stay in the air. The young flyers wanted to make sure the Germans winced hard after this mission.

Once again the flight leader on the mission was Merle Larson, and there was no one in the entire Air Corps whom Joe trusted more. The fearless captain had gotten his pilots out of plenty of scrapes thanks to his cool head and combat experience. Right before the 429th had saddled up, Captain Larson told them that this mission meant a lot: Those planning the invasion of Normandy—which could step off any day—knew the destruction of such strategic bridges like the Bennecourt one would slow or perhaps even halt German troops being sent to reinforce units at the coast.

On this mission, Joe was wingman for Lieutenant Bill Banks. That too was gratifying. You couldn't find a finer flyer than Banks, and Joe was always trying to pick up a few tricks to become a better pilot. He wanted to live long enough to see his family back in Ferndale again . . . and to do so knowing he had done his best to win the war. "If we did our jobs," Joe reasoned, "success might mean many lives saved for our boys who had to get into the water and onto those beaches."

The P-38s flew at eight thousand feet on a clear day. When they arrived in the region west of Paris and over the river, they were, as was usual on missions, greeted with cloudbursts of flak. The pilots by now knew the two different kinds—there was *Fliegerabvehrkanone,* or anti-aircraft fire, and *Flugabwehrkanone,* or flight-defense cannons. If either found its mark, they were in trouble.

Ignoring the flak, Captain Larson pointed down at the target. As leader, he would be first to attack. His Lightning rolled into a deep dive, screaming in at four hundred miles per hour. At fifteen hundred feet, Larson released his bombs and pulled out of the dive. Every pilot in the squadron had to follow the same procedure. Pulling out of the dive too early reduced the chances of a direct hit on the bridge and pulling out too late could mean being caught in the blast from the previous plane's bomb.*

Each pilot took his turn, calibrating his speed and altitude as he dove down, somehow having the fortitude to ignore the dark, smoky flak bursts that appeared to be only inches from the cockpit. When it was Joe's turn, his teeth hurt from gritting them so hard. What a fix this was—do his job right and survive or his last thought could be picturing his mother receiving the dreaded telegram from the War Department.

Joe let the bombs go. Immediately, he felt the P-38 lift up in reaction to the sudden loss of weight. He built on this momentum and pulled the nose up. The first few hundred feet of the climb seemed agonizingly slow and long. During those anxious moments, Joe expected his Lightning to be engulfed in a shattering

---

* This would happen to Lieutenant Moore, one of Joe's good friends in the 429th, the next month. The P-38s were attacking a railroad yard with delayed-fuse bombs. Moore's plane did not pull out of the dive soon enough, and the bomb blast sent it spinning into the ground, where it exploded.

explosion. With any luck, he would have time for one prayer to forgive his sins before all went dark.

But as he looked out of his cockpit, all he saw was blue sky. Joe was not yet able to see what he had left behind. Now he had a different prayer—that there was nothing left of that particular bridge across the Seine.

The prayer was answered, though Joe felt slightly cheated. When he was able to look down, he expected to see smoking, twisted metal. However, the bridge was simply . . . gone. Obliterated. At least he could see the buildings of Paris in the background. A third prayer was that Americans would be there soon, liberating it, and maybe Joe could stroll the streets of a city he could only imagine—or view from the sky.

After Captain Larson led the squadron back across the English Channel and to their base in England, he could report that the mission was a complete success. Not only was the bridge totally destroyed, but while the American pilots were at it, they had hit a handful of nearby railroad tracks. It was a bit frightening what bombs of that size could do.

That night, at the Allied base at Warmwell, the officers of the 474th Fighter Group gathered together and threw a party for themselves. Joe and his fellow flyers celebrated the outcome of the mission and making it through another day. All the pilots had safely returned. The logbook of the 429th Squadron noted that since the last officers' party, "Beer consumption capacity had increased considerably. Those who leaned toward harder beverages could now stay propped up against a wall for hours where before they had been carried off from the field in utter defeat in a comparatively short time."

Joe was not at risk of such an ignoble exit because he was one of the few flyers who did not drink alcohol. No matter, he thoroughly enjoyed the festivities. He was in a room surrounded by friends all focused on a single purpose: defeat the evil Nazis, win the war, go home to the States. Life was not that complicated.

It just hung on a slender thread. In only a short period of time, Joe had lost too many friends. With that thought in mind, he decided to turn in early. There would be another dangerous mission tomorrow and he wanted to give himself the best chance of surviving it. Drifting off to sleep, Joe reflected, "I was very proud to have been selected by Captain Larson for this attack and to have been a major contributor to its success."

More than pride was his reward. Three weeks later, the Distinguished Flying Cross was issued to Joe. And two weeks after that, he was promoted to first lieutenant. He was still only twenty-two years old.

After a mission the following day that involved fifteen planes carrying two 1,000-pound bombs, each intended for the rail lines between Chauny and Tergnier, it was time for the squadron's P-38s to undergo paint jobs. The camouflage design was painted over so that each Lightning had wide, black-and-white, zebra-like stripes. As the 429th's history writer wryly commented, "Such a radical change in the appearance of our planes might have been cause for wonder, but we had already executed so many peculiar orders with no question asked that this was merely another sample of the same." They learned the purpose of these "invasion stripes" was to help identify them to friendly anti-aircraft gunners.

Late on the afternoon of June 5, the 150 or so officers of the 474th Fighter Group were told to gather at the officers' club. Military police had been assigned to the club to make sure that no unauthorized personnel attended. Joe and his fellow officers of the 429th Squadron saw immediately that the walls were covered with maps, and they were told these maps depicted "the most meticulously planned military operation in history"—the invasion of Normandy.

One of the pilots at the meeting was Lieutenant L. C. Beck Jr., who recalled that as an officer stood by a large map, "The silence was unbelievable. Everyone hardly seemed to breathe." The officer was a Major Nute, acting as army liaison, who began by saying, "Gentlemen, tomorrow is D-Day." He then launched into a briefing of what he emphasized was the "greatest military operation in the history of the world." At the conclusion of the briefing, the flyers were given their radio call signs.

Adding to the solemnity of the gathering was the reading of a message from the Allied supreme commander. General Dwight Eisenhower referred to the imminent invasion as the "Great Crusade toward which we have striven these many months. The eyes of the world are upon you." The commander stressed to the men, "I have full confidence in your courage, devotion to duty and skill in battle. We will accept nothing less than full Victory."

The group chaplain, Leon Milner, then offered a very simple and direct prayer: "Give us strength, courage, guidance and understanding in the days to come, and protect us and our fellow men."

The specific assignment given to the 429th Squadron was to patrol the English Channel as the naval armada crossed east toward the beaches of Normandy. There was the possibility the Luftwaffe would try to inflict as much damage as possible before the Allied troops even reached the beaches.

While the P-38 Lightning pilots in Joe's squadron were inspired by General Eisenhower's stirring words and fully grasped the gravity of the moment, they also viewed the upcoming event as "just one more mission, more of the same. It was more significant for the higher-ups, who had to plan and sweat out the results." But for guys like Joe, "All we knew was that we had to climb into our airplanes every day, sometimes twice a day, cross the channel, do our duty as best we could and then hope for luck or the grace of God to get home so we could do the same the next day."

Yet there was a change to the routine. That night, instead of crossing the English Channel to attack enemy positions, the airmen flew above it, patrolling the fleet below. Because the night was dark with a cloud-filled sky, though, the pilots were unable to see clearly enough to fully realize the enormity of the fleet and thus they could not comprehend the scale of the invasion to come.

The 429th and other pilots of the 474th Fighter Group patrolled at 1,500 feet until 11 P.M., maintaining radio silence. The only action was one false alarm, a report of enemy fighters over the beach. When Joe and the others returned and climbed out of their cockpits, they looked up to see all manner of aircraft, including bombers and fighters and even gliders, streaming east overhead. According to the squadron history log, "Hundreds of red and green running lights could be seen as the planes passed overhead in close formation. It was the greatest show we had ever seen." Some of the crafts contained paratroopers, who would be the first American and British troops to land on French soil that day. The airmen hoped that they would soon be joined by many thousands more, thanks to a successful invasion.

For many pilots, June 6 was a long day full of activity. As Eric Hammel's *Air War Europa: Chronology* simply states for D-Day, "The 438th Troop Carrier Group's lead C-47, *Birmingham Belle*, takes off from its base in England at 2248 hours, June 5, with the lead elements of the 101st Airborne Division—and the invasion of France is on." Hammel also points out, "Every fighter group in the Eighth and Ninth air forces mounts at least one mission to France during the day."

Allied bombers continued to attack road and rail networks in an effort to isolate the invasion area and make it difficult for the Germans to bring up reinforcements and equipment. Other parts of northern France were also attacked to keep the Germans guessing as to where the invasion would actually occur. The night before, the Royal Air Force had dropped metal strips, code-named Widow, and dummy parachutists to confuse the Germans' radar and distract their forces.

Thanks to the Allies having secured air superiority over the English Channel, they had been able to collect a lot of information about German coastal defenses. This paid off on D-Day: Allied air forces flew over fourteen thousand sorties in support of the landings and did not have to do so blindly. Because of having been weakened by weeks of dogfights and the destruction of runways in France, the Luftwaffe turned out to be incapable of challenging most of the Allied missions. Later estimates contended that only one German sortie would be undertaken for every thirty-seven Allied ones.

The U.S. Army Air Forces flew almost nine thousand of those sorties, losing seventy-one aircraft. Ninth Air Force medium bombers performed particularly well at Utah Beach, where B-26s and A-20s destroyed most of the German heavy guns and mortars. The attacks were made at a low level with visual bombing, which enhanced their effectiveness. Accompanying the bombers were the pilots of the 429th, knowing they were an important part of one of the most dramatic events in world history. They also went on a dive-bombing mission of their own, led by Major Glass, to take out a bridge just south of Rouen.

There had been nothing like it before for the pilots crossing the Channel on D-Day. "As far as the eye could see," observed Lieutenant Beck, "came strings of ships and boats of every type. I tried to count them but gave up in the attempt. It was simply the greatest armada of ships, planes, paratroopers and men that ever stormed enemy shores."

Joe Moser managed to make it through D-Day unscathed, but at Warmwell there was some evidence of the carnage across the Channel. Some of the C-47 transport planes landed there because damage or dry fuel tanks prevented them from returning to their bases farther inland. Joe noticed one that had "one wing hanging down like the broken wing of a bird." The pilot was dead. Joe learned that during the first pass over the target in France, all but one paratrooper had jumped, so the pilot made a second pass. German small-arms fire from the ground peppered the plane, one bullet finding the pilot. The copilot took over, and the last paratrooper jumped.

As Joe and other members of the 429th Squadron, now safe on the ground, looked on, they saw that their "little strip was filled with broken men and machines, with cranes and ambulances hauling them off the runways so more could land or crash."

They could only imagine the ongoing violence on the other side of the English Channel. Soon, however, they would have a more up-close and personal look.

7

Two days after the Normandy landings, Joe Moser almost had his chance at a dogfight. The entire 474th Group felt liberated that more fighter squadrons than ever before were being unleashed from bomber escorts to attack ground targets in France. Each railroad hub or stretch of track or tank column or artillery installation that the P-38s and other planes hit softened up the German resistance. With luck and persistence, more of the Allied forces would be off the beaches and pushing their way east into France.

On June 8, Joe was on one of those attack missions. The target area was near Avranches, which was just beyond the beaches, and the Lightnings struck railway tracks and gun emplacements. The pilots spotted a tempting sight—three Focke-Wulf 190s flying close to the ground. The German pilots might not see the American birds of prey swooping in from above until it was too late. Whatever fight they put up would be exciting . . . but it would have to be left to the imagination. The P-38 fuel tanks were low, and a victory would sure have been tarnished by winding up in the English Channel.

Day after day, as the aerial attacks relentlessly continued, the Allied ground troops inched their way forward. The toll of men killed and wounded was horrendous, but this was not to be another Dunkirk—slow as they were, the invasion forces were clawing their way inland. Then, on June 16, there was a more personal piece of good news, when Joe and his fellow pilots of the 429th Squadron thought they saw a ghost: Lieutenant Buford Thacker. When last seen on May 7, his P-38 was on fire and going down, then had disappeared into a cloud bank. Yet there he was, strolling into their quarters at the Warmwell base. Thacker bore scars on his face from the heat and flames that had gotten to him before he jumped out of his Lightning, but otherwise he was alive and well.

Thacker told them a remarkable story of survival—first, managing to get out of his burning plane, then not being shot or captured by the Germans after his parachute delivered him to French soil. Members of the French underground had found Thacker before the Germans did. They helped him out of his flight suit and into the garb of a local peasant. After supplying him with food and water, an underground operative took Thacker in tow and guided him on a long journey that included crossing through the mountain range that was the border between France and Spain. On the seemingly endless trip, Thacker walked, sometimes bicycled at night, and even caught rides in horse-drawn carts. Thanks to what was by now a well-coordinated anti-Nazi network that helped downed pilots, within a few weeks Thacker was back in England.

The pilots not only were glad to see Thacker again but also saw his return as a hopeful sign that being shot out of the sky did not necessarily mean death or imprisonment. There was always a chance to survive and be reunited with friends. But sobering news confirmed what they had heard—the Germans had put up posters throughout occupied France that anyone caught helping a downed Allied pilot would be executed.

By this point in the war, Allied pilots had been getting shot down for almost five years and were well versed in what could happen. The first Allied airman to be captured by the Germans was a New Zealand Royal Air Force officer, Laurence Hugh Edwards. He was on a reconnaissance flight over the North Sea on September 3, 1939, when he was attacked by two enemy planes. Edwards became the first of twenty-six British and French airmen to wind up in prisoner of war camps before the end of that year, and there had been hundreds more since.

The 429th was also cheered to learn that Captain Merle Larson, still the squadron's operations leader, was to receive a fourteenth oak leaf cluster to his Air Medal "for his character and leadership." The presentation ceremony was set for June 21. On that day there would be a parade at the Warmwell base, with the medal to be bestowed immediately afterward. But fate intervened.

As the parade was winding down, the pilots were told there was a mission to be undertaken as soon as they could get their Lightnings in the air. A German airfield ten miles northwest of Dreux had to be destroyed or at least damaged enough to interfere with enemy fighter activity. Captain Larson led his squadron aloft and across the water to France. During the raid, his P-38 was hit by flak and caught fire. A sliver of hope was that Bill Banks, Larson's wingman on that day as well as the assistant flight leader, saw his captain parachuting down. Banks circled lower and lower and was able to see Larson land, extricate himself from the chute, and take off for the nearest cluster of trees.

Joe Moser was "devastated," he wrote. What happened was not only a blow to him but to the entire 429th because Larson was "probably the best officer in our unit—and the best pilot.

Somehow, if a crafty, careful and veteran fighter pilot like he could get it, any of us could. We were in a very dangerous game, and I think I felt more vulnerable at that time than any other."

There was a silver lining for the captain's men, in addition to Banks having seen him land safely: They knew that Larson had been shot down before, over North Africa, and had slipped through enemy lines to safety. Especially with the grit Larson had, "lightning" could strike twice.

However much the German positions were being battered, it did not get any easier for the Allied invaders. Hopes that the war in the European Theater might be over by Christmas—not too high to begin with—diminished with each day that the Allies were bogged down. Paris was not getting any closer as the Germans fought to retain every inch they occupied. The 429th Squadron and other fighter and bomber units flew hundreds of sorties.

The cost continued to be high, with no unit of flyers immune to loss. June 29 saw the latest example, when Lieutenant Paul Heuerman of the 429th was shot down. It was not known if he survived.

An encouraging sign that there had been enough of a push into the interior to safely establish Allied air bases in western France occurred at the end of the month, when the squadron was briefed about moving across the Channel. It was discouraging that the Allied ground forces had managed to take only thirty miles of territory in three weeks, yet there was a sense that German resistance might be weakening as the losses in personnel and equipment mounted. The airmen were excited about the prospect of being in newly liberated land, but as Joe mused, they "knew that a forward airfield just behind the lines would not live up to the standards we enjoyed in England."

While the flyers waited for the order to pack their kits, Joe finally was given some time off, having beaten the odds to complete thirty missions against the enemy. The pass for seven days felt like one for a month. He went to the nearby resort town of Bournemouth. The weather that freewheeling week was sunny and warm, and he stayed in a hotel . . . but he did not necessarily have a good time.

Joe could not shake the loss of Captain Larson, noting that it "affected me more than any other of the now frequent losses." Because he had been such a good flight leader, "I felt fearful and vulnerable that he was gone, and while I tried not to let it show, it must have." Overall about his combat service, Joe had a heavy heart: "Too many missions, too many friends lost. How much longer could I last? I could never escape the reality that very soon I would be climbing back into that cramped cockpit and facing a very dangerous and uncertain future."

It was something of a relief to return to Warmwell, where he did not have to pretend to be happy and relaxed. While Joe had been gone that last week of June, the men of the 474th Fighter Group had been cheered by a letter received by General Quesada that was passed along to and shared by Lieutenant Colonel Wasem, the group's commanding officer. It was written by Lieutenant General Omar Bradley, commander of the First U.S. Army. Quesada prefaced the letter by stating, "The Fighter-Bomber boys are doing more to make this campaign a success than anyone ever anticipated. The versatility of our effort is a tremendous contribution. The manner in which each boy has performed his mission and manner in which he has exercised initiative is a source of great pride."

For his part, Bradley wrote that the pilots of the P-38s and other fighters' "ability to disrupt the enemy's communications, supply and movement of troops has been a vital factor in our rapid progress in expanding our beachhead." He added, "I realize that their work may not catch the headlines any more than does the work of some of our foot soldiers, but I am sure that I express the feelings of every ground force commander from squad leaders to myself as Army Commander when I extend my congratulations on their very fine work."

One would think that this July 4th would be more special than most of the previous ones since American independence was declared in 1776. However, given the pace of daily missions, the losses, and the encroaching exhaustion among the pilots, no celebration preparations had been made. This was lamented that night during dinner, which was also attended by several RAF pilots. Even though it was Great Britain that America had forced its independence from, the visitors were not about to let the Yanks mope the rest of the night.

Two of the RAF pilots snuck out of the officers' club and made for the control tower. There they pushed into their pockets Very pistols—a large-bore handgun that discharges flares—and a supply of shells. Soon afterward, the men inside the club heard a commotion and hurried to the windows. As reported in the 429th's history, "A wondrous sight met our eyes." The two RAF pilots were "chasing each other back and forth across the lawn, firing red and green signal flares at each other. As fast as one could reload, he would turn and pursue his friendly opponent until the other could reload on the run. It was a beautiful exhibition!" Not sharing the high spirits was an RAF wing commander who was in a bathroom next to the officers' club when one of the red flares came through the window and began to bounce off the walls. The commander exploded out of the bathroom, his trousers still wrapped around his ankles.

On the morning of July 12, with Joe back in the cockpit of his P-38 Lightning, the squadron hit railroad tracks and yards in the Rennes, Angers, and Laval region. The pilots estimated they destroyed or at least damaged a hundred railroad cars. Two days later, there was another price to pay when a pilot named Moore was killed.

On July 18, Joe missed out on yet another opportunity for a dogfight. He was not on the roster for an early-morning mission that ran into a fleet of German fighters. The army publication *Stars and Stripes* would report that as units of the Ninth Air Force were bombing a railway bridge crossing the Eure River south of Pacy-sur-Eure they were attacked by over fifty Focke-Wulf 190s.

According to the 429th's official history, "Dog fights raged all over the sky above the little town of Merey, on eastward toward Evreux, north toward the Seine. Within a matter of minutes, there were 190s and P-38s too. Wherever one looked, there were P-38s on 190s' tails. Soon, the wave of the attack had been broken, but there was no time to think of the score. Scarcely had the Group begun to reform to set a course for home when the second formation of Germans hit."

Although outnumbered almost two to one, the Lightnings destroyed ten of the enemy, probably destroyed another six and damaged fourteen—and managed to demolish the bridge.

But there would be another pilot missing at dinner that night at Warmwell: Lieutenant Glenn Goodrich. Like Joe Moser, Goodrich hailed from the state of Washington. He had enlisted in June 1942, but during his physical exam in Seattle he was deemed not suitable to be a pilot because his teeth were too crooked to be a good fit for an oxygen mask. Goodrich did not give up and was allowed to be a glider pilot. By December 1943, the army had done enough dental work on him and was getting hungry enough for new combat pilots that Goodrich was welcomed with full wings. He arrived at Warmwell on June 14 to become part of the Retail Gang.

On that morning of July 18, Goodrich had been the wingman of Lieutenant Banks. During the aerial fighting, his plane was hit and began going down. Once it became clear he could not stop the dive, Goodrich should have bailed out. But he could see that his plane was heading right at the village of La Forte and that the impact would be like a flaming bomb to its inhabitants. Goodrich remained in the cockpit and with what little control he had of the P-38, managed to crash it into an open field.* Understandably, Joe had at most a muted celebration when it became official that day that he had been promoted to first lieutenant.

Later that month, he flew in a mission that best illustrated the strength of the Ninth Air Force and General Quesada's mandate of effective ground support. July 25 saw the closest coordination to date between ground and air forces, an operation that the war reporter Ernie Pyle described as one of the major achievements of the Allies in the European Theater.

German resistance had proved to be frustratingly stubborn. Though the Allied troops and their tanks and other equipment had managed to push on from the Normandy beaches, they had not gotten nearly as far eastward as planners had anticipated, or, at least, hoped. The strategy devised was threefold—B-17s and other heavy bombers would hit the area ahead, where infantry would aim to reach; medium bombers would strike west of that; and the fighters of the 474th Group would strafe and drop their bombs closest to the Allied forward positions. This would require precision . . . but to be on the safe side, as the clock ticked down to the attacks, the ground troops marked the edges of their positions with red flares. Bombs falling behind them were the dreaded

---

* Goodrich's parents in Washington did not receive the official KIA telegram until April 11, 1945. The people of Longnes, next to La Forte, had recovered his remains. They were sent to the United States in June 1949 and buried in the cemetery in Ellensville, where he had grown up. For years the Goodrich family received letters from residents of that area in France praising his heroism and sacrifice. A monument to Goodrich stands in the center of the town square in Longnes.

friendly fire. The operation was a big success and was credited with the long-sought breakout from the beaches deeper into the interior of western France.

Two days later, the 429th suffered another hard loss when Banks did not return from a mission. Eerily, in his base lodging he had begun as one of six men occupying its bunks, and on the morning of July 27 he was the only one left. Ever since the loss of Captain Larson, Banks had fretted about the room being jinxed.

On that hot and bright day, elements of the 474th were on an armed reconnaissance mission when two dozen Bf 109s attacked. During the ensuing dogfight, a P-38 from the 430th Squadron struck Banks's Lightning, shearing off part of one wing. Despite his efforts to control the plane, it went into a downward spin. Banks did manage to jump free, and the last the other pilots saw of him was his parachute. When they returned to Warmwell, Banks's friends boarded up the room—no one would risk residing there.

Finally, the time had come: By the end of July, thanks to the breakout from the beaches and the demonstration of how effective close air support of ground troops could be, the Allies had secured enough territory to establish air bases in France. The 429th as well as other squadrons were told to pack up and be ready to head across the English Channel, which the first units began doing on the thirty-first. By then, a second bronze oak leaf cluster had been added to Joe's Air Medal. More important, he noted, "I was alive and still fighting."

Then it was the turn of the 429th Squadron to make the move. The ground crew personnel were ferried across the channel in Landing Craft, Infantry, known as LCIs. It was a rough-enough journey for some of the landlubbers to get seasick, and all were grateful the crossing was being made in early August, not March. For Joe and the other pilots, watching the English Channel pass by below was old hat. In fact, on the day that the big move began, they flew out of Warmwell, attacked the railroad line between Laval and Verneuil, and landed at their new home, even though bulldozers were still working at it.

The airfield was being created in a field near Neuilly-la-Forêt, just inland from the port city of Isigny-sur-Mer. More than half of it had been destroyed by two German bombardments on June 8, but rebuilding was underway. The beleaguered residents had been buoyed six days after the attacks by a visit from General Charles de Gaulle.*

Once the bulldozers had completed their work on the airfield, a steel-mesh landing carpet was laid down, resulting in a functioning takeoff and landing strip. The 429th log observed, "Stray German cavalry horses are pastured along with many cows in the lush grassland around our tents, and fresh milk is delivered to our doorsteps on the hoof. As a matter of fact, the cows are so numerous we often have to drive them away to make room for our equipment. Apples and blackberries now augment our daily diet of K rations."

At first, there was some bad news—their new quarters consisted only of an enclave of tents, making their former accommodations at Warmwell ritzy by comparison. But the next day there was excellent news—two pilots who had been reported missing turned up alive. One of them was Bill Banks. Even better, they were in Allied hands, with Banks already in London. Perhaps boarding up that jinxed room had made the difference. It was assumed that Banks was doing his best to rejoin the 429th.

On the afternoon of August 9, that day's mission having been

---

* Generations earlier, a resident of the town was Jean-Christophe d'Isigny. Over time the last name gradually transformed to Disney, and that line eventually produced Walt Disney.

completed, Joe and the other men of the 429th were back at their
tent camp and "a young man came sauntering down the first road
leading to our Operations tent," the log reports. "He was wearing
a well-tailored, worsted suit of French design, and from a distance
we supposed he was just another Frenchman out looking for his
family. But there was something familiar in his walk." Indeed, he
was another one of theirs thought lost, Roland Levey. After ex-
changing hugs and handshakes, he explained that on July 5, when
his plane was hit, he managed to belly-land it northwest of Châ-
teaubriant. He walked north and came to a large house containing
"an extremely cooperative family." They took him in, keeping him
hidden and fed for four weeks. When Levey heard the Allied front
lines had advanced to only a few miles away, he set off to meet
them.

For Joe Moser, a more personal bit of good news was being
named as flight leader of his group. Thankfully, he was not su-
perstitious about that position previously being held by Larson
and Banks. His view was a pragmatic one: "I was excited but also
aware of the considerable responsibility. The lives of other men
were in my hands." He was still over a month shy of his twenty-
third birthday.

Another drawback to the Neuilly-la-Forêt base in addition to
its sparse lodging soon became apparent. The Germans quickly
caught on that to attack American bases, they did not have to
fly across the English Channel, and they could save fuel too by
striking the new targets in France. As Joe put it, "The Luftwaffe
gave us a little of our own medicine." The members of the 429th
Squadron and other units had to dive for cover during attacks,
when enemy bombs rained down on them. To the pilots, especially, "it was clear to most of us that dropping bombs was better
than having them dropped on you."

Another danger was that the Germans had planted mines in

the surrounding fields before retreating. This was discovered the hard way when an ordnance truck carrying five-hundred-pound bombs to the base drove over a mine. In the explosion, two men were killed and two were badly wounded. The blast was close enough to the base that shrapnel shredded several tents. There were also fears that the base would be targeted by enemy artillery. It was only a mile from the American landing sites of Omaha and Utah beaches, still being hit to disrupt arriving supplies, so shells falling short could hit Neuilly-la-Forêt by accident.

But overriding such concerns was the knowledge that the Germans were beginning to give ground in larger and larger chunks, thanks in large part to the support provided by the aerial missions. Joe noted, "Bombing lines—those lines on maps that indicated where it was safe to bomb without hitting our own troops—had to be changed continually as new reports came in. The pace accelerated, and the general direction was toward Paris." The French capital was 120 miles to the east—a goal that had appeared insurmountable was now becoming, inch by grinding inch, approachable.

The missions of the 429th became even more aggressive, and a new prey was added to the usual fare of bridges and rail lines: tanks. On the afternoon of August 11, the squadron was informed that a cluster of Tiger tanks treading toward the front had been spotted nine miles east of the Normandy town of Domfront. By the time Joe in his P-38 and the other Lightnings arrived, loaded with two 1,000-pound bombs each and led by Captain "Pappy" Holcomb (replacing Captain Larson), the tanks had separated and entered a wooded area to become less visible targets. The pilots did not have to worry about being selective, because with that kind of heavy ordnance, they simply wiped out the entire woods. The Tiger tanks would not be firing on Allied troops to the west.

There was another bonus the following day. When attacking an airfield near Évreux, the P-38 pilots saw a collection of Heinkel 111 bombers that were unable to take off fast enough. They joined the airfield's hangars in being destroyed.

With each day there was more confidence that the enemy, with its dwindling hope of stanching the flow of Allied forces deeper into France and toward Paris, would give ground. The 429th Squadron log crowed that "the Krauts are put on the run. The German armies have finally been crowded out of their foxholes, their hedgerows, their villages and towns. The enemy is dropping back. We receive rapid changes in our bomb lines."

On the next day, August 13, Joe would be part of a reconnaissance run in the Rambouillet area. He had gotten this far without a serious mishap; maybe he would get out of this thing yet in one piece. Every day he beat the odds, he was closer to maxing out on missions—he now had forty-three under his belt—and being rotated back to the States and, eventually, home. Many of the squadron's pilots felt that with the war going so well, it was all right to think that way.

8

O n his forty-fourth mission, Joe Moser would be the leader of F flight with the call sign "Censor Red Leader." The previous afternoon, when he had looked at the list of pilots who would be taking off posted on one wall of the briefing tent at their new base, his name was just one name. Nothing special. Joe and the others were awoken at 6:30 that morning, August 13, by a sergeant shouting from tent to tent. Yawning and stretching, the pilots tugged on T-shirts and wool pants and flight suits and ankle-length leather shoes.

When they left their tents, there was no surprise about the day being hot and hazy. Sweat began to leak under their outfits. Well, what else would one expect in western France in mid-August? The pilots shuffled over to the outdoor tables, where they were served powdered eggs and what was called coffee but was a poor substitute for the real thing. At 8:30, the flyers were inside a stifling tent for a briefing given by Major Burl Glass, still the commanding officer of the 429th Squadron. He would not be leading that day's mission; Colonel Wasem had given himself that assignment. Selected from the 429th and the two other squadrons were thirteen P-38 pilots who would soon be lifting off. No one remarked that this was not the luckiest of numbers.

It was then that Joe learned he would be one of the flight leaders. F flight would consist of four planes. Joe glanced at his wingman, chosen by Major Glass. This pilot had been in the 429th only a couple of months. Joe had flown on a few missions with him but did not know him. For some reason, "I was a little uneasy. It wasn't unusual for me to not know him well, as I am a pretty quiet guy and tend to keep to myself a fair bit." Joe said nothing to Major Glass. If a pilot protested his assignment every time he felt uneasy, the skies over France would be a lot emptier.

The major told the men gathered in the briefing tent that they would be on an armed reconnaissance mission. That plus the possibility of bombing and strafing targets on the ground meant the Lightnings would be flying at only four thousand feet. This would make for some hot and uncomfortable pilots, because unlike when serving as Flying Fortress escorts at thirty thousand feet, that was not high enough for cold air. Add to that what the typical P-38 pilot wore: a flight suit, anti-gravity suit, leather helmet and goggles, an oxygen mask, and a parachute strapped to his back—all on top of the T-shirt and wool pants. It was like being wrapped in a thick blanket. Joe likely recalled the comfort of cool summer mornings back in northwest Washington State.

Their destination was Rambouillet, a town ten miles from Versailles. Previous reconnaissance had ascertained that reinforcements being rushed to the fragile German front lines were coming from that direction. The pilots would observe the number of tanks, supply trucks, and any other vehicles heading west— and if the circumstances allowed, dive down and take some of them out. "If it moves, smash it," Major Glass instructed. Then, referring to the tanks that had been destroyed and damaged on the mission two days earlier, he added, "Let's find some more Tigers."

The hybrid squadron led by Colonel Wasem took off at 10 A.M. Joe reflected, "I never really got over the thrill of putting my hand over the twin throttles of the fighter and feeling the vibration and acceleration as the power of almost 3000 horses pulled me over the rough runway and into the air." Once in formation, the Lightnings flew east.

For Joe, leading his four-plane group generated even more sweat. If the enemy appeared and he had to make decisions, the wrong ones could cost lives. He repeatedly scanned the skies, though he knew, "Invariably, it is the enemy you don't see that will get you." For the most part, that was what had cost a quarter of the 429th Squadron's pilots to be killed or reported missing since the unit had begun operations out of Warmwell that spring. Those pilots and planes had been replaced, but the toll felt like a raw wound.

Unlike in the spring, when the invasion of France was still a vague hope, Joe and the other pilots now knew that the bloody Normandy landing had been successful and that the breakout a couple of weeks earlier was gaining momentum. They all knew the name of General Courtney Hodges, the Georgia native who had enlisted as a private in 1906 and risen through the ranks to now, when he had just assumed command of the First Army from General Bradley, who was being kicked upstairs. It was the First Army that was spearheading the drive toward Paris, and General Quesada was making sure his Ninth Air Force provided every ounce of support it could.

Missions like the ones the 474th was flying this hot August morning were even more important now, with the advancing ground troops needing to know what lay ahead. Even better was if the fighters could put a hurt on the enemy before the troops and tanks got there. Paris was getting closer faster.

The anxiety Joe felt being a flight leader was not helped by the thick haze. He found it hard to see what else was in the air, let alone on the ground. Another reason to be extra vigilant was that the haze raised the risk of the P-38s drifting farther away from one another. They all knew a squadron in a tight formation was the least vulnerable to attack. Radio contact was simply not sufficient; the pilots had to be in visual contact with each other.

Though one day seemed to blend into the next and the routine of flying missions from the Isigny-sur-Mer base was well established, on that morning Joe was aware it was a Sunday. Back in Ferndale, he and his mother and brother and sisters would be getting ready to attend Mass at St. Joseph's. Who knows, if the war had not interfered, he might be escorting a girlfriend or meeting her at the church. Heck, he might even be married. It had been two years since Joe had enlisted in the army, and a lot could have transpired during that time.

From what Joe could see as the sortie cruised at four thousand feet, it appeared to be a peaceful Sunday morning in the French countryside. He saw fields, most of them green, laid out in uneven patches: "They meandered through the countryside, separated by the impassable hedgerows in a way that seemed at once haphazard and still carefully ordered." Joe was not there to sightsee, though, so he kept a sharp eye out for possible targets.

One materialized. He saw a rail line . . . but as he followed it, he could find no trains on it. Then through the haze he thought he glimpsed a gathering of trucks. Joe banked slightly left, and the three other planes in his flight followed their leader. Trucks, all right, a cluster of maybe a half dozen of them. Had to be German because no Allied vehicles could possibly have traveled this far east, a few miles from Dreux. The convoy appeared to have halted on the road leading to the village of Houdan. Whatever the holdup was, the Germans were taking a risk, perhaps counting on its being a quiet Sunday morning and the possibility that the American flyers were giving themselves a break.

They were about to be rudely proved wrong. Joe radioed the three other pilots, "Truck convoy on the road. I'm going in." His wingman would be right behind him, and if all went well, the other two P-38s would follow. Perhaps with one pass each and unloading the five-hundred-pound bombs the Lightnings carried, the convoy would vanish from the otherwise bucolic landscape.

Joe dove and his plane picked up speed. He had the center of the convoy in his windscreen: "My fingers were on the bomb release, and I hoped to see the satisfying explosion as German equipment, ammunition and fuel erupted."

What he saw a few moments later was flak, and plenty of it. Suddenly, Joe understood that he had flown into a trap. His Lightning was surrounded by angry puffs of smoke. There must have been a German battery hidden nearby with the trucks as bait, just waiting for overeager pilots—like him. Since he was almost down to two hundred feet, Joe figured he'd release his bombs anyway and pull up to get out of harm's way. And then his P-38 was hit. Joe felt it shudder and guessed a 37-mm shell had gotten it. The proof was when he saw his left engine on fire.

He managed to climb to the northwest and away from the flak. There was no sign of the other three planes, and Joe prayed they had seen the flak in time to avoid being hit. Some flight leader he was, falling for such a simple ruse. In case they were still in range, Joe radioed, "Censor Red Leader. My left engine on fire. Returning to base." There was no response.

It was a lot easier to radio that he was returning to base than to actually do it with an engine on fire. He shut it down, hoping the air flow from the Lightning would blow the fire out like a birthday candle. He recalled from those countless hours of training what he had to do: "I feathered the propeller, stopping it from freewheeling to reduce drag. Full throttle on the right engine to get as much altitude as possible and head west." And he abruptly realized he still carried the five-hundred-pound bombs under his wings, with a left engine on fire.

Joe saw an empty stretch of road below and no sign of French vehicles or people walking or bicycling. Following it directly above, he let the bombs go. He turned the P-38 west. He sure hoped no German fighters happened to spot him. So far, so good. Well, maybe not so good: "I looked at the engine, praying that the fire would die down or go out. It was growing."

Nothing else to do but keep climbing, scratching and clawing for as much altitude as possible to improve his chances of at least getting to the American front lines. He envisioned the Lightning landing in a field "with American soldiers running up to me, pounding me on the back and personally thanking me for helping take out those tanks and ammunition trains."

But the fire kept growing. Joe kept climbing. He was at 2,500 feet. He felt good about his chances. He'd always had a fair amount of confidence about his abilities and that of his P-38. "Even now, with my plane on fire, I was sure I would get home and see my family again." However, he could feel the heat from the fire getting stronger with each passing mile.

Joe could barely see the engine anymore; it was covered in flames. Now the flames were on the wing too, inching toward the cockpit. He was at three thousand feet. He thought if he could get five more minutes, he might be close enough to the American lines . . . maybe. But then that no longer mattered. The flames were licking the cockpit. Very soon, maybe only a couple of minutes, he would be on fire.

He was out of time. Joe pulled the release, and the plexiglass canopy blew away. The sudden rush of air was burning hot. Joe knew if he did not bail out, he would be roasted alive. But bailing out was not an appealing option—P-38 pilots knew how tough that was and how many Lightnings had crashed with their pilots caught on the tail. But doing so was the only choice left to him.

With his speed having slowed during the climb, Joe figured the best option was to flip the plane over and simply fall out of it. He unstrapped his harness. He may have resented the parachute on his back before when the heat of the morning was uncomfortable, but Joe was very grateful for it now. He yanked the buckles loose from the straps holding him to his seat. The flames had advanced to the cusp of the cockpit. The altimeter told him he was at 3,200 feet. If he could just get a few more miles west . . .

Nope, was not going to happen. There was a sudden explosion as the glass window on the left side of the cockpit burst apart. Burning shards of metal and glass flew around. One of them, as if with cruel intent, managed to get under his flight suit to burn his back. Flames followed through the opening, searing his left arm.

Time had run out. Joe's only choice was to bail out or burn up. He flipped the P-38 over, said a quick prayer, and dropped out . . . or tried to. He discovered that he was stuck, because the toe of his leather boot was caught in the metal plate the canopy had been hinged to. He was halfway out of the P-38 but connected to it by his boot, upside-down and facing forward.

If he could not get his boot free, when the P-38 plunged to earth, he would go with it.

9

With hot waves of wind crashing against him, Joe could not curl his body and reach up to wrench his boot free of the hinge or to unlace it and hope his foot would simply slip out. He tried twisting and turning his leg, to no avail. He wondered how long he could be upside-down with blood rushing to his brain before he would pass out. Crashing, however, would take care of all considerations.

The wind turned out to be his ally. It pushed at him powerfully enough that suddenly his boot was wrenched free of the cockpit. Then the wind betrayed him by trying to force him back to the tail. That offered two unappealing choices: getting his parachute pack caught on it or being knocked unconscious by it and not even getting to pull the cord. His enemy now was the flat blade between the two fuselage booms. Joe craned his neck to a painful angle to see it. The wind buffeted him as he stared, waiting for the plane, with its power shut off, to begin a trip down to the ground. When the tail fell away, he would pull the cord and let go.*

Every second was like an hour as Joe willed the tail to fall away. He held on to the plane with his left hand and with his right clutched the ring of the ripcord. He was suspended over three thousand feet in the air and the wind grabbed at him, urging him toward the tail. He wanted to angrily shout at it: "Why are you taking me with you?" And finally he did shout, "Come on, get out of my way!"

Joe began to panic. He had no other options—either the tail made room for him to fall or he crashed with his plane into the French countryside, possibly burning alive as he descended. "The pressure from the wind felt it could pull my body apart, torso from leg," he later recalled. "Something had to give and had to give soon."

Finally, the nose of the P-38 lowered, causing the tail to rise enough that, he hoped, it would not catch him when he let go. There was only one way to find out, and the flames would not let him hesitate. Joe let go of the plane. In an instant, he was clear of the tail and he tugged the ripcord. As the parachute opened, he glanced down and saw the brown-green ground amazingly close, and getting closer as he fell at 400 mph. Then the silk dome above him filled fully with air and he was almost jerked out of his senses. Adding to the surreal experience was hearing a "crump" sound and seeing an explosion on the ground and then realizing that was his beloved Lightning being utterly destroyed. He had escaped the same fate by only a few seconds.

---

* The tail would not literally fall away. What Joe hoped was that when the nose of the plane angled downward, the tail of the plane would angle upward. Thus, when he let go, it was less likely he would be carried into it; instead, he would fall unimpeded.

There was no time to contemplate this. The ground rose up to greet him and then he dropped onto it, legs first. Miraculously, the bones in them did not shatter. Joe fell backward, first on his butt, then his back. He could not move and prayed he was just stunned, not paralyzed. He was able to twist his neck and head and see that he was in a freshly cut grain field. Easily visible was the plume of black smoke spewing from the burning remains of his plane.

Joe felt a sudden fear—not for himself, but from the realization that when his plane crashed it may have killed any farmers working in the field. He managed to get to his feet, grateful that none of his more important bones, at least, seemed to be broken. His fear doubled as he saw that the blazing debris was next to a farmhouse, making it more likely local people had been at risk. Joe felt a surge of shame: "What if there were kids in there? I should have stayed with that plane. I should have just crash-landed it somewhere where it couldn't hurt anybody. I was trying so hard to save my own life, to get back to the lines, but I might have killed some poor innocent people."

Then it occurred to him that whether or not anyone had been killed or injured, that plume of black smoke was sure to be seen by the Germans. No sense standing in the field agonizing over what could not be undone. Joe slipped out of the harness and began to collect the white silk parachute. When his arms were full he turned to search for a place to hide it and saw that several men were running toward him.

They were not wearing uniforms; instead, they were obviously farmers, and they were grinning. Joe could not understand what they were saying because they talked so fast, but they exuberantly clapped him on the back and took turns shaking his hand. They seemed to be thanking him and all Americans for coming to liberate France from the Nazis. A minute later, the mood changed. Everyone realized they were all exposed in the middle of a field with a P-38 Lightning burning about three hundred yards away. Joe remembered the posters warning that Frenchmen found to be aiding a downed Allied pilot could be summarily shot.

Joe was urged to remove his leather helmet and his flight and anti-gravity suits. They were taken from him along with the parachute. By now there were two dozen farmworkers surrounding the downed American in the field. One man—Joe would later learn his name was François Vermeulen—gave instructions to the others; then he motioned for Joe to come with him. His glance at the dirt road at one end of the field conveyed that any moment German vehicles could appear on it, drawn from the village of Marchefroy by the telltale tower of dark smoke.

The farmworkers spread out, returning to their labors in the field. Joe, wearing only his pants and T-shirt and boots (a piece of leather had been gouged out of the left one), became just another worker gathering stalks of cut grain. He worked alongside Vermeulen. Only a minute later they heard the sound of a vehicle approaching. Joe glanced over his shoulder and saw a moving dust cloud coming closer. There were nervous smiles on the faces of his fellow laborers.

Joe recognized the distinctive sound of a motorcycle. When it appeared, those in the field saw two German soldiers, one driving and the other perched in a sidecar. It turned off the dirt road into the field and, ignoring the French workers, drove directly to the wreckage. The fire was out by now, but black smoke still rose from the pile of twisted and half-melted metal. Joe felt sweat soaking his shirt and pants as he furtively followed the motorcycle with quick glances. After it came to a stop, the Germans got off it and began to slowly walk around the smoldering remains of the Lightning.

After five minutes, the motorcycle started up. Again, as though the French workers did not exist, the soldiers rode past them to the edge of the field, turned onto the dirt road, and headed back toward Marchefroy. Joe felt himself "get weak and at the same time my heart get lighter. Two close calls in one day. Thank you, dear Mother." The dust cloud became more distant, then disappeared.

The hot August sun was directly overhead, indicating it was around noon. It seemed incredible to Joe that he had taken off from the 429th Squadron's base only two hours earlier.

Vermeulen issued a fresh batch of instructions. He told two men—one of whom was his younger brother—to guide Joe through the field to a wooded area about four hundred yards away that separated the field from the one beyond it. However, an older man objected, pointing to another and larger wooded area that had to be more than a mile away. Joe understood the older man—most likely more Germans would arrive soon and they would search the immediate surroundings first. Vermeulen nodded.

Without delay, Joe and the two young men set off at a quick pace. "My years of running nearly five miles every night after football practice from Ferndale High School back to our farm came to mind. This would be easy—even with my banged-up legs and back."

And even wearing leather boots, it felt good to run. Joe found himself smiling. Putting aside that he had been shot out of the sky, he had been pretty lucky so far. It was August, he could hide out in the woods through the night and then be moved along west from village to village until reaching the Allied lines. Or he could be hidden until the lines came to him as the ground troops fought their way deeper into France. Look how Thacker had just showed up that June day at Warmwell after being thought lost for good. "I felt halfway home already just running across that field."

Then he heard the motor of another vehicle. It sounded like the motorcycle once again. The dust cloud reappeared. Without saying anything to each other, Joe and the two men began to run faster. They could be easily seen in an open field, and the only hope to avoid that was to reach the woods before the Germans arrived. But the sound of the motorcycle this time was louder and more urgent. It was closing in on them. Joe heard cries of "Halt! Halt!"

Joe kept running. But the two Frenchmen abruptly stopped. After a few more strides, so did Joe. He could not leave the two others to face the Germans alone. Anyway, he was too far from the shelter of the trees to have a chance of getting there without taking a bullet in the back. Joe turned to find his companions facing the two German soldiers, who held rifles.

One of the young Frenchmen gave Joe a look that meant "Don't talk." He could do that: "We had been trained to pretend to be deaf and dumb if we were captured. No problem. I was a quiet guy anyway. Avoiding the temptation to talk would be easy."

The farmworkers pulled identification papers out of their pockets. After scanning them, the Germans asked questions. To Joe, the answers sounded like they were explaining why he was unable to communicate.

One of the Germans used the barrel of his rifle to push the two workers aside. He stepped up to Joe and searched his pockets. Everything Joe had in them had been hidden under a shock of grain. Then the soldier touched Joe on the chest, feeling metal underneath the sodden T-shirt: dog tags. With a laugh the German reached down, grabbed them, and pulled them up over Joe's head.

That tore it: the tags confirmed he was an American flyer. The same soldier asked, "Wo ist der andere Flieger?"

Joe did not understand and could only stare in response. The question was repeated. Then Joe got it—"flieger" was "flyer" and "andere" was "other." The Germans thought there had been two men in the downed plane. This interpretation was confirmed when Joe looked past the two soldiers and saw the field now filling with more soldiers conducting a search. For what it mattered now, the older French farmer had been right—there were Germans emerging from the smaller and closer section of woods.

The two motorcycle soldiers began to interrogate Joe's companions with a mixture of German and French. Apparently, the wreckage that had survived the flames indicated the American plane had been a big one—and indeed, the Lightning was larger than the Mustang and Thunderbolt—so there had to be another pilot, and possibly a crew if the craft had been a small bomber. Joe, continuing his silence, just shrugged.

Several soldiers arrived and they ordered the two young Frenchmen to come with them. Others took Joe in tow, in a different direction. He prayed for the safety of the two farmworkers as he was prodded through the grain field, now a prisoner of Nazi Germany.

He was urged toward the site of the wreckage. As Joe gazed at the charred remains of his plane, which had shared thousands and thousands of miles of missions with him, Joe was inundated with more questions. He ignored them; plus, he understood next to nothing anyway. He was glad that the crash had not set the farm field on fire. He was even more relieved that his plane had not destroyed the farmhouse maybe twenty feet away. As it was, the ground was littered with roof tiles blown loose by the explosion at impact.

The soldiers grew tired of questioning him, and they all

stood in silence as the search continued. Finally, about an hour later, the Germans, very hot and tired and thirsty, gave up. Joe too felt the peak heat of the day, but all he cared about were the two young Frenchmen and the likelihood that he would soon be in a prisoner of war camp. Already, he was curious whether, wherever the camp was, pilots he knew would be there.

A rifle poked him. It was time to move—he would have to walk to Marchefroy.

His boots kicked up small clouds of dust on the dirt road during the two-kilometer trek to the village. It was just three square miles in size and contained only a couple of hundred people, especially at this time of the war, with many of its men of fighting age gone . . . or killed by the occupiers.

Once in the village, Joe was guided where to walk by pokes of a rifle snout in his back. The group stopped in front of a building in what appeared to be the town square. Joe was escorted into a small office. Once his eyes adjusted to the dark interior, he saw what he believed to be a Gestapo officer sitting behind a desk. The German remained seated as he gazed at the prisoner. Joe gazed back, hoping this would be nothing more than a perfunctory interview before he was shipped off to a POW camp.

At last the officer spoke in English: "Sit down."

There was a chair facing the desk, and Joe sank into it while trying not to reveal how tired he was from the walk to Marchefroy in the heat. He and the young officer—perhaps thirty years old—stared at each other. At last, the Gestapo officer inquired what had been Joe's mission when he was shot down. The query was in English with a heavy accent.

"Joseph Frank Moser. First lieutenant, United States Air Corps, 0755999."

The officer appeared to have expected this response and was amused. He became less so, however, as the interrogation continued.

He asked for the type of plane, where Joe had taken off from, his squadron, and, it seemed, anything else that popped into his head. To each question Joe responded with his name, rank, and serial number.

Joe almost laughed when the officer asked where his fellow crew members were hiding. Apparently, it was driving the Germans crazy that other American flyers were out there somewhere. But Joe answered that particular query—insisting he had been the lone pilot of the downed aircraft—because he did not want the French farmworkers facing questions or worse, especially for nothing.

After as many as fifty questions, the officer paused and resumed the stare from before, but it was a much harder one this time. Clearly, he was angry. At any moment, Joe believed, the officer might order the guards to beat him. In the hands of the Gestapo, anything was possible. However, "I would not give in. I would give them nothing. They could kill me but they would not break me, of that I was convinced as I could be. But I was awfully scared."

After several more questions, the officer became convinced too. He ordered two guards to remove the prisoner. Pokes from rifle barrels coaxed Joe outside, where the bright sunlight was dizzying. The soldiers brought him to a small building made of stone two blocks away. Joe had hoped to find an opportunity to escape. But this building did not look promising. The thick wooden door was opened and he was prodded inside. The cool, damp air was like that of a cellar, perhaps one that had once stored wine. Several seconds later, when his eyes had once more adjusted, Joe saw he was in a single large room with a dirt floor. The only object he spotted was a simple garden hoe. Then the door slammed shut and he could not see a thing.

To further secure his dark isolation, Joe heard a motor start and then the sound of a truck backing up. Once it was against the door, the engine was turned off. There was absolutely no way out now. And he had a very nervous feeling that a POW camp was not what waited next for him, even though that made no sense.

— 10 —

There was nothing reassuring about being a prisoner alone in the dark. Joe Moser was trapped in a building made of stone with just one door that was not only a heavy wooden one but had a truck backed up against it. He had been interrogated once by the Gestapo and could expect another and probably harsher dose of that. Even with his eyes now used to the dark interior, there was not anything to see. But wait, there *was* something to see—the hoe. "If there was one thing a farm boy from Ferndale, Washington, could do," he mused, "it was dig."

Joe sat down against one wall, allowing for time to go by, and hoped he'd almost been forgotten about by the guards. However, "I could hardly stand the wait. I was eager to accomplish my escape." He imagined himself under cover of darkness furtively following the streets to the west that led out of Marchefroy. He would hide in woods, maybe just for a couple of days, and then spot the point men for American troops advancing through the countryside.

After arriving triumphantly at the Isigny-sur-Mer base and accepting the congratulations of his fellow 429th pilots, Joe would be back in the cockpit of a P-38 Lightning. Once his fiftieth mission was achieved—only six more to go—he would be shipped back to the States and the longed-for reunion with his mother, brother, and sisters. He could practically smell the potatoes and other crops soon ready for harvest in the surrounding fields.

Although probably still daylight, it had been quiet long enough that Joe thought it was safe to get to work. He took hold of the hoe and in a burst of pent-up energy dug at the floor for twenty minutes. Dirt flew and sweat flowed. He checked the footings and determined that he would have to dig deeper than three feet to begin a tunnel that would get under the stone wall opposite from the door he had been pushed through. Maybe by sometime during the night he'd be outside the building.

If he did not die of thirst first. He had not had any liquid since breakfast and his mouth and throat were dry. All the sweating was further dehydrating him. But there was nothing to do about it except get out of there. Joe returned to digging, and after what may have been another half hour he could see that the hole was two feet deep. He was tired and even more thirsty but encouraged.

That was when the engine started up and the truck was moved away from the door. Tossing the hoe aside, Joe fell to his knees and used his hands to push piles of loose dirt into the hole.

He was sitting with his back against the opposite wall when the heavy door was dragged open. Harsh bright sunlight was behind a German soldier, and then a second man appeared. He was pushed into the room, and so too was another man. Without bothering to glance inside, the soldier closed the door. The darkness that now filled the room was overwhelming. The truck was returned to its sentry position.

Joe matched the silence of the newcomers. He considered

that they were not fellow prisoners but had been planted in the building by the Gestapo to let their boss know if Joe became talkative or got up to anything—like digging a tunnel. Joe heard their breathing and figured they too sat against a wall, waiting and watching, though they and Joe could not see each other. So much for his escape plan. And he was even more parched than before.

He was hungry now too. Maybe that and the experiences of the long day messed with his mind. For a while, Joe wondered if in fact he had died when his Lightning crashed. It had been a fantasy that he had gotten his boot free and parachuted to the ground. He was, instead, dead. This room was probably purgatory; it was too cool and damp to be hell. Sure dark enough, though. And what better devil overseers than the Gestapo? The two men who entered had just recently met their own ends. His heart ached thinking about his mother receiving the telegram from the War Department and of his brother and sisters never seeing him again.

Maybe it was not too late to pray. Joe quietly recited the rosary over and over again. His fingers twitched as though beads were passing through them. The only glimmer of hope he had was that if he really was dead, he would not be this thirsty and hungry.

It was only when he woke up that Joe realized he had sunk into sleep. He was startled awake by the sudden loud rumble of the truck motor. Sore seemingly everywhere, Joe got to his feet, standing weakly as the heavy door was pulled open. The wan light implied it was near dawn. He could now see the other two men. Farmers . . . in fact, they looked like the two young men who had tried to help him escape by running across the field toward the woods. Before Joe could say anything to them, a German soldier with a rifle strode in and motioned for them to exit. Joe was alone for only a few moments when the door thumped closed once more.

And then he heard a gunshot, followed almost immediately by several more. Joe was certain that, as the posters had promised, those two Frenchmen had just been executed: "I slumped down against the wall and felt that I was going to throw up. I felt as if the shot had gone into my own gut, or that someone had kicked me. They had simply lined these two young men up and shot them. I could picture them, lying against the wall of one of those homes I had walked by yesterday, blood staining the dirt, eyes open."

Joe kneeled and prayed for the souls of those two brave and innocent young men. He knew he would never be able to remove their faces from his mind . . . nor did he want to. They had given their lives to try to save his.

As each minute dragged by, Joe became more convinced that the same fate awaited him the next time the heavy door opened. He had nothing else to do but contemplate that grim prospect for the next hour as he sat in total darkness. Thoughts of escape were gone. The thirst and hunger were gone too, "replaced by a painful vice grip in my gut." He had never felt this frightened before, more so than when his plane was on fire and then when his stuck boot almost robbed him of a chance to survive.

Once again came the sound of the truck engine and the shifting of gears as it moved away from the door, which was opened a few seconds later. A German soldier stepped inside the room, located Joe, and came toward him. This is it, Joe thought. The soldier held a rifle in one hand as he grabbed Joe with the other, steering him to the open doorway. It was indeed morning, and the sunlight seemed even brighter than the day before. Joe glanced around, wondering which wall of which building they were about to stand him up against.

Instead, he was pushed into the back seat of a black sedan. The soldier got in beside him, with his rifle pointed at Joe's chest.

The driver hit the gas, and the sedan leaped forward. In a couple of minutes, Marchefroy had been left behind. Joe was able to tell they were going in the direction of Paris. This was curious: He knew that was where the Gestapo headquarters was, but why was he so important? He was one of many downed American pilots, so why not simply stick him on a train or in a truck with other Allied men recently captured and ship him to a POW camp?

The ride in the hot car seemed endless, but finally Joe could see the city looming in the distance ahead, and soon the sedan was inside of it. They drove down a wide boulevard lined with trees. Abruptly, the driver turned into a courtyard. Joe peered through the window to see what he described as "a handsome, ornate building covered with large Nazi flags." This surely had to be the Gestapo headquarters.

The back door was opened and Joe stepped out of the car. He was escorted into the building and up a flight of stairs. Their footsteps echoed in the wide hallway with a tall ceiling. He was turned into a doorway and found himself in an office large enough to accommodate a huge desk. Sitting at it was an officer scanning some documents. His uniform appeared to sprout decorations, indicating he had done much more than sit behind a desk. He was about the same age as the previous interrogator but had better command of English.

Without preamble, he said, "Lieutenant Moser, we would like to know the names of the men in your airplane."

"Joseph Frank Moser. First lieutenant, United States Air Corps, 0755999."

The officer smiled and asked, "What unit are you in?" He received the same response. "What's your commanding officer's name?"

The questioning continued for close to two hours. At times the officer was clearly irritated. Whenever he stood up to stretch,

Joe expected the Nazi might try to beat information out of him. He was a big man and, aside from there being armed guards only a few feet away, Joe was weak from hunger, so there would have been little resistance.

The questions ceased, and the officer sat behind the desk again. "Joe," he began, as if about to confide something, "you come from a town called Bellingham in Washington State. Your mother's name is Mary." He offered other personal details, and then, "You fly out of a temporary base near Neuilly." Joe was even more astonished when the officer added, "Your fellow pilots include Lieutenants Nolby, Lane, Cobb, Patterson, Mills, Skiles, Schwarzrock, and Hazzard. Your commanding officer is Major Burl Glass."

Joe could not speak, and now it seemed like the officer did not care if he did. He continued to tell Joe about his own 429th Squadron and 474th Fighter Group. He brought up one of Joe's fellow pilots, George Knox, who had been shot down on May 23. "He's a POW," the officer assured him. "Don't worry, he's doing fine." Joe hoped he would reveal news about Captain Larson, but for a few moments there was silence in the room. Joe became aware of how much his back was hurting from standing at attention for two hours. And the thirst and hunger were even stronger.

With a smile similar to the one the officer had first employed, he said, "So Joe, help yourself out here a bit. Tell me what your orders were on 13 August. What was your target?"

There were mixed feelings for a moment: What did it matter, if the officer already knew everything? But Joe said, "Joseph Frank Moser. First lieutenant, United States Air Corps, 0755999."

With that, the interrogation ended. The officer called out and a guard led Joe away. Soon he was back in the black sedan and being driven through the Paris streets. Joe judged it to be about noon, meaning he'd had nothing to drink or eat for at least twenty-seven hours. Eventually, the car passed under an archway into another courtyard. Joe would soon learn he had been delivered to the infamous prison called Fresnes.

Located nearly twenty kilometers south of Paris, Fresnes had been built in the 1890s as an innovative kind of prison, one where cell houses extended crosswise from a central corridor.* Fresnes comprised three large blocks, each containing five stories of cells. Each cell had sturdy metal bars and stone walls. Over the years prisoners had scratched names and dates and messages into the crumbling plaster that covered the stone. It was the largest criminal penitentiary in France. On either side of the huge iron front gate were statues of the Sisters of Mercy, which many inmates viewed as a cruel irony. Over the decades it had housed many of France's well-known criminals.

During World War II, the use of Fresnes was expanded by the Nazis to incarcerate members of the French Resistance, German deserters, and British secret agents. One of the latter had been Graham Hayes, who hailed from Yorkshire. The dashing adventurer—he had once sailed around the globe—was a founding member of the Small Scale Raiding Force, a group of commandos.

In 1942, this daring amphibious unit boarded and took over German ships, sailing them to friendly ports; slipped in behind enemy lines to conduct reconnaissance; and conducted lightning raids to disrupt enemy communications systems. During one mission, Hayes was betrayed by a French double agent and wound up in Fresnes prison. In July 1943, after months in solitary confinement and withstanding the torture aimed at soliciting information about other British agents, Hayes was executed by firing squad.

---

* This "telephone-pole design" would become popular in the United States. The most well-known example is Rikers Island in New York City.

In 1944, the Fresnes prison population further increased when Allied airmen began to be held there instead of being sent to prisoner of war camps.

Now it was about to decrease: By the time of Joe's arrival that second week in August, its Nazi overseers, panicking as the Allied forces drew near, were speeding up executions, which may have come as a relief to some of the inmates, who had endured months of torture in addition to the routine horrid conditions. Among the more prominent prisoners killed were two women.

The fifty-year-old Betty Albrecht, a native of Marseille, had campaigned for women to have access to contraception and abortion, had helped refugees from Germany as the Nazis took control, and cofounded the Combat Network within the French Resistance. She had been arrested by the French police but soon released, which angered their Gestapo overlords, who had her arrested again. After weeks of relentless torture, Albrecht found a way to hang herself.

The day before Joe Moser was shot down, the thirty-nine-year-old Brussels-born Suzanne Spaak was executed. She had lived a life of luxury in Paris, which included having her portrait painted by René Magritte, until the Germans invaded France and she joined the Resistance. One of her achievements was saving 163 Jewish children from deportation to death camps. She had been arrested and sent to Fresnes in October 1943 (leaving her two children in the care of others) and endured ten months of torture before the Gestapo put her up against a wall and shot her.

Joe's first experience with the infamous prison was walking down a hallway so long and dark it resembled a tunnel. The guard stopped him in front of a cell door, opened it, and led him in. The guard stepped out and slammed and locked the steel door. There was no one else in the small cell, which was cool and damp like his previous night's accommodations.

Joe surveyed what he hoped would be only a temporary new

home. The cell was twelve feet by eight feet. Most of the plaster had since decayed and, no doubt, been pulled down. What
remained was covered with fragments of pleading or deranged
messages scratched into it by previous prisoners. Joe prayed he
would not be reduced to that.

Next to the door was a tap and a small enamel basin. Fixed to
the wall was a wooden shelf and a peg to hang clothing. Joe pulled
the concrete bed frame down to reveal a thin and dirty straw mattress. High up the wall opposite the door was a frosted glass window through which thick bars could be discerned. Thanks to a
bulb nearby in the hallway ceiling and the window, there was at
least some dim light. This allowed him to discover that a hole in
the floor was his toilet. Joe launched himself at the tap and thought
he would come close to drinking the prison dry.

He would later learn of a chamber in the prison basement
used for interrogations. After being beaten, naked inmates could
be left for days in the cold and dark room. Worse, though, was
being taken to Gestapo headquarters on Avenue Foch for more
punishing sessions. As the British author Colin Burgess described
them, "Members of both sexes were at the complete mercy of
the Gestapo torturers. If the primary interrogation was considered unsatisfactory further beatings, whippings, burnings and
submersion in icy water followed. Fingernails and toenails were
torn from their sockets. The genital region was a particular fa-
vourite for the attention of the interrogators, and often the mere
threat of severe and even permanent damage brought the desired
response from their victims."

Not quite as bad but also a form of torture were the intervals
between interrogations. It was almost impossible to sleep or force
down a few morsels of the awful food while wondering when
it would happen next—a guard flinging open the cell door and
screaming, "Raus!" Minutes later, physical pain would replace the
mental agony.

Joe sat down on the filthy mattress. There was only the barest cushion between his butt and the concrete. Suddenly exhausted, he stretched out. Almost immediately, he felt insects on him. Joe attempted to ignore them, trying to imagine what his family would be eventually told. He hoped that he would be deemed missing in action, even if no one had seen him bail out: "I wondered what time it was back home. I tried to think about what they were doing, when they would get the telegram, what they would think."

Despite the crawling bugs, especially the bite-happy fleas, after a while Joe fell into a tear-stained sleep.

11

S ounds woke Joe in the morning. He assumed it was dawn as he listened to cell doors being unlocked and then exchanges of words between prisoners and the German guards. The sounds came closer to his cell. Joe heard another sound too—a rumbling in the distance. Then he glimpsed a smidgeon of sunlight out the tiny, frosted window, contradicting the thought that the rumbling was thunder. He had to wonder if it was instead artillery. Were the Allies already that close to Paris?

They were indeed. A desperate Adolf Hitler had ordered the city to be destroyed rather than let it fall into Allied hands. But the Führer had not counted on the defiance of the man who, ironically, he had put in control of Paris.

Dietrich von Choltitz had served in the Royal Saxon Army during World War I and was one of the more respected generals in the German Army during World War II. A veteran of numerous campaigns whose courage and loyalty had never been questioned, on August 7, 1944, Choltitz was appointed the military governor of Paris.

At a meeting in Germany the following day, Hitler instructed him to be prepared to leave no Parisian religious building or historical monument standing. After Choltitz's arrival in Paris on August 9, Hitler confirmed the order by cable: "The city must not fall into the enemy's hand except lying in complete rubble." A week later Hitler, in a rage, screamed, "Brennt Paris?" The translation, "Is Paris Burning?," became the title of a best-selling book in the 1960s and subsequently a film.

On August 15, the Paris police went on strike and four days later a general insurrection was led by the French Communist Party. The German garrison under Choltitz fought back, but was far too small to quell the uprising. He brokered a ceasefire with the insurgents on August 20, but many Resistance groups did not accept it, and a series of skirmishes continued.* On the twenty-fourth, elements of the Second French Armored Division and the U.S. Fourth Infantry Division began entering Paris. The very next day, Choltitz surrendered the German garrison of seventeen thousand men to the Free French, leaving the city largely intact. Because Hitler's directive was not carried out, Choltitz has been described by some as the "Savior of Paris."

Joe Moser was not aware of events transpiring in the city, but they did have an impact on him, as his time as an inmate in Fresnes

---

* Resistance fighters under the command of Colonel Henri Rol-Tanguy secretly operated out of an underground air-raid bunker constructed in 1938. Equipped with its own telephone exchange, the bunker gave staff access to 250 phones around Paris, allowing them to bypass official communication lines believed to be tapped by the Germans. In August 2019, as part of the celebrations for the seventy-fifth anniversary of the liberation of Paris, a restored underground shelter was opened to the public and became part of a redesigned Musée de la Libération de Paris.

was short-lived. That morning, his door swung open, and Joe knew enough that "Raus!" meant either "Get up!" or "Get out!" He could allow himself to think that if the Allies were close by, the best scenario was that the guards were getting out themselves while they could and were turning the captives loose. But Joe refused to be so optimistic. More likely, the Allied officers like him were to be shipped to a POW camp far enough away from the advancing front. Joe thought there he would "receive some Red Cross packages and start to be treated like a captured combatant rather than a common criminal."

He took the first step toward that more plausible scenario by leaving his cell and joining the throng of prisoners in the dank hallway. The first man Joe saw he thought was a figment of his imagination. He blurted out, "Captain Larson!"

Indeed it was: His squadron leader thought lost and now found . . . well, at least by one of his overjoyed lieutenants. The two men embraced. Joe was with "not just a familiar face, but the face of a leader whom I deeply respected. Suddenly, the world felt a different place despite the circumstances."

Each wanted to hear the other's story but the German guards were aggressively prodding and pushing the inmates along the corridor. As the prisoners looked at each other they could see bruised and swollen faces and they knew there were many more bruises beneath the clothing. Only the night before and the nights before that some of these men had been howling and screaming with pain as they were subjected to the cruelest of tortures.

Suddenly, there were the sounds of gunshots. For many of the Fresnes inmates, the immediate thought was that rather than possibly letting prisoners go, the Germans were shooting as many of them as they could before evacuating the city.

However, the gunfire had ceased by the time Joe and Captain Larson emerged from the imposing building. They joined the other prisoners being herded into the courtyard. There were women among them, and Joe noted some of the men were Allied officers like him.* He could not help being curious about why the Allied combatants and native French resistors were held captive together, and why the former had not already been relocated to POW camps.

As Joe was working his way down the hallway toward the entrance, he had noticed that some cells remained occupied. A passing thought was that the Germans had other plans for them. That turned out to be quite true. A total of five hundred men and women remained incarcerated at Fresnes, and the intent was to execute them.

Captain Larson was as much in the dark as Joe was about what was to happen next. And he too could not explain why the Allied officers were still in the hands of the Gestapo instead of the Luftwaffe, who normally would be in charge of Allied pilots and the transfer to POW camps. Perhaps that was about to happen now: They were to be culled from the general prison population. Larson knew there were at least 150 Allied airmen, and he and Joe would later learn the exact number was 168.†

The men heard an ominous sound—more gunshots. One of the captured pilots, Ray Perry, a flight sergeant from western Australia, reported that he could hear shooting going on downstairs. It did not take too much imagination to think that the prisoners were being taken downstairs and shot rather than having

---

* Only later did Joe Moser learn that Fresnes was the prison used for members of the French Resistance until they could be put on trains and sent to concentration camps. Of the 2,500 men and women squeezed together in the courtyard that day, only three hundred would return to France.

† Of that number, there were eighty-two American flyers, forty-eight Royal Air Force, twenty-six Royal Canadian Air Force, nine Australians, two airmen from New Zealand, and one flyer from Jamaica.

it done publicly. An uncomfortable silence fell among the Allied prisoners.

Another sound heard was that of motors and the screeching of brakes. The prisoners could see trucks and buses accumulating outside the courtyard. A Prussian SS officer spoke grimly to a pilot named Spierenburg, a Dutchman who had flown for the RAF, who in turn addressed the Allied pilots: "We are to be taken across Paris and placed on a train for our next destination. I was instructed to tell you that anyone attempting to escape will be shot and a hand grenade will be thrown into the back of the vehicle he came from."

There was a pause that gave the prisoners some hope. Members of the French Red Cross were allowed, with the help of several selected prisoners, to haul large tubs into the courtyard. The steaming bean soup was ladled into cups and small bowls and distributed. The soup was reassuring as well as desperately needed by men like Joe. Plus: Why feed people who were about to die?

Then Gestapo officers brandishing rifles and pistols urged the men forward and to climb into the vehicles. However, after only a short drive the trucks came to a halt and the prisoners climbed back out. They were ordered to march through the streets to a somewhat remote part of Paris.

Especially for prisoners who had been stuck in damp cells for weeks if not more, the hike was difficult, made worse by the sun growing higher and stronger in the blue sky. Two hours later, the weary walkers arrived at the Pantin train station.

More food was distributed to the throng of prisoners—a tin of horse meat, a loaf of bread, and a box of knacker bread, a flat and dry type of bread made mostly from rye flour. Though not as hungry as before, Joe and the others wolfed down every morsel. On the tracks only a few yards away was a very long train consisting of cattle cars. What if their next journey lasted for days? What if this turned out to be their only allotment of food?

Sure enough, the guards began pushing prisoners toward the tracks. With some relief, Joe and Captain Larson discerned that all the Allied airmen would be traveling together. First, the female Resistance members had been culled from the crowd and were loaded onto railcars; then it was the turn of the Frenchmen.

As described by Thomas Childers in *In the Shadows of War*, his book on the experiences of Roy Allen, another American pilot, the railroad siding "teemed with thousands of prisoners. Soldiers darted in and out among them, shouting, shoving, lashing out at them with their whips and the butts of their rifles, goading them into the sweltering boxcars. Some resisted, digging in their heels. They screamed and flailed, fighting against the torrent of prisoners sweeping them toward the already crowded cars. In an instant the soldiers were on top of them, beating them to the ground, while dogs, straining at their steel leashes, snapped and snarled and tore at the stragglers."

The voice of one of the Allied pilots, Phillip Lamason from New Zealand, could be heard above the noise. "We are Allied military personnel," he stated. "And we demand to be treated as such."

The German officer he had addressed responded by sending his elbow into the pilot's face. He fell to the ground. The officer leaned over him and shouted angrily, then yanked a pistol out of its holster. For a moment, it appeared the SS lieutenant was furious enough to begin firing indiscriminately. However, after a few seconds he calmed down and stepped over the stunned pilot to resume herding prisoners into the cattle cars.*

---

* Colonel Lamason had taken on the responsibility of spokesperson rather casually. He would later remark, "From a couple of guys it was determined I was the senior officer. So I began giving orders as to what was what."

Two railcars had been designated to carry the pilots. Once inside, Joe estimated there were at least ninety men in his car. Before climbing in, he had noted "40/8" stenciled on the side of the car, and as a farmer he knew that meant the car's capacity was 40 men or eight head of cattle (or horses). He was standing in the middle of the car, surrounded by dozens of other men, many of whom had already been existing in barely survivable conditions for weeks.

That such crowded conditions could become even more unbearable was apparent as soon as the railcar's doors were closed and locked. The stern August sun baked the car. The interior air was hot and scarce and tainted by the odor of "complete strangers to each other who were now nose to nose, arm to arm, leg to leg," Joe reported. "It was immediately obvious that I was not the only one who had not bathed in days." In fact, having showered just three days earlier at his base, Joe was no doubt one of the cleanest men of the bunch.

There were two "windows" in the railcar, an opening a foot high and three feet wide at each end. These provided the only ventilation, and they were covered with barbed wire. Before closing the car doors, the German guards had shoved inside two five-gallon buckets. One contained water; the other was to be a shared toilet. As it filled and then overflowed with urine and excrement, this bucket would become the epicenter of the foulest stench in the car. For some men it would prove too daunting to work their way through the columns of standing men to get to the second bucket and so they simply let loose where they stood.

The occupants were staggered when the train jerked and began to move forward. All could hear the roar and then chugging of the engine. This train, holding 2,453 men and women and even a handful of children, would turn out to be the last one to leave Paris before its liberation.

No one knew their destination. The airmen could only hope it was a POW camp where they would be treated by the accords of the Geneva convention and have access to Red Cross packages. Thus far, their treatment had been strangely devoid of any humanity. This could be attributed to the Germans becoming desperate and uncharacteristically disorganized as the Allied front approached. Still, the proper treatment of prisoners was supposed to be a priority on both sides.

Oddly, given such miserable conditions, soon after the train journey began Joe met two men who were to become good friends. One was an RAF navigator named Art Kinnis, "a big, blond man with an engaging smile and obvious charisma" whose "strong voice" was heard nearby. He had been shot down only minutes away from where Joe's P-38 Lightning had crashed. Kinnis, a Canadian, had had his right eardrum broken during an interrogation session at the Fresnes prison.

Then Joe heard a conversation near the front of the car in which a man mentioned Anacortes, Washington. Joe squeezed his way through and told the man, whose name was Jim Hastin, where he was from.

"Ferndale?" Hastin said. "That's practically in my backyard!"

Joe asked what was becoming a routine question: "How did you get here?"

"I shot myself down," Hastin replied, explaining that flying a P-51, "I blew up a train that had a little more ammunition on it than I figured. The fireball lit my engine on fire and I bailed."

There were dozens of conversations underway, though over time they petered out as the men became too tired or breathless to talk. As the train clacked along without pause, the men tried to take turns squatting down to relieve pains in their backs and legs but coordinating this was difficult. "After awhile," Joe recalled, "we even gave up this strategy and we all ended up just falling down on each other, two and three deep."

The journey was slightly more bearable when Colonel Lamason once again took charge. He demanded the occupants' attention and said in a clear voice that death was certain if they did not cooperate with each other. "I managed to assert some authority," he later recalled, "and like a chess board arranged people so all could be near the windows for a spell."

Had they known at the time, the weary and worried men would have taken some solace in knowing they were being followed. One of their pursuers was the wife of Pierre Lefaucheux. His incarceration at Fresnes demonstrated that anyone in France could be jailed by the German occupiers. The forty-six-year-old, a descendant of the inventor Casimir Lefaucheux, had received the Croix de Guerre for battlefield bravery in World War I. After that conflict, he worked his way up the ranks in the railway and construction industries. When the next war began, he returned to the military and used his work experience as director of the Le Mans ammunition factory. Once the Germans took over, Lefaucheux became one of the prominent leaders in the French Resistance.*

Alas, Mme. Lefaucheux did not have armed freedom fighters, only determination, with her on her journey. When she had learned that most of the cells at Fresnes were being emptied and the prisoners were to be shipped out by train, Mme. Lefaucheux had taken to her bicycle and rushed to the train station. From there, after the train left, she pedaled furiously behind it mile after mile. She could not, of course, stop the train, but she was able to glean useful information about its direction that, stopping along the way, she passed on to her husband's associates.

---

* Beating the odds, Lefaucheux would survive World War II, and immediately afterward he became president of the Renault car company.

Though not as obvious, members of the French Resistance were also monitoring the travels of the long cattle-car train. They believed the train's only destination was an isolated location far enough from prying eyes in Paris where the car doors could be flung open and the German troops would kill every occupant. As the prisoners had been loaded onto the train cars, messages were sent to Resistance leaders in Nanteuil-Saâcy, who hastily pulled together a plan to stop the train as soon as possible—cut the rail line, if necessary. During an ensuing battle, the prisoners could be caught in the crossfire, but it was believed that without a rescue attempt all would die and in the most merciless fashion.

Given the increasing frequency of aerial attacks on rail lines and moving vehicles—including by Joe's outfit, the 429th Squadron—it was close to miraculous that this last train from Paris was not destroyed and its human cargo along with it. As it was, because of the Allied air efforts, "The train ride was not one smooth journey but a constant series of stops, starts, jerks, waiting and starting up again," Joe recalled. "All the time we were jammed together into a filthy, sweaty, fearful mass of humanity. Every stop and jerking startup shoved us into each other all over again, jarring nerves and threatening what little sense of brotherhood we had together."

"Men and women alike, many suffering terribly from dysentery, had to endure the degradation of performing their toilet functions in the middle of the crowded boxcars," writes Colin Burgess about the train journey. "The stench, compounded by a lack of substantial ventilation, was appalling. As each toilet pail filled it began to slop about in the dark interior, and the clothes of those unlucky enough to be crammed nearby were saturated by the foul wastes."

Once while it was still daylight, the train stopped long enough to allow the prisoners to climb out to relieve themselves and to draw some sweet fresh air into their straining lungs. There was no

opportunity to try to escape—all around them were German soldiers with rifles and machine guns aimed at them. Conceivably, a
coordinated rush by two-thousand–plus people would have overwhelmed the dozens of guards, but the men and women—who,
forgoing modesty, had stripped to their underclothes to endure
the fetid heat of the cattle cars—were too exhausted and disori-
ented to organize such an action. When ordered to, the prisoners
clambered back into the cars, and the train resumed its mysteri-
ous journey.

"Every moment," Joe noted, "was an experience in degradation and horror." There would be much more of both.

12

The sudden plunge into darkness was the most frightening moment thus far for the Allied passengers. The train entered a tunnel at Nanteuil-Saâcy, and before it exited the other end its brakes squealed and it stopped. For those not already suffering from claustrophobia, this would certainly do it. Their fears escalated with every second that the car doors remained closed.

The panting occupants could hear the German soldiers shouting and running, indicating something up ahead had halted the train in such a terrible position. The prisoners did not know that on the other side of the tunnel was a rail bridge over the river Marne—or there had been: The French Resistance had destroyed enough of the bridge that it could not bear the weight of a train.

Conditions inside the cattle cars grew even worse because the train's engine continued to churn out clouds of exhaust. The prisoners began to choke on not only the exhaust but the worsening stench of the cars and the occupants themselves. The darkness

within the tunnel made their experience even more of a nightmare. In only a few minutes, Joe Moser's body was starved for
oxygen, and he was not the only one: "Cries of anguish and fear
from the frightened passengers mingled with the shouts from the
guards. I looked at the faces around me and saw fear and panic."

With lungs so tortured, many of the prisoners could no longer
cry out. By ones and two and threes, they collapsed inside the cars
at the feet of others or fainted where they stood because there
was no room to fall. Finally, the car doors were pushed open, and
the prisoners were allowed to jump and crawl out. The dark tunnel was still dense with exhaust but there was more air available
and over two thousand men and women tried to fill their sore
lungs.

Whether they had the strength or not, they were urged to
hurry along the side of the tracks, toward the rear and from the
direction the train had come, to the tunnel entrance. As the prisoners emerged from it, they hoarsely breathed in as much fresh
air as their lungs could accommodate. Joe estimated they could
have been stuck in the tunnel for as long as two hours and it was
remarkable any of the passengers had survived.

Without any explanation, the guards ordered some of the
men to pick up and carry heavy bags containing the soldiers' possessions. Other men were herded together as hostages, this time
with an explanation from the Germans: "We will shoot every one
of these men if anyone tries to escape."

Also emerging from the smoke-filled darkness of the tunnel
was a woman—incredibly, it was Mme. Lefaucheux. She had left
her bicycle at the tunnel entrance and had ventured in, moving
among the wheezing men and women like a ghost, searching for
her husband. Not finding him, she slipped out again, with the German guards apparently seeing her as only another prisoner. After
this startling apparition had identified herself, the men furtively

passed Mme. Lefaucheux along until she found her husband, a very astonished and admiring Pierre. With the men now being told to move, there was time only for a hug and the message she delivered, that members of the Resistance were following them, seeking an opportunity to kill Germans and take the train.

The prisoners had been told to march, the order emphasized by shouts and rifle prods. Though without details, the men and women grasped that sabotage by the Resistance fighters or the results of an air strike meant the train could not leave the tunnel, and perhaps the plan was to go find another one. Joe expected that many of the prisoners felt like he did—the cool fresh country air and the exercise of marching was infinitely better than the stifling crush of the cattle cars.

The prisoners had been shocked to emerge from the tunnel and encounter daylight. Now, the sunlight felt especially harsh, emanating from a burning orb in the blue sky. They were allowed to rest in a field and the guards gestured for men to trudge to a nearby stream and bring back buckets filled with water. The cool, fresh liquid, combined with the bright warm air drying the sweat on their bodies and in their clothes, was such a contrast to the hell of the tunnel interior that some of the prisoners could not help laughing.

However, none of the Germans were amused. The guards began shouting, ordering the men and women to line up in columns. Clearly, the train was not going anywhere—whatever the Resistance fighters had done on the other side of the tunnel had seen to that. For now, the prisoners stood, waiting, wondering, as the Germans eyed them with their fingers on the triggers of their rifles, machine guns, and pistols.

Finally, they were told to begin walking. It made no sense that one of the SS guards would use a baton to beat prisoners as they walked by, thereby slowing down the column, but there he was.

He swung the thick baton repeatedly with no purpose other than to inflict pain. That was what SS guards could do if they wanted to and apparently this one derived some pleasure from it. He alternately grunted from the effort and shouted curses.

One of the flyers, an Englishman named Philip D. Hemmens, tried to avoid the German because he already had a broken arm, and the pain from the baton would have been indescribable. Suddenly, there was that officer again—word passed that his name was Lamason—pulling Hemmens out of the marching column of men and steering him to another SS officer, one who seemed to be of a higher rank.

"You must tell that guard to stop beating my men," Lamason insisted. "We are prisoners of war and cannot be beaten by rotten bastards like him!"

The senior officer responded in clear English and used a word the flyers did not understand. "You are not prisoners of war, you are *Terrorfliegers*. Child murderers." However, he took note of Hemmens's crooked arm. "The man is injured?"

"Yes, damn it," Lamason snapped.

The officer nodded and walked over to the guard with the baton. After a few words, he lowered it. Lamason and Hemmens inserted themselves back into the column and there were no further beatings.

Urged by the guards and by shouted orders from the German officers, the column continued to move, walking past the rear cars of the idle train and into the countryside. Mile after mile they marched. Some of the prisoners wondered if, with the column of men and women thus exposed, there would be an ambush by Resistance fighters. A few prayed there would not be because of the bloodbath that would ensue. Even if the Germans were wiped out, in all the shooting hundreds of prisoners might be killed and maimed.

At last, they arrived at a pedestrian-only bridge across the Marne River. The prisoners filed across it. The sun's heat was no longer welcome; they felt themselves frying in it. They would have cooled off quick enough if the fragile bridge had collapsed under their weight, dropping them into the river. However, they made it across, where they soon encountered railroad tracks . . . and, miraculously, another train like the first one. There was much déjà vu as the men and women were told to climb into the cattle cars. Then they waited, the interiors of the cars heating up, the foul smell of prisoners packed together like cattle thickening.

Finally, just before sunset, the train's engine roared and spewed smoke and the trip east was resumed. If Resistance fighters still watched, they had to do so from a distance because this was open country, making close concealment and an effective attack too difficult.

There were hours upon hours of travel, with a couple of stops for the prisoners to relieve themselves. In one of the cars an occupant had somehow obtained a hammer. Even the lowliest German soldier would not be ordered to be inside the cars, so in this particular one the prisoners were free to use the hammer to loosen several floorboards. Enough were removed from the bottom of the car that there was a hole that could accommodate men slipping through it. During a relatively smooth stretch of track, seven prisoners willing to take the risk—six Frenchmen and Dave High, a Royal Canadian Air Force officer—lowered themselves through the hole and let go, lying flat on the tracks. Once the train passed over them, they got up and ran away from the train.

Perhaps the entire car would have emptied out . . . except for a sharp-eyed guard. The train had come to a stop soon after the last man had eased himself out and, unwisely, he had tried to run away instead of concealing himself until the train moved on. The guard spotted him and alerted the others. One by one the cattle cars were searched, and the hole in one of them was discovered. A group of guards was dispatched down the tracks to try to catch those who had escaped. The prisoners heard several rifle shots but comforted themselves with the thought that they were just fired out of frustration.

They were wrong. German soldiers returned with five of the seven escapees. Of the other two, one had been shot and killed and the other apparently had escaped. The flyer Dave High was beaten with a rubber hose. "I was struck mostly on the head, shoulders and arms," he recalled, "and was able to move about only with great difficulty for three or four days. I was black and blue for weeks."

The other guards and their officers were more furious than frustrated. The escapees' comrades in the car paid the price for the dash to freedom. Their clothes, water bucket, slop bucket, and any remaining food were taken from them. The train rumbled on, and probably the prisoners in that cattle car believed that was the extent of their punishment.

But at the next stop, they were told to get out of the car. A red-faced Prussian officer began shouting at them, and the Dutch airman, Spierenburg, once more translated: "I have been instructed to tell you that to prevent further escapes, and by way of punishment, 35 RAF airmen and 20 Frenchmen from this carriage are to be shot."

Fifty-five men were selected and told to step forward. Two machine guns on tripods were trained on them. There was some muttering among the men about charging the guns en masse, overwhelming the guards, and using their weapons against the other German soldiers and officers. But no one moved. The prisoners stood naked in the broiling August sun alongside the train. A dozen or so guards lined up opposite them. Some of the men began to pray and everyone waited for the order to be given for the guards to squeeze the machine-gun triggers and begin shooting.

The agonizing wait lasted several minutes. Then the naked men were told to relieve themselves and get back into the cattle car. Pieces of wood had been nailed over the opening in the floor. Spierenburg relayed that the Prussian officer "has decided not to shoot you after all, but the next escape will bring the most severe punishment."

The guards, however, were not done with that car. Maybe to feel the rush of cool air, a French boy of seventeen had snaked his hand out one of the ventilation openings. A German guard sitting atop the next car shot it. At the next stop, one of the car's occupants, Harry Bastable, a Canadian pilot, called out for medical attention for the boy. The door was yanked open, and the boy was ordered out. He held his hands up, and blood continued to flow from the wounded hand down his arm.

The prisoners waited for a soldier with at least a first aid kit to appear. Instead, the teenager was ordered to step away from the train and down a dirt bank. He did, and when he was far enough away from the guards, one shot him in the back and another in the head. His naked body tumbled the rest of the way down the bank. The guards followed and shot him three more times. They then selected two prisoners at random and ordered them out of the car. They were handed spades and told to bury the boy.

After only a few minutes of work, the men were ordered to stop. The French teenager's body was rolled into the shallow grave and covered with handfuls of dirt and gravel from the railroad bed. The two prisoners climbed back in the car and once more the train set off. Peering through cracks and knotholes in the car's wooden walls, prisoners could see the French boy's hands and feet sticking out of the dirt. There was little doubt that roaming animals would ravage his body come nightfall.

For Joe and his companions, the trip east was a seemingly endless series of stops and starts, stops and starts. They coped the best they could: "We talked some and slept in brief moments, our legs collapsing, our elbows, shoulders, armpits, hairy bodies, bony knees and sweaty, hairy heads banging into and poking each other. And, always, the continual stench and heat." Making the journey a bit bearable was the prospect of the POW camp waiting at the end of it.

They had lost count of the days spent packed in the cattle cars and churning relentlessly east, but several of the men in Joe's group knew when they were on a bridge over the Rhine and were entering Germany at Strasbourg. No longer fearing attacks by the French Resistance, the German guards relaxed a bit, and officers ordered that the clothes of the passengers be returned.

The next day the airmen were given a stark view of what their attacks had done to Frankfurt. "The destruction from Allied bombing was almost complete," Joe noted. "The center of the city had been laid to waste and was just a blackened hole filled with rubble. Bare walls were standing as if they were grave markers, with nothing left for them to hold up." True, Germany and its ambitions for conquest and subjugation had brought this destruction on itself, but the prisoners could not help feeling for the civilians and wondering how many of them had perished.

When the train stopped on the following day, the women were unloaded. Word filtered back that they were to be placed on another train, one bound for Berlin.* In a surprising gesture of civility, the guards allowed the French husbands and wives of the Resistance fighters to seek each other out and say goodbye. Then

---

* This rumor turned out to be false. The women were taken to the concentration camp at Ravensbrück.

the men were herded back into the cars and once again the train was on the move.

This last leg of the journey was a short one. The train entered a forest, and soon on either side of the tracks peering prisoners glimpsed men working on the railroad beds and "wearing strange clothing, shirts and trousers with large blue and white stripes." There was anticipation that they were finally about to arrive at the POW camp designated for them. It was strange, though, that the prisoners seen so far certainly did not look like they had been able to take advantages of Red Cross packages and other basic needs. There was a fresh surge of curiosity and excitement when in the late afternoon the train stopped. The long, nauseating, and crippling trip was over.

The cattle-car doors were dragged open, and the occupants were told to get out and line up. They stood in the still-steady gaze of the August sun. Joe's back and legs were stiff and sore, and he expected that was equally true for the two thousand or so other men. They were also filthy and desperately hungry and thirsty as well as utterly exhausted. Many of the men were unsteady as the German guards conducted yet another head count.

As this was being done, Joe and the others glanced around at the train station. Was this a POW camp? They saw tall fences with barbed wire, drab gray buildings, and more prisoners, almost walking skeletons, in the striped and filthy uniforms. And as the arrivals were urged to walk down the road from the station to the camp, on either side were barking German shepherds, straining at their leashes and salivating at the prospect of tearing into human flesh. Ahead was more barbed wire and, beyond it, more dingy buildings. As they marched closer, the Allied prisoners could see faces pressed against the fencing.

What Joe saw "chilled me to my soul. They did not look much like POWs, indeed, with their skulls practically showing through their paper-thin skin, the dim, empty eyes, their meaningless stares, I hardly felt they were human."

Colin Burgess reports: "A few metres from the hissing locomotive, an inadequate army of these barefooted living corpses endeavoured to haul a rough wooden cart overloaded with newly quarried rocks along a dusty incline. As they strained and dragged and pushed the cumbersome vehicle they were dispassionately flogged by two uniformed SS guards. Ferocious dogs snapped and tore at their legs, and they worked with a desperation that only fear of pain or death can induce.

"Eventually the column of prisoners was forced to move out of the station at the double, along a concrete road they would come to know as the Caracho Way, or the 'Street of Blood.'"

The Allied airmen continued to be confused about where they were: How could this possibly not be a camp for prisoners of war who would have the protections of the Geneva convention? But for the French Resistance members there was a sickening understanding. Their mouths silently issued one word: "Buchenwald."

Joe Moser and the other flyers would soon understand that they and everyone else on the train had been sent here to die . . . and to be forgotten.

The training to be a pilot was rigorous but all the effort would allow Joe Moser to realize his dream of flying a P-38 Lightning. *(Courtesy of the Moser family.)*

Joe Moser as a newly minted lieutenant in the Army Air Corps. *(Courtesy of the Moser family.)*

The Lockheed company factories churned out thousands of P-38 Lightnings during the war for use in both the European and Pacific Theaters. *(Courtesy of the Library of Congress.)*

The versatile P-38 in action during World War II. The Germans referred to it as the "fork-tailed devil." *(Courtesy of the Smithsonian National Air and Space Museum.)*

Joe Moser and other pilots in the 429th Fighter Squadron, who dubbed themselves the "Retail Gang." *(Courtesy of the Moser family.)*

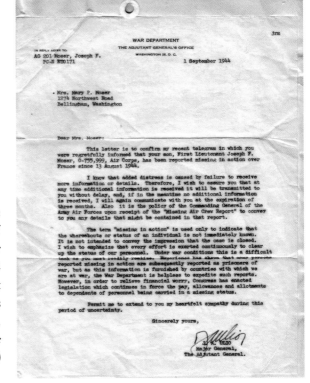

The letter sent by the U.S. Department of War to Mary Moser in September 1944 informing her that her son Joseph was missing in action. *(Courtesy of the Moser family.)*

Immediately after his capture, Joe Moser was kept in a cell in the brutal Fresnes prison in Paris. *(Courtesy of Sueddeutsche Zeitung Photo.)*

Col. Phillip Lamason of the Royal New Zealand Air Force was the senior officer and courageous leader of the captured Allied airmen. *(Courtesy of the Phil Lamason Heritage Trust.)*

One of the most powerful men in Nazi Germany, Heinrich Himmler was head of the SS, which operated the concentration camps. *(Courtesy of the United States Holocaust Memorial Museum.)*

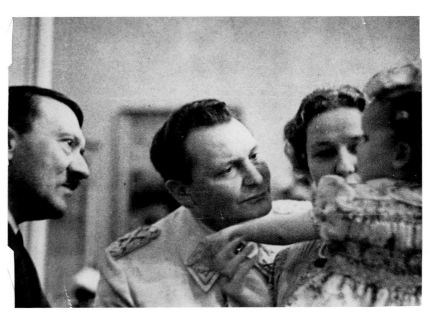

Hermann Goring, shown here with his wife and daughter, was one of Adolf Hitler's most loyal Nazi Party allies and head of the Luftwaffe. *(Courtesy of the United States Holocaust Memorial Museum.)*

The front gate of the Buchenwald concentration camp as photographed soon after it was liberated in 1945. *(Courtesy of the United States Holocaust Memorial Museum.)*

The photograph of Joe Moser taken upon his arrival at Buchenwald, which followed him from camp to camp. *(Courtesy of the Moser family.)*

The Allied flyers were told by amused guards that the only way they would leave Buchenwald was through the crematorium's chimney. *(Courtesy of the United States Holocaust Memorial Museum.)*

The crematorium ovens labored incessantly to dispose of the bodies of prisoners who died or were murdered by the SS guards and kapos at Buchenwald. *(Courtesy of the United States Holocaust Memorial Museum.)*

Karl-Otto Koch was the commandant of Buchenwald until he became too corrupt even for the Nazis. He is second from left in this photograph of SS officers chatting while in the background prisoners stand at attention during morning roll call. *(Courtesy of the United States Holocaust Memorial Museum.)*

Known as the "Bitch of Buchenwald," Ilse Koch (shown during her trial), was the commandant's wife who perpetrated the most unspeakable acts of cruelty. *(Courtesy of the United States Holocaust Memorial Museum.)*

Hermann Pister, who took over from Karl-Otto Koch, was the commandant of Buchenwald when the Allied airmen were prisoners there. *(Courtesy of the United States Holocaust Memorial Museum.)*

Officially, Buchenwald, unlike Dachau and Treblinka, was a labor camp, yet every day dozens of starving prisoners were worked to death. *(Courtesy of the United States Holocaust Memorial Museum.)*

Princess Mafalda of Savoy (show here as an adolescent), a daughter of King Victor Emmanuel III of Italy, died of wounds sustained during the Allied bombing of Buchenwald. *(Courtesy of the Library of Congress.)*

The Ernst Thalmann Park in Berlin is dedicated to one of the many prominent political prisoners tortured and killed at Buchenwald. *(Courtesy of the Library of Congress.)*

The Allied flyers shared the constant hunger which took a toll on all the prisoners at Buchenwald. *(Courtesy of the United States Holocaust Memorial Museum.)*

Some of the children who were prisoners at Buchenwald. Hundreds were killed to make room for adult inmates, including the Allied flyers. *(Courtesy of the United States Holocaust Memorial Museum.)*

The Allied airmen considered themselves fortunate when they were finally housed in barracks like these. *(Courtesy of the United States Holocaust Memorial Museum.)*

Every morning, a wagon was hauled around the camp to collect the bodies of those who had died during the night and bring them to the crematorium. *(Courtesy of the United States Holocaust Memorial Museum.)*

Eugen Kogon, shown here testifying after the war, saved many lives while a prisoner and wrote extensively about the horrors of Buchenwald. *(Courtesy of the United States Holocaust Memorial Museum.)*

During an inspection visit to Buchenwald, Hannes Trautloft, an ace Luftwaffe pilot (shown here as a postwar German officer), discovered that Allied flyers were inmates there. *(Courtesy of Militar Historisches Museum.)*

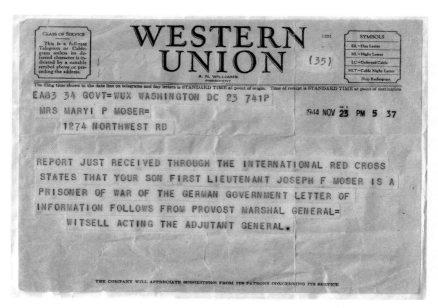

It was only when Mary Moser received this telegram in November 1944 that she knew her son was still alive. *(Courtesy of the Moser family.)*

Joe Moser was one of thousands of suddenly liberated prisoners who mobbed the first U.S. Army vehicles to enter Stalag VII-A in April 1945. *(Courtesy of the Moser family.)*

Once he could bring himself to attend, Joe Moser (right) enjoyed reunions with other members of the KLB Club. *(Courtesy of the Moser family.)*

Jean and Joe Moser in 2007 as he began work on his memoir (written with Gerald Baron) of being a U.S. Army pilot. *(Courtesy of the Moser family.)*

The proud pilot never forgot the thrill of being in the cockpit of his beloved P-38 Lightning. *(Courtesy of the Moser family.)*

One of the last photographs taken of Joe Moser, a humble hero who insisted that his World War II experiences of survival "made life worth living." *(Courtesy of the Moser family.)*

ACT III
THE PRISONER

---◆---

O Buchenwald, I can never forget you
Because you are my fate.
Whoever leaves you, he alone can measure
How wonderful freedom is!
O Buchenwald, we do not lament and wail,
Whatever our fate might be.
But we want to say yes to life,
For someday the time will come when we are
free!

—"The Buchenwald Song,"
by Fritz Lohner-Beda and Hermann Leopoldi*

---

* This song, also known as "The Buchenwald Hymn," was composed in 1938. A
German kapo took credit for writing the song. However, unknown to the SS ad-
ministration, which had commissioned the song, its true composers were Lohner-
Beda and Leopoldi, both Austrian Jews. Lohner-Beda later died in Auschwitz.
Leopoldi survived Dachau as well as Buchenwald, resumed his performing career,
emigrated to the United States, and died at age seventy-one in 1959.

13

Buchenwald remains one of the more well known of the Nazi concentration camps of World War II. However, this is not because it had the highest death toll. To be sure, the Buchenwald facility in the Weimar region of central Germany was a place of almost limitless horror operated by monstrous people. Over 56,000 prisoners died there, yet this terrible toll was far exceeded by the Auschwitz and Treblinka camps, where 1.1 million and 750,000, the vast majority of the Jews, died.* Timing played a role in Buchenwald's infamy in that it was the first major concentration camp reached by Allied forces while still occupied by prisoners. And its sprawling connection of compounds

---

* As is true of the toll in other concentration camps, this figure does not include the thousands more who died after liberation from lingering diseases and other ailments as well as suicide. These people were also victims of the Nazi camps.

made it the largest camp operated by the Nazis before and during the war.

As early as July 1944, the concentration camp at Majdanek in Poland had been discovered by units of the Soviet Army, and the following January Soviet advance units arrived at the gates of Auschwitz, also in Poland. In both cases, though, the camps had been abandoned and partially destroyed. The same was true for American forces when they came to the camps at Ohrdruf and Nordhausen-Dora, both in Thuringia, Germany.

But Buchenwald was an entirely different story: When American GIs arrived there the second week of April 1945, they found an active camp, one containing tens of thousands of skeletal prisoners surrounded by the buildings where executions and inhuman activities had been conducted. The first photographs taken at Buchenwald and those a few days later by the British when they liberated Bergen-Belsen near Hanover would shock officials in the United States and Great Britain and eventually most of the Western world.

In Europe, however, by mid-1944, the reputation of this particular concentration camp had been well established, yet its reality proved even more astounding. "In Buchenwald the Nazis forced prisoners into the most brutal and hideous possible existence," wrote Eugene Weinstock, who had been sent there from Belgium the previous December and became prisoner 22483. "In Buchenwald hundreds of men died every day in the week from two diseases: overwork and starvation. In Buchenwald you found fascism without frills. Buchenwald discipline was famous for being so intolerable that few could bear up under it for very long. Originally, it had been a camp for 'politicals.' It was still that, but the concept of politics was now broader. The Nazis now numbered among political enemies all Jews, trade unionists, liberals, leftists, democrats, professors who would not betray their calling to teach an *ersatz* science, or children who repeated anti-Nazi jokes even if they were too young to understand them."

In August 1944, 168 Allied flyers who had been on the last Nazi train out of Paris became a new category of "political" to be incarcerated in Buchenwald. By then, the camp had been in operation for seven years.

When Buchenwald opened in 1937, it was one of an increasingly intricate series of facilities designed by the Nazis to incarcerate and, with mounting frequency, dispose of the Third Reich's domestic and foreign enemies. The system included the Gestapo, which had been officially established in April 1933 by Hermann Göring, who blended the state and political police in the largest and most powerful German state of Prussia. The purpose of this new police force, according to the law establishing it, was "to assure the effective battle against all endeavours directed at the existence and security of the state."

Soon afterward, as part of the Nazi consolidation of power, all German police forces were combined. By 1934, the Gestapo was headed by SS chief Heinrich Himmler. It became a national agency as a result of the Gestapo Laws of 1936, with Himmler named chief of it. Previously in Germany, there had been no national police organization—each state had had its own. Himmler, for example, had established his version of the Gestapo in the state of Bavaria by 1933. The SS, or *Schutzstaffel*, was essentially the private army of the Nazi Party, and one of its more important roles was to operate the concentration camps that were beginning to be created.

According to *The Buchenwald Report*, a compendium initially produced in May 1945, the purpose of the concentration camp system was that "it is better to put ten innocent people behind barbed wire than to leave a single actual opponent in freedom.

Everything opposed to or inconsistent with National Socialist rule and its theory of state had to be removed."

The first camps—including Dachau and Ravensbrück—were constructed and opened in 1934, the year after the Nazis, headed by Adolf Hitler as chancellor, achieved controlling power in Germany. In preparation for military expansion in 1939 as well as a greater number of people requiring incarceration, there was a boom in camp construction, with Bergen-Belsen, Auschwitz, Riga, and others opening. Early in World War II, the system became more structured with the camps being divided into three categories. The first contained the work camps, the second were for prisoners designated for even more punishing conditions, and the third category was for the *Knochenmühlen,* which translated as "bone mills" and were also simply and more accurately referred to as "death factories." When the revised system was implemented, Buchenwald was designated as a category 2 camp.

Eight decades later, it is still difficult to fathom the remarkable efficiency and depravity with which people, almost all of whom were Europeans, were worked, shot, tortured, burned, and in other ways put to death in the Nazi concentration camps.* How many were there? According to *The Buchenwald Report,* "Even a rough count would be made extraordinarily difficult by the constantly changing population." This refers not only to the ebb and flow of people arriving during the years of the camps' existence but to the constant drain of death. In round numbers, eleven million people died in the Nazi camps, with six million of them being Jews. "From the beginning," the report says, "Jews were

---

* In 1940, the population of Europe was 416 million. During the war, the continent lost 15 percent of its population because of the massive death toll in the camps, other war-related deaths, and millions more who managed to flee.

special targets of the SS will to annihilate." During the war years, they had plenty of company.

Buchenwald began its nightmarish existence with 149 prisoners transferred from the Sachsenhausen camp. As the site continued to be constructed and expanded, at Buchenwald's center was a tree known as the Goethe oak, named for the celebrated German poet who had often visited nearby Ettersberg. For the officials and guards at the camp, it was a symbol of endurance and strength; for the prisoners, the tree represented misery, subjugation, and death.

Over time, hundreds and then thousands and then tens of thousands of prisoners lived within the walls of fencing and barbed wire. Still, especially because of increases in diseases, exhaustion, and dying, there never seemed to be enough labor available to keep up with the work mandated to be done. "The prisoners' living and working conditions were the worst imaginable," states *The Buchenwald Report*. "Work lasted from the first glimmer of morning light until twilight, at times longer. There was a one-hour break at midday that was mostly filled with roll calls. Every day four roll calls took place. Almost no time remained for meals and bodily care. Sanitary conditions were inadequate beyond description; in particular the camp suffered from a constant shortage of water. Between blocks ran a primitive water main into which holes had been bored, allowing a trickle of water that could be caught. For a long time toilets consisted of open latrines."

The first commandant of Buchenwald was Karl-Otto Koch, who would prove to be too corrupt even for the Nazis. He was turning nineteen when he fought for his country in World War I. During one battle, he was captured and was in a British prisoner of war camp until he was returned to Germany in 1919 to receive medals that included the Iron Cross Second Class and a Wound

Badge in Black. Koch worked a variety of jobs, including as an insurance agent, until 1930, when he was jailed for forgery and embezzlement. Back on the street the following year, he saw a better future in the nascent Nazi Party.

He apparently performed his duties well, because he was given higher and higher positions in the burgeoning concentration camp system in Germany, one of them being Dachau. On August 1, 1937, and by then a colonel, Koch assumed the leadership role at Buchenwald. He brought with him his wife of one year, Ilse. At the new posting, the two enjoyed high living and power over the increasing numbers of personnel and prisoners in Buchenwald.

As commandant, Koch's orders had to be followed no matter how inane or aberrant. One example was his idea to increase the amusement capacity of the camp zoo, which included among its four-legged population five monkeys, four bears, and a rhinoceros. When the mood struck him, Koch ordered several prisoners locked inside the bear cage, where they were torn to shreds as the commandant and his underlings looked on as though watching a theatrical production. Prisoners had to compete with the animals for food scraps, with the latter often given priority. The zoo was particularly popular among the children of the SS officers and senior guards, creating the scenario of the youngsters feeding food to deer while only yards away starving prisoners looked on, watching the animals eat more in one encounter than they did in an entire day.

One would not think it possible, but Koch's capacity for cruelty was soon surpassed by his young spouse.

Margaret Ilse Kohler had been born in Dresden, was a good student, studied accounting, and found work as a bookkeeping clerk. She joined the Nazi Party in 1932 when she was just sixteen, and through it met Karl-Otto Koch. They married in

1936. Immediately after she and her husband took up residence
in Buchenwald, Ilse Koch quickly embraced the death camp's
possibilities. A favorite pursuit was to assist a prison doctor in
his experiments. One involved tattoos, and she ordered prisoners skinned—mercifully, they were killed first—to provide the
doctor with fresh material. Using funds taken from inmates, Ilse
had an indoor sports arena constructed. In it she rode horses
with the exercise accompanied by music performed by a band
comprised of SS guards. When the weather and her mood allowed, Ilse rode through the camp wearing only a swimsuit.
Prisoners caught looking at her were beaten or whipped . . .
and those were the lucky ones. When sufficiently enraged, Ilse
carved a path through prisoners, shooting transgressors with a
pistol.

As the commandant's wife, she had the authority to have
prisoners tortured and killed simply because that was what she
wanted. One of her favorite forms of amusement was to order guards to cull a group of prisoners and have them strip-
searched. The guards could keep money or anything else they
found. For however long it pleased Ilse, the inmates stood naked while she and a group of guards' wives pointed and offered
lewd appraisals.

Men other than her husband occupied much of her time. According to *The Buchenwald Report* and other accounts, during her
tenure at the camp Ilse Koch had numerous liaisons, including
with Hermann Florstedt, her husband's deputy commandant;
Waldemar Hoven, the SS captain who was the chief medical doctor; other SS officers; and even several prisoners who caught her
fancy. She was not known to be discreet, yet that did not seem to
matter very much, because Karl-Otto Koch was also not circum-
spect about his homosexual activities. There was also no discre-
tion involved in choosing a prisoner to participate in a threesome

with Koch and his wife, with that prisoner being executed in the morning.

Eventually, Koch had more pressing concerns than securing sexual partners. His rampant stealing, alcoholism, and even the indiscriminate killing of prisoners added up to behavior which attracted the attention of his Nazi superiors, who launched an investigation. Koch was shipped out to another concentration camp, at Majdanek in Poland, in September 1941. He did not acquire better management skills there and was relieved as commandant the following August, when eighty-six Soviet prisoners escaped.

He was ordered to Berlin with the thought that he could disappear into the German bureaucracy. However, Third Reich officials arranged to have Koch arrested and charged with murder and embezzlement—he had been so blatant about it that his behavior had embarrassed the SS. In April 1945, just weeks before the war ended, Koch was executed by a firing squad.

His wife had remained behind at Buchenwald. She had acquired the sobriquet of the "Bitch of Buchenwald," and was appointed an *Oberaufseherin*, an overseer role that gave her a lot of authority during the tenure of Hermann Pister, her husband's replacement. Still, Ilse tried to be unobtrusive, which meant curbing her sadistic tendencies. However, she was arrested in August 1943 and imprisoned with her husband. During their trial, Karl-Otto was convicted, but Ilse was acquitted for lack of evidence. They would have different fates—after Karl-Otto was killed, Ilse was allowed to live with family in Ludwigsburg.

But her life of notoriety was not over. When the General Military Government Court for the Trial of War Criminals was convened at Dachau in 1947, Isle Koch was one of thirty-one people put on trial. The accusation against her was aiding and participating in the murder of prisoners at Buchenwald. One of the more lurid charges contended that she had had lamp-shades and other items made of human skin.* She came up with a novel defense—announcing that she was pregnant. Given her reputation for promiscuity and that she was only forty-one, this was not a shock, but it was surprising because she had been kept in an isolated environment.

In any case, the strategy did not persuade the judges. Ilse Koch was convicted and given a life sentence. After serving two years, the sentence was reduced to four years. There was an outcry, and she was arrested and tried once more with new and revised charges so as to avoid double jeopardy. She was again convicted and sentenced to life behind bars. This time, appeals and requests for pardons were rejected. She was confined to the Aichach women's prison. There, in September 1967, at age sixty, Ilse Koch killed herself, on the night before she was to be visited by Uwe Kohler, the son she had given birth to twenty years earlier, after her first conviction. She and Karl-Otto had had a son, who also committed suicide, and two daughters. To this day, Ilse's grave at the Aichach prison remains unmarked and untended.†

Karl-Otto Koch had been replaced by Pister as commandant of Buchenwald by an order direct from Heinrich Himmler. At sixteen, during World War I, Pister had enlisted in the Imperial Navy. In the next war, he was a member of the Waffen-SS. This

---

* While such tales were disputed, there was also valid, corroborating testimony. Ilse Koch did decorate her desk with two heads shrunken to one-fifth their normal size, which had belonged to Polish prisoners who had escaped the camp but were captured. She also had a table lamp made of human skin and bone. "The light was switched on by pressing the little toe of one of the three human feet that formed the stand," a pathology department worker testified.

† One of the more jarring cultural intersections is the song "Ilse Koch," about her life of sadism, originally written by Woody Guthrie and performed by the Klezmatics on their 2006 album *Wonder Wheel*. The recording received the Grammy Award for Best Contemporary World Music Album.

by itself did not give him a high-ranking position. He was an automobile mechanic. Somehow, when Pister was a member of the Transportation Corps, Himmler took notice of him and thought he was good concentration-camp-administrator material.

Pister was still the commandant at Buchenwald in August 1944 when the train carrying Joe Moser and the other Allied pilots arrived. He managed the gruesome business of a concentration camp well enough to keep his job. Toward the end of the war, Pister burnished his war criminal credentials by packing prisoners into open boxcars pulled by a lumbering train that took twenty days to get to Dachau. By then, many of the evacuated passengers had died of illness and starvation. Understandably, it was dubbed the "Death Train."

Pister was arrested in 1945, and two years later he was one of the defendants who included Ilse Koch at Dachau. He too offered an odd defense, claiming that he did not know of the Hague Convention, which provided some protections to prisoners, and that he was not responsible for the fates of those at Buchenwald because he had not arranged for them to be brought there. And he complained that many of the inmates were "habitual drunkards and vagrants, professional criminals, and Jehovah's Witnesses with Communist tendencies" and thus harsh measures were necessary to maintain order.

His rationalizations were not persuasive. Pister was found guilty, and the sentence was that he be hung. However, the Allies missed out on this opportunity in September 1948, when he died in prison of a heart attack.

While there have been thousands of accounts of being a concentration camp prisoner, a thorough and riveting testimony about Buchenwald in particular was provided by Eugen Kogon. He survived the camp's horrors and devoted years to ensuring the world would know about them.

He was born in February 1903 in what is now Ukraine to an unmarried Russian-Jewish woman, who gave him up for adoption. Apparently, there were no takers because Kogon grew up in Catholic cloisters. His intelligence and studiousness earned him a place at schools in Munich, Florence, and Vienna, where he studied sociology and economics. In 1927, he both completed a doctorate and became editor of *Schönere Zukunft,* a Catholic publication that translates to "Brighter Future." During his ten years in the position, Kogon became active in groups opposing the rise of the Nazis. This brought him to the attention of the Gestapo, who twice arrested him.

Kogon would not be released after his third arrest, which occurred in March 1938, in Vienna. In September 1939, when the war in Europe began, he was sent to Buchenwald. He became one of the very few prisoners to survive nearly six years there. Certainly, a factor was the position he held, which was clerk to the camp doctor, Erwin Ding-Schuler. Even in Buchenwald, where evil was commonplace, Ding-Schuler managed to distinguish himself.

He was still only in his twenties when he was an officer and surgeon at the camp. Born in 1912, he joined the Nazi Party twenty years later and the SS in 1936. The following year, Ding-Schuler received a degree in medicine. It probably came in handy when he murdered Paul Schneider at Buchenwald with an overdose of strophanthin. Perhaps as a reward, in 1939, Ding-Schuler was assigned to head the division for spotted fever and viral research of the Waffen-SS Hygiene Institute at Buchenwald. Until 1945, he conducted extensive medical experiments on some one thousand inmates, many of whom lost their lives, in Experimental Station Block 46, using various poisons as well as infective agents for spotted fever, yellow fever, smallpox, typhus, and cholera.

Though the surgeon was a monster, Kogon was able to form a friendship with him. In addition to the relationship helping keep

the clerk alive, Kogon was able to use his office and the unwitting
Ding-Schuler's authority to save the lives of other inmates. As
detailed later, this would include British special operatives imprisoned at Buchenwald.

And as it turned out, Ding-Schuler was directly responsible for
saving Kogon's life. In April 1945, with the liberation of Buchenwald imminent, the surgeon informed his clerk that he was one
of forty-six prisoners on an SS execution list. Kogon was packed
into a crate that was smuggled out of the camp and shipped to
Ding-Schuler's home in Weimar, where he was set free.

After the war, Kogon returned to journalism and was a volun-
teer historian for the U.S. Army, collecting eyewitness accounts
about the German concentration camps. His writings in maga-
zines, newspapers, and books were indispensable in trying to understand the depths of depravity achieved by the Nazis, especially
in their concentration camp system.

Given the hundreds of examples, it would be difficult to cite
just one representative of that depth. But surely a good candi-
date at Buchenwald was Walter Gerhard Martin Sommer. He was
born on a farm in Schkölen, Germany, in 1915. He was just sixteen
when he joined the Nazi Party, and he became a member of the
SS when it was first formed. In 1935, Sommer was recruited to the
so-called "Death's Head" unit of the SS that was assigned to run
the emerging concentration camps. His commander was Colonel
Theodor Eicke, who preached the doctrine of "inflexible harshness" in treating prisoners, which required that the guards have no
sympathy for inmates.

The Sachsenhausen camp was Sommer's first stop. Then in
1937, at age twenty-two, he was assigned to Buchenwald. The next
year, after *Kristallnacht*, the German onslaught against Jews and
their properties in Germany, thousands of Jewish prisoners began
arriving at Buchenwald. Among those to greet them was Sommer.

He had been put in charge of a cell block, which gave him complete authority over its occupants. His techniques with prisoners were so effective and entertaining to superiors that Sommer was elevated to oversee the punishment bunker and later became chief penal officer.

What were these "techniques"? Implementing them showed that Sommer did possess a unique sort of sadistic genius. One was to suspend prisoners from trees with their arms tied behind their backs and then raise them up off the ground. Gradually, shoulders were dragged from their sockets and shoulder and wrist bones broke. As if this were not painful enough, Sommer would direct guards to beat the suspended prisoners in the face and groin. Their screams of pain inspired the bemused guards and their officers to nickname the area of trees as the "singing forest."

Another torture technique was to have prisoners' backs rubbed with steel brushes hard enough that there would be gaping wounds, into which he would pour acid. A particularly bizarre practice was to have a prisoner brought to his quarters at night. Sommer injected carbolic acid into a vein. After the resulting embolism killed the prisoner, the murderer pushed the body under his bed and stretched out to sleep.

Far from being appalled, superiors were impressed by his inventiveness and promoted Sommer to master sergeant. They were especially amused when, on one brutally cold night, Sommer had a German pastor suspended naked by his arms in a courtyard. Every few minutes, a bucket of water was thrown at the pastor until he froze to death.

According to Eugen Kogon, Sommer's sadism was inexhaustible: "His greatest sport was to herd all his prisoners into the corridor, about four feet wide, where he had them do kneebends and hop about until they dropped from exhaustion. He would then trample them with his heels, until the blood spurted from ears and noses and at least a few were left dead. On one occasion he crowded fifteen prisoners into a single cell, giving them only a children's chamber pot which they were not permitted to empty for days. The floor of the cell was ankle-deep in excrement. Subsequently Sommer murdered all fifteen men."

The growing demand for troops on the German front lines spelled the end of Sommer's sadistic reign at Buchenwald. He was assigned to a tank unit in France. When Karl-Otto and Ilse Koch went on trial for corruption, Sommer was implicated and, for a time, was a prisoner himself at Buchenwald. He was saved again by manpower demands, when he was once more sent to a tank unit in the front with the promise that through combat he could redeem himself. Soon there was less of him to redeem when an explosion took off his right thumb and right leg. His left arm and abdomen were hit by grenade splinters. He was hospitalized for the remainder of the war.

In an ideal world, one would be able to report that Sommer received the punishment he deserved, and then some. Indeed, when the war was over, he was identified as a Buchenwald guard by former prisoners. However, medical examiners determined that he was unfit to stand trial, and he was confined to a hospital in Bayreuth. By 1956, Sommer had married his nurse, they had a child, benefited from free health care, and received a monthly pension of 280 marks. His undoing, two years later, was filing for 10,500 marks in back pension. That was when the German government put Sommer on trial and he was found guilty of thirty-eight murders.* He was given a life sentence.

---

* Certainly, this was a gross undercount. However, prosecutors did the best they could given that few witnesses were available or able to provide testimony in 1958.

Sommer was freed in 1971. He died seventeen years later, at age seventy-three, in a nursing home.

It has been estimated that at any given time during 1944, the fences of Buchenwald confined 20,000–25,000 prisoners. Every day, 150–200 prisoners died—however, this is likely an underestimate because the always-active crematorium had the capacity to burn up to four hundred bodies a day, and even the über-efficient Nazis did not count every death by incineration. In addition, there were deportations to other labor camps as well as to the extermination chambers in Auschwitz. Still, there were always enough laboring prisoners to go around as long as the trains continued to arrive outside the gates.

It was into this version of hell that Joe Moser and his fellow Allied flyers were thrust in the third week of August 1944.

14

T he dogs were the first thing I saw after getting off that train,"
Joe Moser recalled of that broiling day, August 20, 1944,
when the long journey from the Fresnes prison finally ended at
Buchenwald.

The relief of being out of the packed, foul cattle cars immediately vanished when the passengers were confronted by German
shepherds. The men were made to stagger through the terrifying gauntlet of two rows of snarling dogs. The dogs' teeth were
bared, froth was dripping out of their mouths, and it appeared
that the guards were barely able to restrain them. Later, the airmen would learn that these animals had been trained to, when
released, jump for a man's throat and bite through the windpipe.

Well over a thousand prisoners jumped out of, fell off, and
were dragged out of the cattle cars. Those who could not initially stand and walk were kicked by the boot-wearing guards
until they either managed to get to their feet or slipped into

unconsciousness. The newcomers were herded into columns and ordered to march quickly. The ones who did not skip or stagger fast enough were beaten with fists—or received worse treatment, when approached by guards with whips.

As frightening as this experience was, it was also puzzling. No reports had gotten back to England or the Allied bases in western France of such a reception at German prisoner of war camps. The Allied pilots, according to Moser, "knew nothing of concentration camps or death camps and certainly had no reason to believe any such thing would be our destiny." Because they had come through a side gate where the train station was, the prisoners had not seen the sign on the front gate that read BUCHENWALD KONZENTRATIONLAGER. If they had, not only would they have been better informed but a few might have noted the irony of Buchenwald meaning "Forest of Beeches" because of its bucolic surroundings. Also on the entrance gate was JEDEM DAS SEINE, which translated to "To Each His Own," a phrase which would only have added to their befuddlement.

The column of prisoners marched ten abreast, stumbling to keep up with each other. A few vaguely noted a sign that read CARACHOWEG. They were unable to appreciate the grim humor of "caracho" being Spanish slang for "double time," a carryover from when Buchenwald housed Communists who had fought against the Fascists in the Spanish Civil War.

For Joe and the other arrivals, with each step came a daunting reality: "As we were marched toward the main camp I could see beyond the line of dogs and guards an imposing fence and the dull gray-brown weathered wood of factory buildings. There was a dinginess and heaviness to the buildings that filled me with a sense of foreboding. There was a heavy dread deep in my gut when I looked beyond the guards and through the fence."

What Joe and the other Allied pilots saw were faces staring

back at them, "hundreds and hundreds of empty, vacant, bony skeletal faces. Nothing recognizably human in those faces. Just empty, dead stares."

As the men moved along "skeletal figures seemed to materialize from nowhere, lining the roughly paved street," writes Thomas Childers. "Their faces were drawn and ashen, scarred with sores and blisters. Their emaciated limbs swam in the filthy threadbare uniforms. Most shambled along in stiff wooden clogs; others had bundled their feet in rags or newspaper tied with string."

Even with what he was seeing, Joe's mind could still not grasp that they were somewhere other than where the captured pilots had expected to be: "If this was a POW camp, it was far, far worse than anything I imagined when trying to prepare myself to be a prisoner."

However, with every minute that passed the new and horrifying reality became more apparent. The Allied prisoners caught a glimpse of the camp zoo on one side and the crematorium to the west, blocking out the sun sinking lower in the blue sky. The men did not know immediately that the building was a crematorium; on that late afternoon, they noticed only that smoke was wafting out of the chimney and there was a peculiar smell in the air, one Joe associated with fried bacon. But as the men were marched past the building, one of the German guards grinned and said in English, "The only way you leave this place is as smoke." As the remark was passed among the flyers, the terrible truth began to be understood.

As it dawned from man to man, they and Joe realized that they were in "something far worse than anything we could have imagined. It was a place where men and children were starved, worked to death and executed. We had found ourselves in the deepest, darkest part of the heart of Nazi evil and hatred."

The men trudged past the crematorium and several other buildings. They were told to halt outside one particular structure, larger than many of the others. The guards did a count of that last section of the column, and it totaled 168 Allied flyers. There was some small comfort that one or two of them had not fallen by the wayside, probably to be beaten or even shot by the guards or ripped apart by the dogs.

There was a pause, during which Phillip Lamason stepped forward. This time, instead of protesting the treatment of the airmen, an act likely to result in immediate death, he addressed the men. During their journey it had been confirmed that the colonel from New Zealand was the senior ranking officer of the Allied group. His directive to the flyers now was that for as long as they were illegally incarcerated in the camp, they would conduct themselves as officers and would be a disciplined, unified group of prisoners. In the meantime, he would continue to protest the abusive treatment and their presence in a concentration camp in violation of the Geneva convention.

The sneering guards looked on until it was the flyers' turn to enter the large building. The next order was for them to remove their clothes. The naked prisoners were told to form a line. One by one, the flyers stepped up to a man wielding black electric clippers. Though the blades were already clogged with hair, the barber attacked each head in the same aggressive manner. Like the others, Joe found the hairs on his head and face ripped out by the clippers, leaving the skin raw and bleeding. Moments later it was the same for his armpits and groin.

That each prisoner's head was not shaved identically was an indication of the carelessness or perhaps cruel sense of humor of the "barber." On some heads, hair had been left "in American Indian style [with] a strip about two centimeters wide which ran over the middle of the skull from the brow to the nape of the neck," reported Weinstock. "Others had hair growing on either side of the skull while the crown of the head was shaved to the scalp. In some circumstances the prisoners might have been weird or even comical, but in Buchenwald the sight was another affirmation of the carefully nurtured sadism of the Nazis." He added, "This also made escape more difficult."

The next station was a shower. The men stumbled through the cold spray, washing themselves as best they could with thin slivers of soap. After the sweat and filth of the train journey, the experience was almost an enjoyable one, even with the water stinging fresh wounds.

The next line was for the newcomers to be disinfected. A man sat on a stool holding a brush. As each prisoner was presented, he dipped the hard bristles into a tub of lye and scraped from head to toe, causing more pain as old and new wounds were torn open. "My underarms and crotch burned like I had been stuck with 1000 burning cigarettes or stung by 100 angry bees" was how Joe described the sensation. "Try as I might to keep it inside, I too yelped out in excruciating pain."

Through the sweltering heat of the late afternoon the men were marched naked to another building. Once crowded inside, prison uniforms were handed out. None of the men were measured or matched, they simply had to make do with what they were given. Weinstock recalled about his experience: "We were given clothing turned in by other prisoners, the flimsy rags of hundreds of thousands of anti-Nazis who may have worn them ten years or more before their incarceration. They were civilian clothes, offering a panorama of the styles of the past fifty years, so variously patched that I saw trousers of which one leg was black, one yellow; blue pants with red patches; red pants with a huge white patch on the seat; ancient rabbinical frock coats with one tail missing; jackets with sleeves which fell off when we inserted our arms. Those who received pants too wide in the waist were particularly unlucky. Since they had neither string nor belts they had to hold their pants up at all times."

What the flyers were handed was less flamboyant. For most of them the clothing consisted of dingy gray shirts and pants with broad, darker-gray stripes. Joe was somewhat fortunate that the pants thrust at him fit well enough, but the shirt was so large it came down to his knees. (He would learn that this was an advantage.) A few especially fortunate prisoners received pairs of wooden clogs, but the rest remained barefoot.

The last item distributed was one of great importance: a small tin bowl. If for some reason they did not present the bowl at mealtime—it did not matter if it had been lost or stolen—the inmates did not eat.

When this introductory regimen had been completed, the flyers were pushed outside. There were sixty barracks to house prisoners in the hundred-acre Buchenwald compound, and the men expected to be directed toward one of them. However, time passed as they stood on open ground and darkness overtook the camp. The ground where they stood consisted mostly of gravel and rocks, an unpleasant surface for the majority of the men without shoes. It would come to be known as the "rock pile." Guards arrived and handed out thin blankets. There was not nearly enough to go around. Apparently, it was to be three men to one blanket.

In groups of two and three, the Allied flyers sank to a sitting position on the ground to await further orders. As more time passed, it became evident that this was to be their barracks. The German guards indicated there was no room for them elsewhere in the camp, so this would be where they would sleep, or attempt to. And, they were finally informed, there would be no food as well as no shelter because they had missed dinner while being processed.

As they sat on the harsh ground, some of the men returned to wondering why they were at a facility that could not possibly be a POW camp. There had been reports circulated, many based on the accounts of escaped Allied prisoners, of what a German POW facility was like . . . and this sure was not it. Buchenwald was obviously a camp to which people were sent to die. From what the flyers had seen of other prisoners, they died from overwork or starvation or disease or a combination of all three. The smoke spewing out of that one building's chimney meant there were quicker and more efficient ways to die. Here, prisoners were deliberately being murdered, and few, if any, people cared. At this facility, the only purpose was death.

But why the Allied flyers? Over time, they would learn they had been sent to Buchenwald because they were considered terrorists. That was why their transportation papers informed the administration at Buchenwald upon their arrival, "Not to be transferred to another camp." In other words, this was to be the end of the line for the Allied airmen because of how they had been designated by the Germans.

During the Battle of Britain in 1940, the focus of the Luftwaffe was to attack airfields to hurt the Royal Air Force enough that it could no longer adequately defend England when there was an invasion or, even better, Prime Minister Churchill would offer to surrender. It had been the intention neither of the Luftwaffe nor the RAF to attack the civilian populations in Great Britain or Germany. However, one night a German bomber unloaded on an oil depot and its payload also hit a neighborhood in London. There was a similar incident the same week. Though civilians had been killed in error, the RAF took the gloves off and sent bombers to attack Berlin and civilians there died. This shift to targeting nonmilitary sites resulted in the British and Germans accusing each other of being "terror bombers."

The Americans, at first, escaped this label after the United States entered the war in 1941, by design. "The United States Army Air Forces did enunciate a policy of pinpoint assaults on key industrial or military targets, avoiding indiscriminate attacks on population centers," writes Conrad C. Crain in *American Airpower Strategy in World War II*. "This seems to differentiate US policy from the policies of Germany, Great Britain, and Japan, all of which resorted to intentional terror attacks on enemy cities during the war."

The accusation of terrorism had become more specific before the United States entered the war. Because the puppet Vichy government had signed a treaty with Nazi Germany after the fall of France in 1940, there was officially no longer war between the two countries. Of course, the French Resistance did not accept this and continued to fight the Germans and aid the Allies' efforts, which included helping downed pilots avoid capture and, ideally, be smuggled out of France to fight again. Because the French freedom fighters were civilian and not military opponents, and they employed lethal measures, the Germans considered them to be terrorists. By extension, Allied pilots who continued attacks that could harm civilians in France and Germany were *Terrorfliegers*, and this sort of went double for those pilots shot down and aided in any way by Resistance fighters. To the Germans, the flyers had lost the protections of the Geneva convention and thus could be treated like Resistance members.

There was, however, a crucial difference. Apprehended Resistance members or even those who had offered the slightest help to an Allied airman could simply be lined up and shot—as Joe believed had happened to the two young French farmworkers who had attempted to help him escape arrest. However, the Germans knew doing that to a captured pilot was crossing a line. And not only would it be viewed internationally as a war crime, the powerful

Luftwaffe and its leader, Hermann Göring, had to accept the possibility that the Allies would do the same to their pilots.

The Gestapo and SS were left to come up with a solution—quietly, *Terrorfliegers* would be imprisoned, such as in Fresnes, and then, if necessary, shipped off to a camp in Germany. If they died there, they died. No one in America or England or elsewhere would know; they could be listed as missing in action forever, the assumption being they most likely died the day they disappeared.

And so, as the Allies approached Paris that August, Joe and the other 167 *Terrorfliegers* had been lumped in with the French Resistance fighters, supporters, and suspects and put on a train. Buchenwald was the designated destination. What happened to them there was of no more concern than was the fate of the thousands of other emaciated and exhausted inhabitants of the work camp. There was very little chance of survival and no way out—except, as the guard had confided with a grin, as smoke and bits of ash propelled up a chimney by the crematorium's incessant burning.

Still, Joe was one of the men who wondered if the encroaching darkness would offer an escape opportunity. To such newcomers at Buchenwald there was still hope. But a barbed-wire fence about sixty yards away enclosed their compound, and every fifty yards along it stood a fifty-foot-tall watchtower. Each one contained an SS guard whose eyes roamed the compound below. The inmates had to assume that searchlights were ready to be switched on if there was any suspicious activity and that, moments later, machine guns would sweep away any escapees.

Though the movements of prisoners were usually observed and followed carefully by the guards, over time, from their own observations and talking furtively to other prisoners, the Allied flyers were able to form a layout of their camp, which covered forty square kilometers. They were within the section surrounded by both barbed-wire fencing and a sentry line. Specifically, the area where the flyers were "housed" was known as Little Camp, differentiating it from the Prisoners' Camp, also called the Large Camp, where conditions were not quite as primitive. Within this enclosed and well-guarded area were the poultry yard, pigsty, rabbit hutches, horse stables, a hospital for prisoners, sewage facility, a whipping block, crematorium, dog kennels, an execution facility, the Goethe oak, and Appellplatz or "roll-call square."

The airmen would become very familiar with this four-acre area. They and the other prisoners were forced to it at least twice a day for attendance to be taken. They faced a whipping block and almost every day they had to witness it being used for punishment, which consisted of an inmate being bent naked and beaten with a cane. On what the grinning guards called "special occasions," a gallows was rolled into the square and one or more prisoners were hung. The appalled inmates would not be allowed to leave Appellplatz until the victim's arms and legs had ceased twitching.

Another section of the camp, also surrounded by a sentry line of watchtowers, contained the camp headquarters, SS barracks, the SS officers' houses, the commandant's private residence, entrances to manufacturing plants, a stone quarry, and a falconry.

There was even a brothel. A year earlier, Heinrich Himmler had issued a directive establishing "special buildings" in concentration camps, including Buchenwald. They housed brothels, which were occupied by as many as two dozen female prisoners provided by the Ravensbrück camp. The women had volunteered after being promised that the reward for their services was to be freed after six months. Sometimes that promise was honored, but most of the women were returned to Ravensbrück or shipped elsewhere. Jewish women were not eligible to serve as prostitutes and Jewish prisoners were not allowed to visit the camp brothels. If a prisoner in good standing could not pay for a brothel visit with money or another acceptable form of currency, the camp administration sent an invoice to his family.

The officers posted at Buchenwald did not have to spend months at this somewhat remote location away from their wives and children. Many had been joined by their families, who, according to Weinstock, "could look out after dinner to watch the smoke from the crematorium's chimney make a pattern against the sunset. An officer's children grew up in that house; there he ate and drank, slept with his wife, listened to his phonograph."

Every prisoner wore a triangle with its color indicating that man's category. Red meant a German political prisoner, green for common criminals, gray with the letter K superimposed was for murderers, violet meant a Jehovah's Witness or other specific religious denomination, black was for gypsies and what were referred to as "shiftless elements," and a pink triangle was worn by homosexuals. Jews wore a yellow Star of David. Apparently, there was no color or symbol to accurately identify the 168 Allied flyers, and it was assumed, or at least hoped, that they would soon perish in the harsh conditions anyway. There was one other group, though, without identification: Russian soldiers, but they still wore their uniforms.

All the wooden barracks in the Large Camp were exactly the same. Each had a capacity of 300 men, with the true number of inhabitants at any given time ranging from 400 to 480 prisoners. They could find some elbow room when allowed to visit the library, which had thousands of volumes extolling the Nazi philosophy and achievements, or the five-hundred-seat movie house that offered the visual equivalent of the same material. The most impressive structure in Buchenwald, made of stone with the walls inlaid with mosaics and rugs covering the floor, was known as Block 51. Especially unlucky prisoners would learn that here Germans who regarded themselves as scientists performed experiments.

The boundaries of sadism were frequently reached and then

exceeded by the Nazi practitioners in Block 51, who justified their actions by claiming to be searching for medical innovations and cures for various ailments. Prisoners brought there to be guinea pigs were usually relatively healthy ones because serious health issues like chronic exhaustion or disease might skew the results. As Weinstock recorded: "Nazi scientists removed hearts from the bodies of men to see how long those organs would function outside the body. They took out a prisoner's lungs and tested artificial lungs in their place. They injected the helpless, writhing prisoners with a variety of experimental serums. They removed the genitals or the liver from living humans to test the reaction."*

Another structure that inspired as much fear as Block 51 was the crematorium. The thirty-five prisoners who worked there had two primary responsibilities. One was to burn the bodies provided throughout the day, beginning with the morning shipment of prisoners who had died during the night or were so close to death they merited efficient disposal instead of a futile hospital admission. The other was to extract and turn over to German clerks any pieces of gold or platinum found in the mouths of the dead. If a worker were found to have tried to keep a valuable piece for himself, he was tossed into the flames of the eight furnaces totaling sixteen ovens, which blazed twenty-four hours a day.

The execution facility was another testament to Nazi efficiency, being contained within the crematorium building. Columns of prisoners designated to die were shoved into this room and one by one were forced down a chute. A bloody chamber awaited them, and when they emerged from the chute, their heads were

---

* How many prisoners died in such a horrid manner is not known. This was apparently beyond the record-keeping abilities of even the Nazis. However, when the Allies liberated the camp, they found thousands of organs preserved in jars of formaldehyde and labeled with prisoners' names, ages, and ethnicity.

crushed by a club-wielding crematorium worker. The prisoners, even those not killed outright by the blows, were dropped onto a conveyor belt that carried them into another chamber, this one housing the furnaces. With alacrity, workers stripped them of their clothes and yanked out teeth containing gold. The prisoners were then tossed into the ovens. Some trial and error and much observation had helped the Nazis to arrive at the knowledge that it took twelve minutes for a prisoner—whether alive or dead when inserted into an oven—to become nothing more than ash.

Ashes drifted down onto the airmen as they faced their first night at Buchenwald. To try to sleep, there was nothing else to do but pair up—actually, triple up—and hope to nod off while covered by only the thin blanket. Joe had Jim Hastin and another pilot next to him, and they immediately found the filthy coverlet inadequate for three men no matter how close together they squeezed. Cruelly, the cool air of the night inexorably replaced the daytime warmth. Any smidgeon of comfort Joe and the other Allied flyers felt by imagining that Buchenwald was only a nightmare would be dispelled with the first light of dawn.

15

J oe Moser described the flyers who woke up the next morning as "a confused, angry, fearful and terribly hungry gray mass." And still cold too. Accompanied by blaring whistles, the guards and kapos had begun waking the men in Little Camp at 4 A.M., so there was not yet a sign of sunrise. Groggy and shivering, the prisoners were ordered from the "rock pile" to Appellplatz.

"On a signal the prisoners from each barracks fell in on the camp street and marched eight abreast to the roll call area," Eugen Kogon wrote. "Thousands of zebra-striped figures of misery, marching under the glare of the floodlights, column after column—no one who has ever witnessed it is likely to forget the sight."

Specifically, *Appell* was the roll call to discover how many were missing, either because they had attempted an escape or they were too ill and weak to walk or even be carried to the square. Many inmates would come to feel that those poor wretches who had perished were the fortunate ones. On this first morning for the Allied flyers, they answered when their names were called and, thankfully, no one was missing.

"We faced south, and on our right, just past the machine shop, stood the crematorium with its dirty, thick, acrid air pouring out continuously," Joe reported. "As bits of heavier ash floated down on us, so did our hopes for a life beyond this misery."

Clouds in the sky were touched by the glow of the approaching sunrise when coffee was distributed from large iron urns. The newest prisoners learned the definition of coffee at Buchenwald was different from elsewhere, at least for inmates. The liquid being poured—precisely a third of a liter to each man—was cold and the source of its odd taste was identified as being from acorns.* Still, after the seemingly endless ordeal of the train journey and the night spent in the chilly air, the so-called coffee was welcomed.

For a time there was nothing for the prisoners to do but to mill about. The flyers chatted among themselves and then mixed with other inmates who had been at Buchenwald for weeks or months or had somehow managed to survive even longer. Finally, close to noon, with the sun now burning high in the sky, the flyers were allowed to return to their patch of rocky ground and told to line up. One by one, they stepped up to a kapo ladling soup into tin cups and then to another kapo handing out an inch-thick slice of black bread. Most often, they would find that the soup consisted of dehydrated cabbage, at times including bits of turnip or what at first appeared to be white meat until the wriggling motion betrayed them as worms. A bonus would be bits of kohlrabi, whatever had not been eaten by the zoo animals, which had first dibs on the vegetable.

The flyers would also learn that although the kapos too were

---

* If a guard saw or believed any prisoner received an extra ounce of coffee, the entire work detail was beaten.

prisoners, they were not any more merciful toward their peers than the guards. In fact, many were worse. Any evidence of kindness by a kapo toward other inmates would be punished, possibly by taking away his special status and its lenient treatment. To lower the risk, most kapos overcompensated, outdoing the guards in cruelty and currying further favor with sadistic behavior.

Some of the airmen would learn a little about the levels of the German command structure at the camp, but all soon figured out how the prisoner hierarchy worked, which had more impact on their day-to-day existence anyway. There was at Buchenwald *Lageraltestes*, the three senior camp inmates. They were selected by the SS and their function was to represent the prison population. Mostly, they were to communicate orders from the SS to the inmates, and it was assumed that they would in turn convey to the SS news of any trouble, such as escape plans or other plots being formed by the prisoners. For this, of course, the senior camp inmates received special privileges.

At the next level down were the labor records office and the prisoners who worked in it. Such men, essentially clerks, took care of much of the daily detail work that would have taken guards away from more important tasks. This meant that the clerks had a significant impact on the camp population. As *The Buchenwald Report* points out, the position carried with it "much positive or negative influence that could be exercised on behalf of the prisoners. Hundreds of valuable people could be saved only with help from the labor records office, in part by secretly striking them off the lists of death transports, in part by smuggling them into external work details when their lives were in danger inside the camp."

Below them were the senior block inmates. A prisoner was nominated for this position in each block by a senior camp inmate and approved by the Buchenwald commandant's office. In turn, a senior block inmate selected two or three inmates to serve as "room attendants" for each dormitory wing. The responsibilities included maintaining order in the entire block and receiving and distributing food. Clearly, the latter responsibility afforded them a lot of power in the block, as the senior inmate and his assistants could starve uncooperative prisoners while hoarding extra food for themselves.

There were other inmates who served in various supervisory capacities, currying favor with the guards or happy enough to not be one of the "regular" prisoners whose survival was always more precarious. Quarry foreman was one example. One of the worst details to be assigned to was quarry laborer. Not only was it brutal, backbreaking work digging out huge stones, but the foremen could demonstrate Nazi-like sadism, either to impress the guards, with extra rations as the reward, or out of boredom. A frequent trick was to grab the cap off a worker's head, toss it toward one side of the quarry, and tell the man to go fetch it and be quick about it. The prisoner would run a few steps and then be shot by a guard for attempting to escape. In general, guards were rewarded with money, like a bounty, for thwarting escape attempts, even though this was less challenging than skeet shooting, and compensated guards would in turn share their reward with the foremen who had made it possible.

Then there were the kapos. "A few shining examples stand out from the many depraved characters who functioned as kapos," states *The Buchenwald Report*. "There were a number of older prisoners who, insofar as they remained alive, served as models of purity, humanity, and personal courage from beginning to end."

However, they were the exceptions. Especially this far into the war, with manpower strained to the limits, there were more kapos than guards to run the camp, and they enjoyed exercising their power over the other prisoners. A few of them may have pondered that Germany would lose the war and there would be a reckoning, but overall, survival at Buchenwald was day-to-day. There might not even be a tomorrow.

Most of the flyers felt the same way Joe Moser did: The soup was disgusting, but it was the only thing between them and starvation, so they might as well get used to it. He tried to push the worms on the surface of the soup away so that when he tipped the tin cup only the thin gruel underneath would pour in. But it was no use; the wiggling worms were the dominant ingredient. Joe kept spitting the soup out and finally tossed the rest on the ground. He would realize very soon how foolish that was. The bread was not much better. The cooks at the camp used as little actual batter as they could, and the rest was sawdust. The flyers could only get a bite down accompanied by a sip of the foul soup.*

With the meal, such as it was, completed, the flyers were left alone in what had become their barracks. Suddenly, Colonel Lamason stepped forward. In the clear light of midday the airmen could see that he was a tall, handsome man with blue eyes and a nose that had previously been broken (from rugby matches). He called "Attention!" and the men rose to their feet and faced him.

Over a decade later, Allied flyers who survived Buchenwald would find a literary and cinematic representation of Colonel Lamason in the character of Lieutenant Colonel Nicholson, created in the novel *The Bridge on the River Kwai* by Pierre Boulle and portrayed by Alec Guinness in David Lean's screen version—but without the madness. Phillip John Lamason was still shy of his twenty-sixth birthday in August 1944 yet the Royal New Zealand

---

* In contrast, the camp dogs' midday meal consisted of one kilo of meat each. Once the German shepherds had finished eating and trotted off to rejoin their masters, prisoners fought over whatever traces of gristle and bone the satiated dogs may have left in the bowls.

Air Force squadron leader already had the aura of command and leadership that immediately earned the respect of the other flyers, whatever their country.

Lamason's early background might not indicate an inclination to be a leader of men. Born in September 1918, he grew up in the coastal city of Napier. The degree he earned from Massey University was in sheep farming. However, like many of the subjects of King George when Great Britain was fighting for its life, he joined the military in September 1940. By April 1942, Lamason was an officer and pilot seeing action against the Luftwaffe in Europe. He earned the Distinguished Flying Cross the following month for piloting a bomber that had been badly damaged in a raid over Czechoslovakia and was on fire as he wrestled it back to its base in England. He received more honors early in 1944 for leading attacks on Berlin and other targets that were heavily defended. Returning from one of these missions, Lamason had to make an emergency landing. On hand to greet him when he clambered out of the wounded bomber was the American Air Forces officer Clark Gable. A few observers remarked it was hard to tell who was truly the movie star.

Beating stiff odds, and displaying heroic endurance, Lamason was still flying combat missions into June. On the eighth, he was the pilot of a Lancaster heavy bomber participating in a raid on a railroad yard near Paris. His plane was shot down, but he and several crew members managed to bail out. Lamason and his navigator, Ken Chapman, were found by members of the French Resistance. During the next seven weeks the two men were moved to various secret locations. Then they were handed over to an operative who was to help them escape to Spain but instead turned them in to the Gestapo. As would happen with Joe Moser and the other airmen, Lamason and Chapman were interrogated, classified as *Terrorfliegers,* and confined in the Fresnes prison.

Many of the men Lamason addressed that August 21 morning in Buchenwald were still astonished that the German officer had not killed the colonel when he had protested the flyers' treatment on the way from the Fresnes prison. They realized once again that they would be even worse off now if that officer had chosen to murder the Allied colonel despite the many witnesses.

Once the flyers were upright and focused on him, Colonel Lamason said, his New Zealand accent evident, "Gentlemen, we have ourselves in a very fine fix indeed. The goons have completely violated the Geneva convention and are treating us as common thieves and criminals.

"However," Lamason continued, his voice rising, "we are soldiers! From this time on, we will also conduct ourselves as our training has taught us and as our nations would expect from us. We will march as a unit to roll call, and we will follow all reasonable commands as a single unit." He also advised the airmen to stay together and not to provoke the guards to react in a way similar to what they had experienced during the train ordeal.

Straight away, Lamason organized the flyers by national service—RAF, Royal Australian Air Force, etc.—and he appointed the commanding officer for each group. Joe could not say it was like old times, but it was reassuring in this hateful place to be serving under his old CO, Captain Larson, again. And most likely, the other members of the Army Air Corps echoed Joe's sentiments: "From this moment on we once again became soldiers, now in a tightly knit group experiencing what very few Allied soldiers would experience. It boosted our morale and gave us hope. We might be in these awful prison uniforms and be in the dirtiest, filthiest, most degrading place on earth, but we were soldiers, American soldiers, the best, proudest fighting force on earth."

The Allied flyers also understood that maintaining discipline and unity offered better odds of success should there be an opportunity to escape. If they allowed themselves to be dulled and become hopeless by their situation, and perhaps even to fight among themselves for food scraps or an extra inch of blanket, they were dooming themselves to Buchenwald for as long as it operated . . . or they lived. The war could go on for another year, or more—how many of them would still be alive then if they did not survive together?

Until some of the questions could be answered, all of the Allied officers would remain united in one group. Each nationality had its own subgroup, but cooperation and mutual support were the top priorities. Marching and otherwise acting as a military unit would make a formidable impression on their captors. And they had a leader in Colonel Lamason. How effective a leader he was became quite clear later that day.

Just outside the concentration camp were factory buildings. The larger operation was the Gustloff Armament Works, which had been constructed the year before specifically to make use of the slave labor Buchenwald provided and was funded by money stolen from Jewish businesses. The other was Deutsche Ausrüstungswerke, a general armaments and radio factory owned by the SS. The reservoir of labor was constantly being replenished—if a prisoner died of overwork, there was always another to replace him as long as the trains kept arriving at the side gate. And they worked cheap—for nothing, in fact, because whatever the factories' owners paid went directly to the SS (with a healthy slice to Commandant Pister). This system was a gold mine for the Nazis, with the factories employing as many as nine thousand of the eighty thousand prisoners who had been crowded into the camp by late summer 1944. Every day, they were herded from the camp to the machinery that produced rifles, pistols, aircraft parts, and even motorized vehicles.

To refuse to work at the factories meant a beating or torture or a bullet in the brain. Yet that was exactly what Colonel Lamason did: refuse.

Nazi officers informed the New Zealander that the next day he and his fellow airmen would begin working side by side in the factories with the thousands of other prisoners. Colonel Lamason responded that this would not happen. He explained that, yes, obviously they were prisoners, but they were soldiers and could not be required to participate in war-production activities— especially manufacturing weapons to kill other Allied soldiers. If the circumstances were reversed, German prisoners would not be ordered to work in such factories.

The SS officer's immediate reaction was to grab a rifle from a guard's hands and strike the impudent prisoner with the butt of it. Lamason almost collapsed; then he waved off help from his fellow officers and straightened up. He and the Nazi officer gazed at each other. The airmen expected that at any moment the order would be given for their leader to be shot. Perhaps they would all be shot. But after a few moments, the Nazi officer shrugged and dismissed them.

But this was not the end of the matter. The next day, a different SS officer at the head of a contingent of guards and a German shepherd marched into Little Camp and confronted Lamason at the rock pile. Though believing he was about to die, the colonel quipped, "I didn't realize it took twenty guys to shoot me."

The unamused officer ordered Lamason to tell his men to get to work in the factories. To further persuade him, the dog rose up and snapped repeatedly at the New Zealander's throat. "No, we don't work," Lamason said. "We don't do this. We are servicemen, we want out of this place."

The officer told his men to take aim. With twenty rifles trained on him, Lamason looked the German commander in the eye. One more question was asked: "Are you going to work or not?"

Lamason shook his head and the two men continued to gaze at each other. Finally, the German officer barked an order and the guards ground arms and the group marched away.

These acts of defiance and the solidarity of the Allied airmen offered the barest glimmer of hope that they might survive their imprisonment. But as they were to learn, hope was forbidden in Buchenwald.

16

B eing in such an unfamiliar and frightening environment, the
Allied airmen had no idea what would happen to them next.
They certainly did not expect that they might be killed by their
fellow flyers.

On August 24, units of the Eighth Air Force undertook a massive strike against targets across Germany and areas outside of it
that were still occupied by Nazi forces. More than 1,300 bombers
were sent aloft. Among the targets were the two factories connected to the Buchenwald camp.

For the Allied prisoners, it was just another morning in their
painful and somewhat surreal surroundings. The shouts of the kapos greeted them before dawn. Few of the flyers had to be woken
because of the impossibility of getting any sleep on the insufferable stony surface of the plaza. They were hurried to *Appell*, where
they stood rubbing themselves in the early-morning chill. Several
of the men had already begun to wonder what it would be like

for them to spend nights outside when the colder air of autumn arrived. It was with some relief that the morning quickly became hot and humid.

It was a typical day for the nine thousand or so other prisoners at the camp who, after *Appell* was finally completed, were marched to the factories. They actually considered themselves and were viewed by fellow inmates as the fortunate ones. First of all, they were healthy enough to go to work and, hopefully, survive a full day of it. There were perhaps dozens of prisoners who had died during the night. There were others too weak or sick to work who were waiting to die, which might be hastened by impatient guards or kapos. There were work details more onerous than the factories, such as wheeling the carts that collected the dead and the very sick and delivered them to the crematorium that relentlessly generated smoke and the ash that fluttered down onto the camp and its inhabitants. And hundreds of prisoners trudged off every morning to the quarry, some never to return and others who would but with broken bones that either healed by themselves or eventually resulted in a cart ride to the crematorium.

Another reason why the factory assignment was coveted: It offered an opportunity to hurt the German war effort. There were furtive acts of sabotage committed by the workers that slowed production. There was pilfering too, with prisoners smuggling weapons, radio parts, and other useful items out of the factories. The goal was to have enough material hidden away that when the inmate uprising occurred—next month, next year—it had a better chance of success.

For the Allied flyers, thanks to the resistance of Colonel Lamason, there was no marching off to the factories. They were still assigned work because there was no such thing as being idle at Buchenwald, but the jobs they were given had to conform with their special status. "The camp administrators knew the airmen were in Buchenwald illegally and could not be presented with an opportunity to escape," explains Colin Burgess in *Destination: Buchenwald*. "No one beyond the camp perimeter could even know they were there. For the airmen, this at least meant they were assigned to such simple domestic duties as cleaning, carrying, and interior road maintenance."

So it was, ironically, that their illegal status saved their lives that day.

Joe Moser and the other flyers first heard the sound shortly after noon—a rumble in the distance. It could not possibly be artillery this far into Germany. As humid as the day was, the sky was clear with no sign of storm clouds. The men were sitting or lying on the harsh surface of their "barracks," hoping for the appearance of something to eat. The rumbling sound seemed to be getting nearer. One of the flyers, listening intently, speculated that they were the engines of Flying Fortresses.

And soon, a formation of B-17s came into view. The prisoners estimated they were at twenty thousand feet because at the usual thirty-five thousand feet they would have been barely specks in the sky. These bombers were easily visible as they approached. One was a short distance ahead of the others. Known as a "pathfinder," this plane's purpose was to drop a flare or sometimes a bomb on the target to let the other pilots know they had arrived at the destination.

As the Allied airmen watched, the pathfinder B-17 came right at the Buchenwald camp and let loose a bomb.

"I turned and ran and saw my fellow prisoners trying to find a direction to run to," Joe remembered. "We were completely enclosed. Barracks to the west, electric barbed wire fence to the north and east and completely surrounding the camp. The bomb screamed down."

The men realized there was nothing to do but to fall flat and cover their heads. The bomb crashed into the armaments factory. The mild concussion as it exploded told them it was a marker flare bomb and by itself would not cause much havoc. But that also told them it was the first of the large payload about to be released. The airmen cowering on the rocky ground realized that even at twenty thousand feet the bombardiers could only be so precise.

Sure enough, as some of the men glanced upward, they saw dozens of five-hundred-pound bombs being released and raining down from the Flying Fortresses. In all, there were 129 bombers on the attack that day.

There were explosions inside the factories. Petrified prisoners rushed out the doors only to be greeted by another form of death as guards raked them with machine-gun fire, ceasing only when the Germans feared for their own lives and ran away from the expanding carnage.

There was a moment when the flyers paused to wish they were the ones up in the sky doling out such destruction, but then the desire to survive took over. To Joe, the bombs "all seemed headed right for my head. 'Mother of God,' I prayed, and I knew that in mere moments I would be in her presence. There was no doubt."

Eyes squeezed shut, the airmen tried to melt and leech into the rocky ground. Each expected the next bomb to land right on top of him. The thunderous concussions of the bombs as they landed shook the ground with incessant violence. "The debris was flying in all directions, and now I could feel things hitting my body." Contemplating death, Joe managed to muse in the midst of the maelstrom, "The German guard was wrong. Looks like I'd leave here as wet dust sifting into the air."

That air had suddenly become much hotter because of the sweeping heat of the explosions and the fires they were creating.

There would be a few seconds when there would be a halt to the horrific noise and heat, and the pauses offered hope that the barrage was over. But each time, with a deafening roar, it would resume. During one pause, Joe allowed himself to look around and then up. First, he saw the other flyers lying exactly like he was. Second, he saw another wave of B-17s approaching.

The attack was being carried out by the 401st Bomber Group. Its Flying Fortresses had taken off that morning from a base sixty miles northwest of London. If the Allied prisoners had known the specifics, there would have been total astonishment that any of them survived the assault, which consisted of 175 bombs weighing 1,000 pounds, over 500 bombs weighing 500 pounds, and close to 300 incendiary bombs. In total, the planes conducting the raid dropped over 600,000 pounds of bombs on the Buchenwald factories and their immediate surroundings.

It was with disbelief that the Allied prisoners realized the raid had ended. There were no more roaring concussions. But there was still a roar, this one emitted by the raging fires. "For once," Joe noted, "the fires and smells of the crematorium were overtaken by something much stronger." In twos and threes, the heads of the men came up off the ground. They knew thousands of prisoners were in those factories, which had become another kind of crematorium.

The relief that all of the Allied prisoners had survived soon gave way to awe at the extent of the destruction—and admiration for the pilots and bombardiers who had managed to leave most of the camp unscathed. From what the airmen observed and later learned, both of the factories were so badly damaged that they were knocked out of the war effort. Close to a thousand prisoners were killed and wounded, with most of the casualties in the factories and a handful from a stray bomb landing in the rock quarry. By design or accident, bombs had also fallen on the SS barracks and quarters for officers and their families just south of the camp, killing scores of German soldiers and guards and over two dozen of their family members. These included the wife and daughter of Hermann Pister, the camp commandant.

Casualties also resulted from bombs damaging the I Barracks. This was a stone building surrounded by a ten-foot-high stockade fence and continuously guarded by SS soldiers. In this structure were housed more prominent prisoners the Germans wanted to isolate from the general population. Among those killed that August afternoon were Rudi Breitscheid and his wife. The seventy-year-old, born in Cologne, had worked as an economist and journalist, and following World War I he had been a member of the German delegation to the League of Nations. Breitscheid had opposed the Nazi Party at its very beginnings but, like many others, could not stem the tide of fascism in Germany during the 1930s. He eventually had to leave, going first to Switzerland and then to France. The Nazis caught up with him, though, and the Gestapo arrested him in 1941. He joined thousands of other political prisoners at Buchenwald.

Breitscheid's wife died from wounds the day of the Allied raid, but he lingered for four days before succumbing. He would be honored after the war with a plaza named for him in Berlin.

Another well-known casualty of the August 24 attack was the forty-one-year-old Princess Mafalda of Savoy. She was the second daughter of King Victor Emmanuel III of Italy, and in 1925 she had married Prince Philipp of Hesse, a grandson of German Emperor Frederick III. She and her husband, who became a member of the Nazi Party, would have four children and, for a time, live a life of privilege.

In the 1930s, because of his wife's connections, Prince Philipp was appointed by Hitler to be a liaison between the German government and the Fascist government in Italy. Once the war began, however, the couple, especially Princess Mafalda, fell out of favor with the Führer. One of the phrases he used to describe her was the "blackest carrion in the Italian royal house." The Nazis' chief propagandist, Joseph Goebbels, went one step further by saying she was the "worst bitch in the entire Italian royal house." Such declarations, merited or not, did not bode well for her future.

Soon after Italy surrendered to the Allies in 1943, her husband was placed under house arrest in Bavaria. He had managed to ferry their children to the Vatican, where they were given sanctuary.* Princess Mafalda was in Bulgaria attending the wedding of her brother-in-law, King Boris III, when she was summoned to the German embassy. There, she was arrested by the Gestapo. After interrogations in Munich and Berlin, she was sent to Buchenwald.

Princess Mafalda's experience during the air strike was particularly gruesome. Her living quarters were adjacent to the factory complex, and during the attack she was buried up to her neck in smoldering debris and consequently suffered severe burns. She contracted an infection and died three days after the raid. Her naked body was dumped in the crematorium but a priest found it, covered her up, and arranged for a quick and immediate cremation.† He also cut off a lock of the princess's hair, which was smuggled out of Buchenwald and after the war would be given to her family.

There was another high-profile political prisoner who died as a result of the bombing . . . only he didn't. Ernst Thälmann, who was fifty-eight in August 1944, was one of the earlier targets of

---

* Prince Philipp and his children would survive their confinements and the war. He would afterward live in Italy, where he became a successful interior designer.
† The priest was Father Joseph Thyl, who was head of the crematorium work detail that day.

the expanding Nazi Party. The farmworker from Hamburg had served in the German Army during World War I. Wounded twice while serving on the Western Front, his honors included the Iron Cross Second Class. After the war, Thälmann returned to Hamburg and became a laborer and then an employment inspector. He also joined the Communist Party and, during a visit to Moscow in 1921, was introduced to Vladimir Lenin.

An unsuccessful assassination attempt the following year did not curtail his efforts on behalf of the Communists in Germany. He helped organize the Hamburg Uprising in October 1923 and ran for German president in 1925. Seven years later, by then one of the most visible Communist Party members in the country and an ally of Josef Stalin, Thälmann ran again for president, this time against the incumbent Paul von Hindenburg and the insurgent Adolf Hitler. The latter and his Nazi Party took over in January 1933, and two months later Thälmann was arrested.

He would be held in solitary confinement for over eleven years. A change of scenery occurred when he was transferred to Buchenwald in August 1944. Any hopes that Thälmann might be able to interact with other political prisoners there were dashed on the eighteenth, when he was put up against a wall and shot. The bombing six days later conveniently allowed the Nazis to announce that both Thälmann as well as Rudolf Breitscheid had died from wounds sustained during the Allied raid.

There was one other significant casualty—the Goethe oak. During the raid it had been so damaged that it would have to be taken down. There was some satisfaction among the camp inmates to see what remained of a mighty tree denoting German pride was nothing more than a blackened stump.

The Allied airmen in the camp had escaped the wrath of the bombs but would not escape the wrath of the Germans. Suddenly, as they gazed at the blazing ruins of the factories, SS guards streamed into Little Camp. Only the flyers were ordered to Appell-platz. As had already become routine, they lined up by units be-hind Colonel Lamason and the other senior officers and marched to the plaza. Waiting for them there was a manned MG-42 ma-chine gun. Immediately within every flyer was the fear that they would pay the ultimate price for the catastrophic air raid.

The men were told to form a line facing the machine gun. A German officer stepped forward and addressed them, his anger evident. The airmen were told, in passable English, that they had a choice—die immediately here in the plaza or assist those fighting the fires in the factories. At first, the men exhaled, relieved to have any choice. Then, they wondered how they could be of any use, being barefoot and barely clothed and with no other protection from the flames. But the furious officer was not about to engage in a discussion. He demanded that they get moving and salvage what they could from the battered structures. After a few seconds, Col-onel Lamason gave the order and they marched out of the plaza.

They came to a halt outside the Gustloff Armament Works. For Lamason and the flyers, the basic problem remained: not do-ing anything to help the enemy war effort, including salvaging equipment that could possibly be used again. It took only a few minutes to figure out what to do.

As Joe Moser recalled: "I entered a building that was only par-tially destroyed and found some machining equipment and tools that were undamaged. I picked up the heavy gear and made my way through the rubble back to the outside, as did several of my fellow prisoners. When we were outside, we looked at each other and I saw they had the same thought I did."

With no guards or kapos supervising them, the Allied airmen hoisted the same pieces of equipment they had just brought out-side and carried them back inside. This chore was repeated for the next few hours. Whenever a guard or kapo did come by, the flyers looked busy enough, always lifting and carrying. If a man was spotted heading toward the smoldering building, he pretended to be navigating around debris and then resumed walking the "right" way.

The carelessness of one of the flyers might have blown it for the whole team if not for Colonel Lamason's intervention. One young airman had come across a dead German soldier inside the factory and, unable to resist, had taken off the shiny boots and tugged them onto his own feet. They were quite noticeable when he next emerged from the burning building.

Fortunately, the colonel encountered him before an SS guard did. "You bloody fool!" Lamason told the abashed flyer. "Get those off and get rid of them." Within seconds, the flyer was again barefoot.

The "work" continued for the rest of the afternoon. "The almost meaningless effort to contribute to the damage caused by our fellow warriors from above gave our morale a huge boost," Moser wrote. "We continued the charade until we were called for the evening *Appell*."

17

The airmen got to experience a truly long *Appell* that evening. The camp guards were unusually disorganized, still processing the humiliating insult and destruction of the Allied air raid. They needed extra time to complete their paperwork because of the dead, wounded, and otherwise missing prisoners.

Bolstered by their sabotage that day, the airmen felt pretty good during the hours at Appellplatz. And the regimen Colonel Lamason insisted upon was easier to follow. "We stood together," wrote Joe Moser, "as still and military-like as our weakened and tired bodies would allow. We were Americans, and Britons, and Canadians, and Aussies and New Zealanders and more. We would win this fight. We might no longer be able to contribute much, but by God, we would do all we could. They could starve us, treat us like dogs, humiliate us and torture us, but they could not break our fighting spirits."

Incredibly, the morning following the destructive air raid,

with portions of the manufacturing plants still smoldering, the airmen were asked if they would help repair them. Initially, after the roll call had been completed, an SS officer harangued the flyers as though they had been responsible for the raid and that such miserable and vile creatures as themselves represented the vermin who made up the Allied forces. But once the officer got that out of his system, he calmed down and through a translator asked for volunteers. Specifically, he wanted to know who among the airmen had skills as a plumber, carpenter, or electrician to offer.

Fortunately, the men managed not to laugh. When no one raised a hand, the officer, translator in tow, stepped from one prisoner to another, asking the same question. He received the same response every time: name, rank, and serial number. The officer finally gave up, tossing several last insults at the airmen before ordering them back to their rocky barracks.

For the following two weeks the Allied flyers continued to share thin blankets and sleep, as best they could, on the stony surface. Once it was lights out (except for the tower searchlights) the rocks offered at least some comfort, having been warmed by the day's sun. However, as the nights wore on into September, they shed their remaining warmth and "the night chill nearly overcame the increasing pain in our stomachs."

Thomas Childers writes that "the men sank gradually into the brutal routine of the tent camp: the endless roll calls, the savage beatings, the starvation rations, the filth, the vermin, the disease." Conditions became more crowded within the barbed-wire-enclosed Little Camp, yet every day "new prisoners—Poles, Czechs, Hungarians, Jews—were tossed into the already horribly crowded tent camp. They wandered around the barren compound, trying to find a place to sit or sleep, a place to escape the surprisingly brutal sun. It was impossible to take more than a few steps without bumping into another dismal soul, and vicious fights broke out over scraps of food, draining away even more energy from the starving men."

As best they could, the men tried to tolerate their cruel surroundings. They could at least continue to communicate with and sometimes comfort each other. And share their experiences of how they wound up at the Fresnes prison. Many of the flyers had been captured by Germans immediately after they landed on French soil. Others had been found by French Resistance members or at least French families willing to hide them. Joe Moser's freedom had lasted only minutes, but for some of the airmen, like his friend Jim Hastin, it had lasted days or even weeks. Also by sharing their stories of combat and being shot down and attempts at escape, they realized the full treachery of the man known as Captain Jacques.

As the airmen related their experiences, the tales had an infuriating familiarity. Whoever had kept them safe would receive word that it had been arranged to turn the hidden flyer over to the next person in the underground chain. Most often, this was a man named Georges Prevost, described as a "portly" Frenchman. The experience of Colonel Lamason and his navigator, Ken Chapman, was all too typical.

During the last week of July, the two downed flyers had been turned over to Prevost in Paris. He led them across the Seine to an apartment in a building across from Moy's Restaurant. Waiting for them upstairs was a young man with thick glasses. He was a French intelligence officer whom Prevost referred to as Captain Jacques, whose full name was Jacques Desoubrie.

"A short, stocky man with piercing grey eyes set behind a pair of moderately thick-lensed spectacles, Desoubrie dressed quite smartly, and his light brown hair was always immaculately combed," writes Colin Burgess. "An easy smile revealed bright gold fillings in his front teeth. Many an evader was taken in by his excellent English, oily charms and smooth reassurances."

Captain Jacques explained that there was an escape route to Spain known as the Comet Line, and he had successfully led Allied airmen along it at least seven times. He then introduced Lamason and Chapman to a pleasant woman named Geneviève, who would care for them until it was time to leave and who was the sister of Georges Prevost.*

Lamason and Chapman ate and slept well that night, with their meal accompanied by the champagne provided by Geneviève. In the morning, Captain Jacques was back and with him was an RAF officer named Bob. All three flyers were asked for the names of people who had helped them get this far. Jacques explained that, as the men had observed, such people were often poor farmers or had other low-income occupations and the French Resistance wanted to give them money in gratitude. This seemed reasonable, so what names were remembered were offered.

The next day it was time to move on, or at least for Lamason and Chapman. Georges Prevost was back, and he and Captain Jacques brought the flyers to meet Madame Orsini, a thin, short, red-haired woman wearing dark-framed glasses. She in turn led them through city streets to the Place de la Concorde. An hour later, a black Citroën containing two men stopped. The flyers were invited, in English, into the car.

The car sped through a dizzying array of streets with the two men discussing their years of living in the United States before the war, which explained their perfect English. The Citroën halted in front of another apartment building, and Lamason

---

* Georges and Geneviève Prevost were genuinely trying to help downed Allied pilots. They would later be betrayed to the Gestapo, and it is believed that both died in concentration camps.

and Chapman were escorted into separate rooms. They were told they would have dinner together but then were to return to their rooms and try to get to sleep early. Tomorrow would be a big day—they would be joined by other flyers on the journey to Spain.

Sure enough, the next morning there were six airmen eating when Lamason and Chapman entered the kitchen. The half-dozen downed flyers in turn would wait for their own departure day. Lamason and Chapman were instructed to take separate routes—the colonel escorted via Metro and Chapman on the back of a motorcycle—to a rendezvous point near the Champs-Élysées. When they did find each other, the location was next to a barracks containing German soldiers, which seemed to the two flyers an unnecessary risk. Lamason's escort took them to a nearby café, where they drank beer until a car stopped outside. The airmen got in, and after five minutes the car pulled into a driveway. The building in front of them was the headquarters of the Gestapo. Lamason and Chapman were arrested.

Joe Moser's own commanding officer, Captain Merle Larson, had fallen victim to the scheme coordinated by Captain Jacques. When German anti-aircraft gunfire had shot down his P-38 Lightning, he had landed unnoticed. For a week he negotiated the French landscape without being detected, and then when he was found, it was by members of the French Resistance. For two weeks they kept him hidden; then Larson and several other downed pilots were turned over to a colleague, a woman with red hair who worked with Captain Jacques, who had to be Madame Orsini. The next step after that was not toward freedom but toward arrest and imprisonment.

"We were caught in civilian clothes," Larson said in an interview many years later, "so they called us spies. We had our uniforms and flying suits on underneath, of course, and our dog tags too, but the Germans took away our uniforms and tags and gave us back our civilian clothes and took us up for interrogation."

Another pilot betrayed was the idealistic and patriotic Levitt C. Beck. The young lieutenant had been fulfilling his dreams of being a fighter pilot, dueling in the sky with the Luftwaffe and doing his part to damage Germany's war machine. His optimism was not diminished in June when, on the twenty-ninth, he was shot down over France. Beck bailed out in time and was found by friendly French, who hid him on the third floor of a café in the village of Anet, southwest of Paris.

He lived there for three weeks. While Beck did his share of staring out the window, he also put pen to paper and wrote about his life, training, and combat experiences. A dream was to have his story—which, no surprise, he titled "Fighter Pilot"—published after the war, but his main motivation was so his parents back home in Huntington Park, California, would know about his thoughts and experiences. On July 16, Beck had to safeguard the manuscript because he had been informed arrangements had been made to escort him to a field where a plane would return him to England. That night, Beck put the manuscript into a hand-made pine box that in turn was placed inside a tin box that was buried under a shed behind the café.

Captain Jacques, or someone following his mostly successful strategy, was responsible for Beck's capture. It is known that a Gestapo officer posing as a French Resistance fighter betrayed the lieutenant during his attempt at escape, and Beck became one of the airmen kept at the Fresnes prison and shipped to Buchenwald that August. His manuscript survived the war. After the liberation of Paris, his parents were contacted by the French Resistance about their son's capture and the existence of the manuscript. It indeed was sent to them, via the War Department, and *Fighter*

Pilot was issued by the Wetzel Publishing Company of Los Angeles in 1946.*

To the Allied airmen at Buchenwald, Captain Jacques immediately came to represent a particularly despicable form of Nazi collaborator. For most of them it would not be until years later that they learned the story of Jacques Desoubrie, the illegitimate son of a Belgian doctor who was just twenty-three in 1944. He was working as an itinerant electrician when the war began, and he quickly embraced the Nazi philosophy and ambitions. Adopting the "Captain Jacques" identity, he managed to infiltrate the French underground and become a trusted member of it while simultaneously being a member of a Gestapo group led by Prosper Desitter, whose goal was to betray and capture dozens of downed Allied flyers and arrest and execute the many French patriots who had assisted them. In 1943 and '44, his team was very successful.

Eventually, though, that success jeopardized Captain Jacques. Suspicions were raised by the alarming number of flyers who began the journey along the Comet Line and then disappeared. His position became more precarious when Paris fell. Desoubrie thought it prudent to have one less close associate to incriminate him, so he stabbed Madame Orsini. However, she survived the attack, was arrested by the Allies, gave up Desoubrie under questioning, and was herself sent to the Fresnes prison. After the war, Desoubrie was tried for treason, found guilty (thanks in part to Orsini's revelations), and in 1949 was executed by firing squad.

It was also during the first two weeks at Buchenwald that many of the airmen met, after initial contact was made with Colonel Lamason, other Allied prisoners, several of whom had impressive

---

* Lieutenant Beck did not live to see his book published. He died in Buchenwald of disease and starvation on November 29, 1944.

reputations as spies and saboteurs. They were members of an exclusive and ultrasecret service in the British military.

As John Grehan and Martin Mace put it in their book on the service, "The Special Operations Executive was born out of the ashes of defeat." That it was created at all in the summer of 1940 was a testament to either Winston Churchill's confidence in the ability of Great Britain to survive the German onslaught or his sheer stubbornness. Even in the midst of the Blitzkrieg, the prime minister envisioned a means of attacking Germany from within its occupied territories, if not within the fatherland itself. On July 22, Churchill accepted a proposal titled "Set Europe Ablaze" that created the Special Operations Executive that would instigate and supervise subversive activities on the other side of the English Channel. The initial phase of the SOE focused on recruiting and training secret agents.

While many of these men already had military experience, the training was especially rigorous in unarmed combat, explosives and other tools of sabotage, techniques for enduring interrogations, spying tactics, the sending and receiving of messages without being detected, and whatever other skills that would not only come in handy but might keep them alive as commandos. Early on it was realized that women SOE agents were also needed, particularly as couriers, because in occupied countries German soldiers routinely stopped and questioned young men, whereas, at least at first, young women were not viewed with suspicion.

Because of the location of its headquarters and Sherlock Holmes, SOE administrators and senior agents were known as the Baker Street Irregulars. The wry reference was to the young boys used by the famous fictional detective to "go everywhere, see everything and overhear everyone." The first wave of agents began to be deployed in 1942, and at its peak during the war the SOE consisted of ten thousand men and three thousand women. It can only be estimated how many of them died in action or were

tortured to death or died in prison from wounds and disease. As
Grehan and Mace point out, "France was the most important
SOE arena, and the most dangerous for its agents. Almost a quarter of [the] agents in France failed to return and estimated losses
incurred" were roughly equal to that of an infantry regiment.

Each agent knew that to be captured was to face a gruesome
fate. Once aware of the existence of the SOE, Hitler ordered that
its agents were to die by being hung with piano wire. As Heinrich Himmler explained, the Führer's outlook was, "They should
die, certainly, but not before torture, indignity and interrogation
had drained from them that last shred and scintilla of evidence
which should lead to the arrest of others." And, presumably, as
word spread of the horrific experiences of SOE agents, fewer
men and women would sign up and fewer of those who already had would undertake missions behind enemy lines. However, Churchill's special secret service remained a very effective
weapon against the Nazis up until the collapse of Germany, not
shutting shop until 1946.

Of the SOE agents imprisoned at Buchenwald, perhaps most
prominent was a British wing commander with the extended
name of Forest Frederick Edward Yeo-Thomas, who for simplic-
ity was called Tommy.* Forty-three years old in fall 1944, Yeo-
Thomas had been born in London but spent most of his school
years in France. Though a bright student, he had discipline issues,
and his parents had to keep finding new schools that would take
him. He left the system for good at age sixteen, when, claiming to
be eighteen, he enlisted in the British Army and served through
the end of World War I.

---

* Yeo-Thomas's life story is worthy of an entire book. Fortunately, the author
Bruce Marshall thought so too decades ago, and his *The White Rabbit* is a well-
researched and riveting tale.

Yeo-Thomas felt cheated that hostilities had ceased before he could fully experience them, so he moved on to Poland to aid its war with the Russians. He was captured and sentenced to face a firing squad but managed to ease out of his cell before dawn arrived. That near-death adventure apparently satiated his wanderlust, because when Yeo-Thomas made his way to Paris, he stayed there and became a businessman, which would include serving as an executive at the Molyneux dressmaking company. But in the 1930s he began to miss the military life and joined the Royal Air Force as an interpreter. When World War II got underway, he signed up with Special Operations Executive.

With the code name White Rabbit, Yeo-Thomas parachuted into France in 1943 to assist underground operations there and gather intelligence about the German occupation. He returned to England with useful information as well as an American pilot handed over by the French Resistance. By September, Yeo-Thomas was back in France. There were several close calls with the Gestapo during the ensuing eight weeks, but once again he went home to deliver top-shelf intelligence. On his third mission, he was betrayed and then arrested by the Gestapo.

Though believing him a spy, the Nazis did not know what an important agent they had, and Yeo-Thomas was determined they would not find out. For two months he was tortured and interrogated but he managed to maintain that he was Kenneth Dodkin, a downed RAF pilot.* Because Yeo-Thomas had known Dodkin and his background, the few details he offered were checked by his captors and found to be factual. Finally, either the Gestapo

---

* Among the methods used on Yeo-Thomas was what is today known as waterboarding. In his case, with his arms and legs in chains, his head was thrust repeatedly into a trough of ice-cold water. He contracted blood poisoning from the chains cutting into his left wrist. Miraculously, the minimal treatment available was enough to eradicate the infection before his arm had to be amputated.

believed him or grew weary of torturing him, because Yeo-Thomas—who had twice tried to escape—was patched up and transported to the Fresnes prison.

After four months of enduring the awful conditions there, he was sent to the Compiègne prison to join thirty-six other SOE men who had been caught and survived interrogations.* The agents made two attempts to escape before all were shipped off to Bu-chenwald, arriving on August 17, 1944. They were met by other SOE agents, including Christopher Burney and Maurice Pertschuk. They immediately began cautiously reaching out to other factions in the camp and forming plans to escape. The arrival of Colonel Lamason and his Allied airmen was encouraging indeed . . . or even more than that.

A surreptitious meeting was arranged between the New Zea-lander and "Kenneth Dodkin" and Burney, who had been cap-tured by the Germans for spying and had access to the various networks at Buchenwald. Burney was another one of the colorful characters who filled out the SOE ranks. The upper-class English-man born in 1917 had been one of the early Special Operations Ex-ecutive branch recruits. Already a lieutenant in the British Army with commando training, Burney, who spoke perfect French, was parachuted into France in May 1942. He worked with the French Resistance for several months but, being tall and blond, began to arouse suspicions. It was decided that Burney should be secretly removed to Spain, but before that happened he was arrested by the Nazis.

Burney's first imprisonment was for fifteen months in Fresnes,

---

* It was revealed in 2012 that Sophie Jackson, author of *Churchill's White Rabbit*, another book on Yeo-Thomas, had discovered a written connection between her subject and a young naval intelligence officer named Ian Fleming, leading her, and eventually others, to conclude that Yeo-Thomas was the model for Agent 007, James Bond.

in solitary confinement because of his resistance to torture and refusal to provide information about SOE operations. Then he was sent to join other SOE agents at Buchenwald. He and Yeo-Thomas became leaders in the underground movement at the camp. And they were eager to meet Lamason and bring him and his men into the fold of inmates hoping to one day take over the camp.*

When the get-together began, Lamason was instantly alarmed—he had known Dodkin, and this first man was *not* him. He warned Burney of betrayal and that the camp's underground networks were compromised. His fear was immediately put to rest when the true identity of "Dodkin" was explained.

Yeo-Thomas had learned, according to Bruce Marshall, that "twelve kilometers from Buchenwald was a small and poorly guarded airfield called Hohra. Provided they could fight their way out of Buchenwald, there would be little to prevent their attacking the airfield, seizing the bombers and flying back to the Allied lines. Lamason, as hot-headed as Tommy, readily agreed."

However, there was a big obstacle to overcome, and soon. The SOE agents had learned there were weapons hidden within the camp, but only the Communist leaders knew where they were. Thus far, they had refused to share the location.

Suddenly, that knowledge became crucial: On September 9, an announcement was made that sixteen of the imprisoned SOE agents (though not including Yeo-Thomas or Burney) were to report to Admission Block 17 in the camp. There was, of course, much apprehension among the Allied inmates as the group was

---

* Unlike many of his fellow SOE agents, Burney was still alive, though barely, when Buchenwald was liberated in April 1945. After the war, he worked for the United Nations and became a manager of the British and French Bank. The MBE recipient died in 1980.

gathered together by SS guards and set off. Yet there was bravado too, because as the men marched they sang, "It's a Long Way to Tipperary."

When they arrived at the building, they learned they were to be executed the next day and were locked inside for the night. A priest made his way to Admission Block 17 but was refused permission to see the condemned men. He lingered, hoping the camp administrators would change their mind. He later reported hearing the sounds of beatings coming from inside the building.

The next morning, Hitler's order was carried out. The sixteen men were paired up back-to-back and their hands tied together. As Burgess describes the ensuing scene: "Nooses made from piano wire were placed around their necks, and each pair of men were hoisted aloft until the nooses engaged over steel hooks protruding from the walls. They died a violent, agonizing death, thrashing about as the nooses bit deeply into their necks." Once their movements stopped, the SOE agents were lifted down and carted off to the crematorium.

The total death toll was actually seventeen, because there was one man who apparently the Germans could not wait, even just one more day, to kill. The forty-nine-year-old Robert Benoist had achieved fame in France first as an infantryman and fighter pilot in World War I, then as a championship race-car driver. He won the French Grand Prix in 1924, and three years later earned immortality in the sport by winning the Spanish, Italian, and British Grand Prix trophies in addition to capturing the French title again. There was a period of retirement in the early 1930s, then Benoist returned to win the twenty-four hours of Le Mans in 1937. He was lionized as one of France's greatest sports heroes.

As the Nazis overwhelmed his country, Benoist and two other top racers fled to England and changed occupations, becoming agents with the Special Operations Executive. The next time

Benoist was in France, arriving by parachute drop, it was as a British Army captain as well as an SOE special agent. The dashing former racer helped to organize cells of saboteurs and to hide caches of weapons for French Resistance fighters. In June 1943, when the Prosper Network of spies was compromised, Benoist was one of several top agents arrested. Unlike most others, however, this did not end his activities, because while being driven to Gestapo headquarters in Paris, he jumped out of the moving car and managed to escape. Benoist reconnected with the French Resistance and was smuggled out of the country.

Back in England, after such a close call, Benoist could certainly have passed on more spying missions. But in February 1944, he was in France once again as an SOE agent. Four months later, while working with the underground in the Nantes area, Benoist was found and arrested. This time, there would be no daring escape, and he became a Buchenwald inmate. Though arrangements were in place for other British and French SOE agents to die on September 10, the impatient Nazis executed Benoist the day before.*

When word filtered among the Allied airmen on September 9 that sixteen of the British officers had been transferred to a building known as Admission Block 17, they saw that for the grim news it was. "A call without warning meant either interrogation and torture or death," Joe Moser wrote. "On that day the call came."

The next day, after Colonel Lamason informed his men of the executions, "life became even more grim," according to Joe Moser. "I kept thinking about what the guard had said when we first came into camp, about not leaving except as smoke through the chimney. When you are young, all of life is ahead and it is not

---

* A year to the day after his death, on September 9, 1945, the Coupe Robert Benoist car race was held in Paris.

easy to face the likelihood of death. That's why they send young men and women to war; we think nothing bad can happen to us. Yes, it's very possible to be scared, but there is always this innate belief that everything is going to be alright. Now, despite our youth and optimism, we weren't so sure."

It was becoming increasingly evident that the only sure thing about Buchenwald was death.

O ur uncertainty and heavy dread grew along with our hunger and the long days in camp," recalled Joe Moser. "Although we couldn't see a lot of the other prisoners except during *Appell*, the horrors of this place became more and more evident."

Optimism was in increasingly scarce supply as October took hold. Eugene Weinstock recalled that it "began the nightmare within the nightmare—a terrible winter during which the SS committed at least forty thousand murders in Buchenwald. This figure is so gigantic that it is almost meaningless, but every murder involved a man, an anti-fascist, who bled and suffered agonies in one of the weirdest bursts of mass sadism in the world's entire history."

Weinstock further explained, "Other concentration camps in the path of the Allied armies were closed or dismantled, or fell before conquering troops. In each case the Nazis herded the prisoners out. Transport followed transport. There was no place to put prisoners, no food to give them, no medicine, no doctors, no work. There could be only one solution to this problem from the Nazi point of view. That solution was death."

Death became more routine even without the SS lifting a finger. With food and medicine becoming almost impossible to obtain and diseases running rampant in Buchenwald, no one was immune.

"Every day we saw bodies," Moser remembered. "Those who died during the night were taken out of their barracks and dumped outside the door so the kapos could pick them up and haul them to the crematorium. Frequently the bodies were stacked high outside the crematorium as the supply for its fires was greater than the capacity."

Though it had become a routine sight every morning, the Allied prisoners still found it hard to look at the handcart making the rounds of Little Camp. The physical condition of the prisoners pulling it appeared barely better than its cargo—the bodies of the men who had died during the night. Many mornings the handcart had to make two or three trips to the crematorium and back because the pile of bodies, even as emaciated as they were, became almost too heavy to push. And the crematorium could get backed up if it had been a particularly deadly night and more deaths occurred throughout the day. The facility's workers did the best they could. They knew almost to the second how long a body took to become ash, and the process could not be rushed. When piles of bodies lingered for days, they attracted rats, which not only feasted on the remains but further spread disease throughout the camp.*

---

* As coal became scarce with the approach of winter and Germany's resources continued to dwindle, the crematorium's efficiency was affected and there were more and larger piles of bodies in the camp. The Buchenwald commandant, Hermann Pister, begged permission from Himmler to conduct mass burials. When this was finally granted, such graves were only for German prisoners to avoid the risk of those bodies being buried with those of Jewish prisoners.

Often, death came quicker than disease or starvation. If a prisoner looked at a kapo the wrong way or that kapo was in a bad mood, the prisoner was beaten severely, and on occasion the beating got out of hand. The SS guards would not interfere; in fact, the sudden outburst of vicious violence was a break from the repetitive routine of camp life. What was one less inmate when some amusement was derived? And what could be a death sentence was being forced to work in the rock quarry. The noncommissioned airmen were ordered to do so, and there was nothing Colonel Lamason could do to stop that. It was a relief when those men returned late in the day, and they brought with them harrowing stories of prisoners crushed by huge stones or beaten to death by guards wielding small ones.

A welcome diversion for the Allied airmen was the sight of children. Yes, there was much sadness that there were inmates at Buchenwald who were so young and innocent but seeing them made it easier for the flyers to remember their own younger siblings, and for the fathers among them, their own children.

To the Nazis, housing children at the camp made sense. They could be forced to work hard too and they required less food and space. Housed together at Buchenwald were 877 boys who were mostly between seven and ten years old, though several were younger. There had been more of these Jewish boys, but from time to time bunches of them had been culled and transported out of Buchenwald, presumably to one of the death camps. Having the children there served another purpose: propaganda. The Nazi government proclaimed that the young boys were in protective custody and being kept safe from the ravages of war in bucolic surroundings inside the fatherland itself.

The children lived in what was known as Block 58, which held a total of a thousand prisoners. Their beds were wooden cubicles that were like stacked crates. Each cubicle was four-by-four feet and housed five inmates. There were thus fifteen prisoners, most of them the young boys, in a column twelve feet high and four feet wide. Just as well, some inmates ruefully thought, the inhabitants were as thin as they could possibly be and still be alive.

Starvation takes a terrible toll on everyone, but it weakened the Allied flyers faster. Until being shot down, most, if not all, had been accustomed to living in a fixed base camp where hot meals and cold beer were common. Now as the cooling weeks of September passed and with October having begun, the men continued to try to survive on the ration of the lukewarm soup flavored with cabbage or turnips with worms for protein and the thin slice of sawdust bread. Rounding out the daily diet was the disgusting coffee served in the morning and again at night, and a bonus was that once or twice a week leftover boiled potatoes were tossed toward the prisoners to fight over.

"Many of the prisoners we saw were starving, and we too started to take on the gaunt, empty, desperate look that we saw on so many faces when we first walked into camp," Joe observed. "Although we tried to preserve our energy, I could feel my body using up all its reserves and starting to eat into my muscles. The constant ache of hunger grew almost daily, along with a shaky weakness and pain from muscle loss."

As a consequence of their weakness and their filthy surroundings, more of the Allied airmen became ill, and those already ill—some dating back to the agonizing train journey from Paris in August—became sicker. Fever, severe abdominal cramps, vomiting, and diarrhea were sure signs of dysentery, and soon most of the flyers suffered from it. Most distressing, as Moser somewhat daintily put it, was "pardon me, explosive, bloody diarrhea."

The facilities at the camp were of course not adequate for so many men with worsening ailments. For the airmen, toilets existed only in their memories. What they had to use instead was a hole in the ground twenty feet long and three feet wide and seven feet deep lined with concrete. A thin stream of water moved through the hole that connected it to the camp's overall sewage system. This system had been constructed to accommodate twenty thousand prisoners, and there were four times that many now at Buchenwald. Often, the sickest of the men did not make it to the hole before letting loose. Moser compared it to the area outside the barn containing cows at the farm back home, "a special kind of smelly, sticky, clingy muck. And remember, most of us, including me, had no shoes."

It could be worse: There were a few guards and kapos who, when sufficiently enraged or bored, would toss prisoners into the hole. Most managed to scrabble their way out. One time, however, as one of the flyers sat on the wooden plank that crossed the rudimentary latrine, he was petrified to be tapped from below. He discovered a French prisoner who needed assistance getting out.

Describing the experience of one of the pilots, Roy Allen, Childers wrote about the latrine that "the smell was overwhelming. There was no space. Men were already squatting shoulder-to-shoulder over the pit. Some wavered unsteadily on the edge. Weak and tormented, their bowels gripped by violent spasms. They seemed ready to topple in. Some had terrible appendages, hemorrhoids that hung like grapes, balls swollen as big as oranges from disease and beatings."

Late one day when Colonel Lamason arrived at the latrine he looked down to find two naked bodies floating in it. He returned to advise his men to wait a couple of hours, if they could, before relieving themselves there.

It was at this time that Joe Moser and some other airmen realized how lucky they were to have been given clothing too big or too long for them. In the absence of toilet paper or anything that could substitute for it, pieces of torn cloth would suffice. On the other hand, each week brought these flyers closer to winter and to being completely naked—they acknowledged the cruel irony that the days and their shirts were getting shorter simultaneously.

The much less appealing alternative was that they would not even survive until winter. Disease or starvation would kill them, or the Nazis might suddenly decide to do so. The latter appeared probable one day when the Allied airmen were ordered to line up outside a drab, gloomy building and, one by one, enter it. This is it, they thought, time to die.

Once inside, however, each prisoner stepped in front of a man who may have been an inmate or camp employee and was flanked by guards. Either way, he seemed to have little to no experience giving injections, yet that was what he was doing. The syringe he wielded contained a bright green liquid. As each man stepped in front of him, the orderly jammed the needle into his chest and pressed the plunger. There was no explanation, so the flyers were left to wonder if they were being inoculated against or treated for disease, being used as guinea pigs for an experimental drug, or being poisoned. Least of their worries was that the same needle was used for every man.

Moser's experience was especially excruciating. When the syringe was used on him "the obviously dull needle hit a rib bone. I nearly buckled under the pain. He attempted to pull the needle out but it was now buried into bone and was stuck. He pulled and turned and the needle broke off from the syringe, sticking out of my chest. He grabbed a needle-nose pliers, clamped unto the needle, put a strong arm on my shoulder and yanked the needle out, tossing it to the ground. He fixed another needle on and proceeded to jab that one viciously into my chest again, this time missing bone. The same needle went into the next guy and the next until I saw him break it again."

With the condition of his men deteriorating, Colonel Lamason saw it as absolutely necessary that discipline be maintained and that further lines of communication be established with other prisoner groups and the camp administration. He continued to have the Allied airmen march in an orderly fashion to and from Appellplatz. He created a guard detail at their rock pile to prevent pilfering by other inmates. Lamason noted that such signs of unity appeared to result in fewer incidents between his men and the guards and kapos.

Another form of unity came from the men themselves when the Konzentrationlager Buchenwald, or KLB Club, was born. One of the founders of this sort of fraternal organization was the Canadian Art Kinnis, who would take notes at the surreptitious meetings. Of course, there was little the KLB Club could do except further motivate its members to help each other survive, but the men did express the hope that they would all gather together again after the war.

To that end, Kinnis compiled a list of the Allied prisoners' service numbers, numbers assigned by the SS upon their arrival at Buchenwald, and their home addresses. It may have been only a pipe dream that such a postwar reunion would ever take place, but it was a harmless one that may have lifted a few spirits during the darkest hours.

As much as Lamason despised Hermann Pister, he realized he had to establish some kind of dialogue with him. The camp commandant, of course, could simply have had the impertinent and troublesome colonel shot with a hand gesture, but he knew how irregular and to some extent high-profile the 168 Allied airmen were at Buchenwald. Additionally, by the fall of 1944, with Germany ceding territory to the Allies and Russians on both fronts and in ever-greater swaths, Pister had to be contemplating his own future. Such a blatant war crime would certainly endanger it.

In his meeting with Pister and other senior camp authorities, Lamason relied on Splinter Spierenburg, the Dutchman who had been flying for the Royal Air Force and spoke fluent German. The top priority for Lamason, he explained to Pister via Spierenburg, was that the airmen be transferred immediately to a prisoner of war camp. They were not spies and they were certainly not terrorists and thus had no business being in a concentration camp.

After several of these meetings, Pister may have felt like putting the flyers on the train to a POW camp himself just to be rid of the irritating New Zealander, but he had to keep rejecting the demand. The authority for such a transfer could come only from Himmler himself in Berlin, and there was no indication that would change. Unspoken was the possibility that if Himmler decreed anything about the 168 inmates, it would be that they be executed and their bodies burned, leaving no trace of their existence at the camp.

And through Yeo-Thomas and Burney, Lamason met other men who aided in the effort to keep the Allied flyers alive. Two of them were Russian colonels who were senior members of what was called the International Camp Committee. Lamason learned this was an underground resistance group including members from as many as a dozen nationalities who hoarded supplies and weapons for the eventual takeover of the camp. This group approved the release of blankets, clothes, footwear, and some food to the airmen, which no doubt saved at least some of their lives.

Two other prisoners, Alfred Balachowsky and Jan Robert, proved to be of much value. Each had developed good relationships with members of the Buchenwald administration and were able to pass along information either confided or overheard to Lamason as well as other inmate leaders.

Balachowsky, a Russian-born French scientist specializing in insects, joined the underground Prosper Network of spies in Paris during the war. Betrayed, he was sent to Buchenwald. He avoided the harshest treatment by being placed on a team of scientists at the camp led by Germans to develop a vaccine for typhus. Balachowsky used this position to continue spying, this time on behalf of the International Camp Committee. Jan Robert, who had also managed to ingratiate himself with administration personnel, was a Dutchman who before the war had trained athletes for competition in the Olympics.*

A sense of some unity with other prisoners at Buchenwald helped the spirits of the Allied airmen. At this point, anything would help. It was very difficult to avoid contemplating that no one knew where they were or if they were alive at all. Most likely, they had initially been reported missing but then had not shown up on the rolls of any prisoner of war camp. There were no Red Cross visits or even arriving packages at Buchenwald, so presumably that organization had no knowledge of the flyers. It was even possible that because there had been no word about the airmen weeks and months after being downed, as far as the War Department—and by extension, their families—were concerned, by October the missing men were most likely dead.

Finally, though, there was a genuine piece of good news. One of Colonel Lamason's protests, at least, appeared to have had the desired effect. The airmen were informed that they would no longer need to sleep on the cold rocks in the open air but would be given accommodations in Little Camp. Space in Block 58 had opened up. Apparently, the children and possibly the entire population of that barracks had been relocated.

---

* Both men survived Buchenwald. In the case of Balachowsky, he continued in his profession, and in 1948 was elected president of the Société Entomologique de France.

The move indoors was welcomed by the men, who had begun to experience new levels of misery. They had just endured a three-day rainstorm with intermittent thunder and lightning. During the storm, the flyers expected to be fried by a bolt out of the raging sky at any moment. While this did not happen, being lashed by cold rain and wind and not sleeping at all was awful enough. "On the rock pile the shivering men, soaked from head to foot, huddled under their few blankets, their shirts, anything that might shield them from the relentless drenching," wrote Childers. "They stood for hours at roll call, their bare feet submerged in the muck. They waited in line for cold soup and watery tea. And still it rained."

Taking up a crowded residence inside the wooden barracks was a godsend. However, it turned out that the children were still there. The Allied airmen were replacing the adult inmates who had been moved elsewhere. Suddenly, the flyers were not as fond of the youngsters as before. After moving in they "quickly found that anything left lying round, such as our food bowls or blankets, would almost instantly disappear," Moser reported. "It wasn't long before we couldn't decide if living in the ridiculously overcrowded and tumultuous barracks was worse than braving the elements outside."

Thankfully, the annoying situation turned out to be temporary. After only a few days, the boys were told to grab their few possessions, however they had been acquired, and move to another building. The airmen luxuriated in the extra space, and in the evening, with every night colder than the last, they took turns congregating around the small wood stove. Another luxury was toasting the sawdust bread against its sides, making it slightly more palatable.

After a couple more days, the flyers noticed something—the children were not at *Appell* that morning, that evening, or the morning after that. A concerned Colonel Lamason asked about the boys' whereabouts. Barely hiding his amusement, an SS officer reported that all 877 of them could still be accounted for—in the choking smoke spewing from the chimney and the ashes wafting to the ground.

19

The Allied airmen had blended in with the tens of thousands of other prisoners in Buchenwald, and not at all in a good way. The lack of nourishment made them almost unrecognizable to each other. Joe Moser was typical in that he estimated he had lost thirty-five pounds. His thoughts often turned to how much more weight he could lose before passing a point of no return.

"I was now one of those empty human sacks, eyes staring out lifelessly behind deep sockets with sunken cheeks and the filthy striped uniform sagging over my skeleton." The harsh realization for Joe and the others was that they now resembled the inmates who had stared at them when they had gotten off the train from Paris.

While the barracks they inhabited offered some protection from the cold air and rain, the wooden building was also infested with fleas and bedbugs. As maddening as the irritation could get, the flyers resisted scratching as best they could. As Colin Burgess explained, "The smallest open sore invited infection. With no medicine or nutritious food these wounds would not heal and became weeping, open sores. The men soon learned to stuff any such holes in their flesh with small wedges of paper to soak up the matter." Adding to their discomfort was that the hardness of their bunks became insufferable as the flesh on their bodies thinned.

Morning and evening *Appell* had become even more of an ordeal because the men, at times, had to stand for hours as they grew weaker and as the dropping autumn temperatures in central Germany took full hold. A beating delivered by a guard or kapo hurt more than ever and required extra time for recovery. No one wanted to take his chances at the camp hospital. It was extremely rare for someone to return from there having been successfully treated for anything.

In reality, the hospital was the last stop on the way to the crematorium. When there were no longer beds available, patients had to be removed to open some up. The men there the longest, who were most often the sickest, would be designated for death. A pill or needle would be administered and within a few hours their bodies were being hauled to the crematorium. Many of the patients were weakened by pneumonia as well as dysentery and to accelerate their decline they would be dropped into barrels of ice water and left to die.

Ed Carter-Edwards, an RCAF flyer, knew from frightening experience how thin a thread one's life in the hospital hung on. He had developed pneumonia so serious that he was brought there. His survival depended on "strangers moving me around so that when the German doctor came in he wouldn't recognize the same guy and stick the lethal needle in me. I'd watched it happen to others: If the doctor didn't think you were going to make it, he'd stick that needle directly in the heart."

Every hour of every day, death was present. Executions could be ordered for any real or imagined transgression, but the SS administration and guards had a special enthusiasm for killing Russian soldiers. They feared the Russians more than any other ethnic group, and there was some safety in keeping that population in check. Roy Allen, the American B-17 pilot, later told of a horse stable that was converted into an execution chamber tailored for killing Russians efficiently.

Stripped of their uniforms, the soldiers were brought into the small building and told to line up with the backs of their heads and necks directly in front of holes in one of the walls. Perversely, jaunty music from a radio or record player was blared to obscure the murders. In a room on the other side of the wall, a German guard went from one hole to the next, firing through it with a rifle. Once he reached the end of the room, dead (or close enough) Russians were dragged out through a different door and through another room, then tossed onto an idling truck. Water pipes had been installed in the former horse stable so that the spray from several ceiling showerheads would wash the floor of the execution room, the water and blood sluicing toward a floor drain. The next batch of victims was brought in, and so on. Once the truck was piled high enough with bodies, it was driven to the crematorium. Only on days when the facility was overflowing with bodies would the murders be halted, to resume as soon as the backlog was resolved.

Word spread that there would be even more executions, and Russian soldiers would not be the targets. Orders had come from Berlin to kill another batch of the captured SOE agents—this time, all of them and be done with it, if possible. A desperate Yeo-Thomas approached Eugen Kogon and Alfred Balachowsky, who continued to work side by side under Dr. Erwin Ding-Schuler in Block 50, where medical experiments continued unabated. The two prisoners banked on their longtime association with the Nazi doctor to make a bold suggestion—use the facility to save lives, in a more direct way than possibly developing an anti-typhus vaccine.

Ding-Schuler was receptive. However morally corrupt he was, he was not a stupid man. As the Allies swept further eastward, they were collecting prisoners and, inevitably, ones like him who had personally murdered hundreds of people in his abominable medical career would be put on trial, if even allowed to live that long. Perhaps it was not too late to save himself.

He and his two inmate assistants devised a scheme. There were three French patients with typhus at the hospital who had no chance of survival. Ding-Schuler agreed to switch their identities with those of three British SOE agents. However, he had one condition, which was nonnegotiable: One of them had to be the man known as Dodkin. The doctor's reasoning was that with Dodkin the recognized head of that group, if and when Ding-Schuler was arrested, the British agent's request for mercy would have the most weight.

Yeo-Thomas accepted the sense of this. However, suddenly forced upon him was an awful decision of who would live—just two men other than himself—and who would die. He could not agonize for long, because final orders for another round of executions could be issued any day. Yeo-Thomas passed along to Balachowsky the names of Harry Peleuvé and Stéphane Hessel. Both men spoke fluent French, reducing the chance of the scheme being discovered. Further insurance was persuading Arthur Dietzsch, a German kapo, to assist in the ruse, with his compensation being the same that Ding-Schuler expected.

Hessel was not a British SOE agent but a member of the French Resistance, and much more. He had been born in Berlin in 1917—the son of the writers Helen and Franz Hessel—but by the time he was twenty-two, he was a French citizen.* When the war began in 1939, Hessel joined the French Army. With the fall of France, he then joined the French Resistance. It was while helping to organize underground communications networks that he was arrested by the Gestapo and eventually sent to Buchenwald.

The three French patients were transferred to another building and were replaced in the hospital by Yeo-Thomas and the two others.† The switch took place just in time. On October 4, there was another announcement, and fourteen SOE agents were marched off. They were murdered the next day in the same depraved fashion. Miraculously, the execution orders had not included the names of four agents—Maurice Southgate, Alfred and Henry Newton (twin brothers), and Christopher Burney. They continued to survive in Buchenwald, as did the three "French" patients, who,‡ after their startling recovery, were assigned by Kogon and Dietzsch to work parties.§

Berlin's bloodlust for Allied prisoners at Buchenwald was apparently not yet satisfied. It was Yeo-Thomas and Burney who

---

* Hessel's parents were the models for the title characters in *Jules and Jim,* a novel written by Henri-Pierre Roché that became a film directed by François Truffaut.

† The three men had been informed of the scheme and, because they knew they would indeed die, agreed to participate.

‡ Several months after avoiding execution, Stéphane Hessel escaped during a transfer to the Bergen-Belsen camp and soon encountered advancing U.S. Army troops. In the decades after the war, he worked for the United Nations and for other organizations dedicated to world peace. His book *Time for Outrage!,* published in 2010, when he was ninety-three, has sold close to five million copies worldwide and inspired numerous international political-protest movements, including Occupy Wall Street. In 2011, he was named by *Foreign Policy* magazine in its list of top global thinkers. Hessel died in February 2013.

§ After the war, Arthur Dietzsch was not executed but was given a life sentence in prison, with a letter from Yeo-Thomas part of the court's consideration. In September 1945, soon before his trial was to begin, Ding-Schuler committed suicide.

first passed on the word about the next round of executions. This time, they told Lamason, those designated to die, in whatever cruel way the Nazis determined, were the *Terrorfliegers*. Even the exact date had been decided by Heinrich Himmler: October 24. The camp commandant, Pister, was informed that there were to be no exceptions, that every Allied airman, even those in the hospital, and even those who could not walk, was to be killed.

Lamason made his own decision: He did not tell the men under his command that they were soon to be killed. Joe Moser later learned the colonel "did not reveal it to us at the time out of fear of what we might do that would jeopardize our position."

That was a mild way to put it. The airmen would have been pushed to a desperation point had they learned of the preparations being made, which included a bureaucratic ruse to ensure it would never be known that they were executed, let alone that they had been at Buchenwald at all. As Burgess elaborated, "The airmen were certainly an embarrassment to the Germans, but their deaths would have enormous ramifications if the British found out. The killings would have to be concealed by the issue of false certificates stating that each death was the result of natural causes."

Lamason could hope that in the days leading up to October 24 there could always be a miracle. However, by now, even the resilient colonel had ample evidence that miracles were in very short supply in Buchenwald. All he could do was keep his men occupied and together as a military unit while he searched for a way to stop or at least delay the new round of executions. Unaware that the day of their execution was fast approaching, the flyers remained full and eager participants in Lamason's discipline and brotherhood program.

According to Joe Moser, "Our marching as a unit back and forth from *Appell* helped us to remember that we might be filthy, starving skeletons, but we were still soldiers in the greatest uni-fied military organization in the history of the world. We be-lieved that while we might not see the day itself, we had no doubt that the outcome of this great struggle was certain and that the world would be freed from the unbelievable nightmare of Nazi control."

There was another advantage to the flyers' ongoing display of discipline. According to Lamason, "Marching in unison upset the guards terribly."

The days when the Allied flyers would be able to march back from morning and evening *Appell* to their barracks dwindled down to a precious few. It began to appear to Colonel Lamason that the only option his men might have to avoid dying as hor-ribly as the SOE agents was that the SS guards would have the decency to simply shoot them.

ACT IV
THE SURVIVOR

———— ◆ ————

Christmas Eve will find me
Where the love light gleams
I'll be home for Christmas
If only in my dreams

—Written by Kim Gannon and Walter Kent,
first recorded by Bing Crosby in 1943

20

Despite the best efforts of the Nazi hierarchy and Hermann Pister and his administration at Buchenwald, the presence of the *Terrorfliegers* at the camp was not a complete secret. There were other inmates who knew that there was an unusual sub-category of prisoners, downed Allied flyers who, curiously, were not in a prisoner of war camp. Buchenwald was full of enemy soldiers sent to work and die there, ones who had inconveniently not perished on the Western and Eastern Fronts.

But the *Terrorfliegers* were different. It was almost as if the Nazis did not know what to do with them, other than wait for them to die from disease and starvation. But that window of time was closing because of the Allied and Russian forces advancing rapidly from two directions. Hence, the order to execute them.

The presence of the downed flyers at Buchenwald was also known by some German pilots. In fact, members of the Luftwaffe had been aware of imprisoned enemy pilots while they were still at Fresnes. There were several senior Luftwaffe officers who were displeased that Allied pilots were there, knowing how poorly inmates were treated, including torture and even outright murder. It was disturbing that the Allied men were under SS control and not the conventional military authorities.

A German pilot or crew member who was shot down and captured would be processed and become a prisoner of war at a so-designated camp which would be operated according to the tenets of the Geneva convention. The Luftwaffe expected no less for their Allied counterparts. Fresnes was at best an ill-advised detour and could by itself be a dangerous if not fatal destination. If word got back to the Allies, there could be reciprocal treatment of German captives as retribution.

Conceivably, if this displeasure had risen high enough in the Luftwaffe ranks, something might have come of it. The commander in chief of the Luftwaffe, Hermann Göring himself, may have intervened, not only to protect his own airmen but to assert there was a code of honor—*A Higher Call*, as Adam Makos titled his book about the encounter between American and German pilots—among flyers, whatever uniform they wore. However, time ran out for the Allied inmates of Fresnes as the American, British, and Free French forces approached Paris. Once they left the prison and were forced into the cattle cars to be shipped east, the Allied flyers were out of sight and out of mind to the Luftwaffe, who had plenty of other matters to attend to, including their own survival.

This was even more true when the flyers were at Buchenwald. By mid-October they were only 168 men out of the tens of thousands of woeful and mostly forgotten inmates. They might as well be Russian soldiers or political prisoners or Communists or Jews or any other group for whom Buchenwald was built. The Germans hoped that murdering them on October 24 would result in just another batch of bodies to be immolated at the crematorium. Over time few if any people would remember they had been at Buchenwald at all.

After the war . . . well, at most there might be a rumor about flyers from the United States, Great Britain, and other Allied countries who had been kept captive in a concentration camp in Germany. Or not. Of the many millions who died during the war, how much attention would really be spent on the deaths, under whatever circumstances, of fewer than two hundred men?

So Joseph Moser and his companions faced the twin curses of what seemed to be successful subterfuge and ultimate indifference. And then the Luftwaffe found them again.

A week after almost all of the SOE agents had been executed, two Luftwaffe officers paid a visit to the Buchenwald camp and were given an escorted and very selective tour. One of the visitors was a particularly distinguished German pilot, Johannes Trautloft. It was because of this officer, whose colleagues called him Hannes, that the Luftwaffe was allowed to visit at all and was treated with fawning courtesy. He was a much-decorated career Luftwaffe officer, a true national hero, and had connections to the government in Berlin. Whatever the reason, even just for amusement, if Colonel Trautloft and his adjutant wanted to visit the Buchenwald camp, they could not be refused.

And so it was that the two men in crisp Luftwaffe uniforms arrived at the imposing entrance. If Pister had known the true purpose of Hannes Trautloft's visit, the commandant would likely have concocted a reason, however inane, to postpone it. Pister was unaware that Trautloft had heard about Allied airmen being among the Buchenwald inmates and he was there to confirm this. However, it was also possible that Trautloft's visit would be only a tragically missed opportunity.

He may not have been happy that Buchenwald existed at all.

Trautloft was a local product, born in March 1912 near Weimar in Thuringen. At nineteen he began pilot training at the German Air Transport School and graduated ten months later. In February 1932, Trautloft began special training as a fighter pilot, and the program included four months at a secret facility in the Soviet Union. He became recognized as one of the more talented and promising flyers in the German military, which apparently was already looking ahead to another war.

Trautloft gained his first combat experience during the Spanish Civil War, when he and five other pilots were sent to Cadiz. There, in August 1936, in Heinkel He 51 biplanes, they flew missions in support of the Fascist forces of Francisco Franco. Trautloft shot down two Republican planes before he himself was shot down. He survived the crash landing, eluded capture, made his way back to the Fascist front, and was soon once again roaming the skies.

Trautloft was viewed as a rising star in the Luftwaffe when World War II began. He flew missions during the invasions of Poland and France. He scored victories during the Battle of Britain. His successes and daring not only earned him promotions but the favor of the German high command, especially Göring. As a major, Trautloft was given command of JG 54, an elite Luftwaffe unit. It became known as the *Grünherz-Geschwader,* and Trautloft had his pilots wear the green heart symbol of Thuringen, which he had begun wearing during his adventures in Spain.

His stature within the German military increased, and his responsibilities expanded in addition to his success as a pilot, having recorded fifty-eight victories by the summer of 1943. A few months later, the now-Colonel Trautloft was put in charge of all German day fighters. His devotion to the German military was more a matter of personal pride and love of country than a loyalty to Adolf Hitler, whom he believed was sacrificing German lives for what he viewed as a lost cause.

It was not just happenstance that Trautloft heard about Allied airmen being prisoners in Buchenwald. With the deadline for the next mass execution looming, a desperate Phillip Lamason and Christopher Burney devised a plan to get a note into the hands of a Luftwaffe officer at the nearby Nohra airfield. Of course, even if the plan worked, nothing could come of it. With the steady advance of the Allies, which included relentless strikes from the air into the fatherland, the Luftwaffe certainly had higher priorities than the fate of less than two hundred enemy soldiers.

But Lamason had no other credible ideas. Burney knew of a Russian inmate at Buchenwald who was part of a work detail that went to and from Buchenwald and the air base, and, equally important, he could be trusted. A brief note was written.* It requested that news of the presence of Allied pilots at the death camp be passed up the Luftwaffe chain of command to Berlin itself. Lamason was banking on a kinship between air forces being stronger than any animosity between enemies. This was a gamble, indeed, because at any stop along the way, including the very first Luftwaffe officer who read it, the message could be dismissed.

Incredibly, the note was received and passed on and found its way to Hannes Trautloft. He gave it enough credence that he arranged to go with his adjutant on a visit to Buchenwald. The reason the senior Luftwaffe commander gave was perfectly legitimate—to assess, two months after they were bombed, the ability of the two factories adjacent to the camp to contribute to Germany's military efforts, some of which Trautloft personally supervised.

---

* We must assume that Lamason or Burney relied on a fellow prisoner fluent enough in German to compose the message rather than risk its coming into the possession of an officer at the airfield who did not speak English.

Thus, on that October day, he was at Buchenwald. As a genuine war hero of Germany whose reputation and courage were beyond reproach, Trautloft was treated with deference. He feigned keen interest in the factories and then asked to look over the camp itself. Trautloft did not display the distress he felt seeing the wretched conditions of the prisoners. Ironically, he concluded none of them were Allied pilots because they could not possibly have been treated so horribly and not be distinguishable from Jewish, Communist, Russian, and other inmates. Finally, he told the escorting guards it was time for him to leave.

Joe Moser, Merle Larson, Phillip Lamason, and the other airmen had watched silently as the eminent Luftwaffe officer walked past them, glancing from face to face. Moser noted about Trautloft and his adjutant, "The disgust they felt for their fellow German SS officers was clear. It was also certain that they did not approve of the way we were being treated and the conditions of the camp."

Colonel Lamason knew what the stakes were—without the deus ex machina that Trautloft represented, he and his men would most likely die. This moment was their last and best chance. But it was clear that if any commotion was made, they would either be shot immediately or severely punished later after the Luftwaffe officers were hustled away. Surely, Pister had instructed his guards to be extra vigilant. The frustration Lamason felt soared. The plan had actually worked to this point. . . .

Trautloft turned away, then he halted when a voice called out to him. One of the airmen, the tail gunner Bernard Scharf, had taken it upon himself to risk his life and perhaps dozens more. What separated him from the others was that by now he spoke fluent German. Being addressed this way from the other side of the fence made Trautloft pause, then wheel about.

Immediately, SS officers intervened, pressing Trautloft to

exit the compound. He hesitated, and when the officers became more insistent, Trautloft began to believe that the contents of the smuggled note were indeed true. He pointed out firmly to the SS officers that he outranked them and could not be ordered about. He told them to step back, and he faced the man who was in such desperate condition.

Trautloft was appalled by what he heard. The words spilling out as fast as he could utter them for fear of being shot, Sergeant Scharf revealed that he was one of 168 Allied flyers sent to Buchenwald instead of a prisoner of war camp. Trying to hide his shock, Trautloft asked if the group had a commanding officer. Lamason identified himself and echoed what Scharf had said. The colonel resisted the desire to inform Trautloft of the October 24 execution date. While that could have made even more of an impression on the Luftwaffe officer, the news could also panic his men and perhaps lead the Germans to consider moving the date up.

Trautloft and his adjutant both nodded at the airmen to acknowledge having heard them. Then it was time to leave. As his car drove away from Buchenwald, Trautloft decided that if his duties allowed, he would speak to Göring about the illegal and obviously dangerous imprisonment of fellow flyers.

After Trautloft left, the airmen returned to their usual routine, which by this point was simply trying to remain alive. Perhaps something would come of the Luftwaffe officer's evident interest in their incarceration. It was a good sign that during the rest of that day there was no punishment for having drawn the visitors' attention. However, it was also possible that the level of interest diminished with every mile the Luftwaffe vehicle put between it and Buchenwald.

There was something else to worry about . . . that is, if the Allied flyers had known about it. Trautloft could communicate what he had learned at the camp to Hermann Göring. However, by this point in the war the *Reichsmarschall* might not be able to do anything.

The head of the Luftwaffe had once enjoyed an excellent relationship with the Führer, thanks to both his impeccable military credentials and loyalty. Göring had been an ace pilot in World War I, was awarded the honor known as the Blue Max, and he had taken over the Jasta 1 fighter wing commanded by the legendary Manfred von Richthofen. Göring became an early member of the Nazi Party and had scored points with the young Hitler by being injured during the violent and unsuccessful "Beer Hall Putsch" in 1923.* A decade later, when Hitler was elected the German chancellor, he rewarded the longtime loyalty of Göring by anointing him Minister without Portfolio. During his first year in the new cabinet, Göring created the Gestapo, then turned it over to Heinrich Himmler.

Göring continued to accumulate power and influence in the Third Reich. When the war began he was at the height of both in addition to serving as commander in chief of all of Germany's air forces. After the triumph of overtaking France and pushing Great Britain's back to the wall, Göring was made *Reichsmarschall*, an invented rank that gave him seniority over all other German military officers. Additionally, he was acknowledged as the successor to Hitler should any misfortune befall the Führer.

Then the gradual fall from grace began. The Battle of Britain did not result in a knockout blow forcing that country to surrender. After the United States entered the war in Europe, the combination of its strengthening air force and the recovering British one made for heavier losses for the Luftwaffe, and eventually there was decreasing opposition to the bombing missions the

---

* As a result of his subsequent medical treatment, Göring became addicted to morphine and would remain so until after the war.

Allies were conducting deeper into Germany. The first thousand-bomber raid on the fatherland, with Cologne the target, came as early as May 30, 1942, which also had a psychological ripple effect. More and more, Göring was being held responsible by Hitler—and thus, the German public—for the failure to protect the homeland. The overmatched Luftwaffe's poor showing on D-Day was attributed to a lack of adequate leadership, which ignored the harsh fact that on that day over Normandy, Germany could put no more than three hundred planes in the air.

By October 1944, the German military was retreating on both the Eastern and Western Fronts, and the Luftwaffe had been decimated by losses of both personnel and equipment. Göring had also retreated from public view, spending more time at the several private residences he owned, and Hitler now routinely excluded him from strategy meetings. The power and influence he had wielded just three years earlier were severely reduced.

If Hannes Trautloft chose to, he could easily relay the message to Göring about the illegal imprisonment of the Allied flyers . . . and yet nothing might be done. Previously, no one other than SS administrators knew they were at Buchenwald. Now, the ominous fact was no one would care.

21

Hannes Trautloft did not know about the date set for the execution of the Allied flyers. In addition to Colonel Lamason not revealing it in front of the men during Trautloft's visit to Buchenwald, Commandant Pister and his SS officers had certainly not volunteered this information as the Luftwaffe officer prepared to depart. Trautloft really had no right to stick his nose in their business, so Pister felt justified in having done only the minimum required by professional courtesy.

With luck, after Trautloft left the camp he would be so distracted by the burden of his routine duties that he would give little or no further thought to the skeletal Allied airmen in the filthy clothing, and the SS could do what Berlin obviously believed needed to be done. Thus, no matter how determined Trautloft might be to have the flyers transferred to a POW camp as a matter of honor, not knowing that he had only days to do this could result in an intervention that came too late.

However, the Luftwaffe colonel felt he needed to write a report on his visit to Buchenwald while the details were fresh in his mind. The report sent to his superiors in Berlin included a description of the wretched condition of the Allied flyers who were being imprisoned there illegally and that most if not all would die. Trautloft insisted the men were not spies and were certainly not terrorists and thus there was no reason for their continued incarceration in a concentration camp. Further, their ongoing captivity was a stain on the honor of the Luftwaffe. There was still a World War I Red Baron–like attitude that enemy pilots saluted each other's skill and gallantry. It was an appalling insult to this philosophy that fellow pilots, whatever flag they flew under, were in Buchenwald.

In Berlin, after the report had reached his desk and he had read it, an infuriated Hermann Göring agreed. Though his position in the Third Reich had weakened, he still packed a political punch. He issued an order that control of the Allied flyers at Buchenwald be transferred from the SS to the Luftwaffe. It is not known if Himmler protested and possibly brought the matter to Hitler's attention. If so, the Führer did not countermand Göring's order. The next step was to inform Pister of the change in the airmen's status and arrange for them to be sent to another camp.

At Buchenwald, the flyers knew nothing about Trautloft's report and any consequences it might have. After the Luftwaffe officers had left the camp "we felt some renewed hope," Joe Moser stated, "but even that was mixed with the realization that we remained in the hands of the SS and that anything might happen."

In fact, as the days passed, Pister heard nothing from Berlin. As far as the Buchenwald commandant was concerned, as time passed Trautloft's rather inconvenient visit could be viewed as only a minor bit of interference in an SS matter, to be forgotten. Apparently, as the SS officers had hoped, Trautloft had moved on to attend to more important concerns, and the execution was still scheduled for October 24. That date was now just a week away.

Other than attempting a breakout—sure to fail without the cooperation of others at the camp—Colonel Lamason was out of ideas. Not one of his sleepless nights changed that.

It was possible that some of the airmen might not live long enough to be killed. Cases of dysentery were now worse, and only a handful of the men did not have it. Malnourishment had become critical, thanks to the combination of little more than the worm-infested soup to live on and some men being too sick to keep it down. Joe Moser's weight continued to drop off—he was about to dip below 110 pounds—and he felt a constant lethargy. Being the men's commander did not make Lamason immune—he had lost forty-two pounds and was suffering from diphtheria as well as dysentery. Should he die, it would be catastrophic to the morale of the men—even if only for the few days they had left.

Every morning was the same, as if there had been no visit from the two Luftwaffe officers—the shivering flyers staggered off to *Appell* and staggered back. Those who could not even limp along were half-carried by others who themselves had only the barest ounce more of strength left to give. It would not have surprised any of the flyers if, while standing at attention during *Appell*, someone simply dropped dead. Lamason may have considered if being executed could be a blessing compared to ongoing misery leading to the same fate. Still, to maintain discipline and to stick it in the eye of the SS guards, the colonel had his men march and stay in formation as best they could.

Finally, one morning was different. The men were in their barracks, trying to keep warm, when a group of SS guards appeared. There was at first fear: Was this the day they would be lined up and shot? Or worse? Lamason wondered if the date had been moved up. If so, then all was lost.

The flyers were instructed to collect their meager possessions. As Moser reported, "This caused an immediate increase in our blood pressure as such a summons at Buchenwald was a virtual death sentence. I remembered again the warning we received when entering, that the only way we would leave the place was as smoke through the chimney—the smelly, dirty, horrible chimney that never stopped spewing dark, choking, acrid smoke."

Though barely able to stand, Lamason again took command. He ordered the airmen to once more—and perhaps for the last time—form into columns. With the guards escorting and directing them, the men marched as a unit. They recalled how the doomed British SOE men had defiantly broken into song as they were led off that awful afternoon. Now, though, it was all the flyers could do to stay in step with each other let alone belt out a tune.

Soon, however, it was with great relief the men realized they were not being steered to the execution block but to another building. This turned out to be a storehouse. It was stunning enough for the nearly naked prisoners to see shelves filled with clothing, but what happened next was at first impossible to believe—each man was handed the clothes he wore when he had first arrived at Buchenwald. For Joe, that included the left shoe with the missing piece of leather that had been torn off when he wrenched free of his P-38 Lightning cockpit. That hot August morning now seemed like years ago.

Tentatively, then more broadly, the airmen grinned at each other. This bizarre example of Nazi efficiency had to mean they were being spared. "There were smiles on our skeletal faces," Joe recalled. "We were pretty certain that if they were going to cremate us, they wouldn't bother to give us our clothes back only to take them away again. Still, we hardly dared to breathe, hardly dared to hope too much."

But their steps were livelier as they exited the building. The guards now steered them away from Little Camp and out toward the main gate. It was raining, but now nothing about the day was bleak.

They were told to halt near the main gate. Stepping through it to address them was a Luftwaffe officer. The 153 Allied airmen who had been able to leave their barracks listened incredulously as they were told they were now considered prisoners of war and would be treated according to the Geneva convention. They were to be transferred to a camp where there would be visits by Red Cross personnel and that accepted Red Cross packages. The Luftwaffe officer had more to say, but the minds of the airmen were overwhelmed.*

When the speech was concluded, Colonel Lamason brought the men to attention. There was almost a skip in their step now as they resumed marching and passed through the gate. The Allied airmen could feel the staring eyes of the thousands of inmates left behind. "I looked back at them with a deeper understanding of their pain and suffering than I could have imagined earlier," Joe noted.

When the flyers arrived at the train station, there was a sense of déjà vu as they saw the forty-by-eight cattle cars. This time, though, only three dozen men were herded into each one. Ironically, once the train started off, and even with their clothing back on, the occupants of the cars crowded together for warmth. Nothing felt better, though, than leaving the horror of Buchenwald behind.

---

* Fifteen of the men had been either too weak or in the hospital and unable to march with the others. Several of them would later be reunited with their fellow flyers; others would remain at Buchenwald. Two of the latter group would die— Beck and Hemmens, the man Colonel Lamason saved from a savage beating during the train journey from the Fresnes prison. His body was also tossed into one of the crematorium's furnaces.

When word reached Himmler in Berlin that the Allied flyers had left the Weimar concentration camp and that indeed Göring had pulled rank on him, the chief of the SS went into a rage that included hurling a wineglass at the wall. But there was nothing he could do. The *Terrorfliegers* were finally on their way to a POW camp.

22

This train ride was much less of a nightmare than the one back in August, but it was still a grueling one. Huddling together to combat the cold air, the Allied airmen were immediately reminded how long it had been since their last shower and that they had been living in incredibly filthy conditions since. And many of them were ill. There were, once again, just the two five-gallon buckets in each car, one containing water and the other for waste. At least, because there was more room, the weaker men could sit or lie down on the cold wooden floor of the boxcar.

As foul as the air inside the cars soon became, "I certainly was not complaining," Joe Moser reported, "because once out of the wind range of Buchenwald, the everlasting smell of the crematorium was finally behind me." The men were also comforted by the belief that wherever they were going, it would be a better place. Not only had they been told this, but it was encouraging that the guards on this train belonged not to the SS but to the Luftwaffe.

As the train clacked noisily on the tracks, Joe felt for the first time since entering Buchenwald a flicker of hope that he would see his family again. Anything could happen; death could not be considered a stranger, but Joe entertained the possibility that he and the other airmen would arrive at a POW camp, be housed there in endurable conditions, Germany would not hold out too much longer as its men and material became exhausted, and when the war ended the flyers would return to America, Great Britain, New Zealand, and the other Allied countries. However, it pained Joe to think that his family might think him dead.

It was just as well that he did not know what had transpired since he had been shot down on August 13. Eighteen days later, Mary Moser had answered a knock on the door of her Northwest Road home in Ferndale to be greeted by a messenger who handed her a telegram. It informed her that her older son was missing in action. As distressing as that news was, the silence that followed was worse. With each passing day when there was no further word from the War Department, an ounce of hope was lost.

Still, Mary Moser tried to cling to a best-case scenario—Joe had survived the downing of his plane and had been found by friendly forces, and he was being sheltered in secret until it was safe for him to be returned to the Americans. Cautiously, she waited for that notification or perhaps even word from Joe himself. But after a few weeks, when that did not happen, she switched to another, less optimistic scenario: He had survived the crash, been captured by the Germans, and was in a prisoner of war camp. Once the Red Cross made contact with Joe, it would convey this information through its system and then Mrs. Moser would be informed.

Over more time, when that did not happen, she could not help thinking the worst: Not only was Joe dead, but his body had not been recovered. There might never even be a killed-in-action telegram.

The flyers were in transit for two days. It was October 22 when the train came to a stop in Sagan, a town in the province of Lower Silesia, two hundred kilometers southeast of Berlin.* The wooden doors of the cattle cars were rolled open, and the men were told to get out. Their exit made for a pitiful sight, as Joe described it: "Our starving bodies were cramped and stiff from the two days of bouncing on the rough wooden floor, and we gingerly jumped from the train, most of us sitting on the edge at the door to get off like old men rather than jumping with a springy bounce as we would if we were still the 24-year-old boys that our ages said we were."

The guards at the train station were taken aback as the arrivals formed a ragged line. According to Colin Burgess, "The Luftwaffe authorities, who had no love for the SS and Gestapo, were genuinely shocked at their latest prisoners' condition."

The new home for the Allied airmen was Stalag Luft III. The first camp compound, later to be known as the East Compound, opened in March 1942. From its inception, this was a Luftwaffe camp intended to contain captured flyers from England and other British Empire countries. By October 1944 the camp had expanded to five compounds on sixty acres and contained ten thousand prisoners. The entire camp was enclosed within electric barbed-wire fencing and guard towers were spaced a hundred yards apart. Escape would be a very challenging exercise. To make it even more challenging, there were English-speaking guards who mingled among prisoners dressed like them, listening for conversations that included escape plans. Called "ferrets," these guards were usually detected and rendered ineffective.

---

* This town today is Zagan, and it is within the borders of Poland.

The huge irony about Stalag Luft III was that it had been built on sandy soil so that escape tunnels would be more difficult to construct. Yet by the time the Allied airmen were transferred to it, the camp had acquired a reputation opposite of what it had striven for because of what would, over the years, become one of the more famous—or infamous, depending which side you were on—events of the war.

The German hierarchy pointed to Stalag Luft III as an example of escape-proof prison design. In addition to the difficulty the sandy soil posed, the inmates' barracks were raised two feet off the ground to give guards a better view of any tunneling activity. The camp administration, headed by the commandant, Friedrich Wilhelm von Lindeiner-Wildau, had also installed seismograph microphones around the perimeter in the belief they would detect digging activity.

The camp expanded with a North Compound in March 1943 and with a South Compound in September of that year. By then, captured American flyers were also at Stalag Luft III. It was, as POW camps go, one of the more humane ones in the German system. Its "amenities" included a well-stocked library with programs that actually allowed inmates, with tests administered by the Red Cross, to earn degrees in such areas as law and engineering. A theater constructed by prisoners offered plays and concerts. A radio station with the call letters KRGY—for the German word for prisoners of war, *Kriegsgefangener*—broadcast music and camp news items. Not one but two newspapers, the *Circuit* and *Kriegie Times,* were published every week. (*"Kriegie"* was the nickname for a prisoner, short for *Kriegsgefangener*.) There were readily available recreation activities that included basketball, touch football, soccer, volleyball, and even fencing.

Almost all of the Allied prisoners at Stalag Luft III were officers and were treated accordingly by the Luftwaffe administrators and guards. The officers were even given the equivalent of their pay in camp currency to buy items at a shop offering goods considered surplus by camp staff. Each prisoner received a food allowance totaling around sixteen hundred kilocalories per day. A normal man required twenty-five hundred kilocalories a day but helping to make up some of the shortfall were the contents of Red Cross packages that arrived regularly, plus what could be purchased with the camp currency.

Most important, especially to the new prisoners, was that the purpose of Stalag Luft III was not to work prisoners to death and execute them. Commandant Lindeiner-Wildau and his Luftwaffe guards operated under the provisions of the Geneva convention.* When an inmate died—usually from disease, not mistreatment—his funeral was conducted with full military honors. If a flyer had to sit out the rest of the war, this was the place to do it.

However, this apparently was not the complacent outlook of Roger Bushell, who would become Stalag Luft III's most famous prisoner. It was he who organized what we now know as the "great escape," thanks to several books on the event and especially the movie of that title.†

Bushell turned thirty-three in August 1943 while an inmate at Stalag Luft III. He had been born in South Africa, but at fourteen he was in England, studying at Wellington College, and after that he studied law at Cambridge. One of his nonacademic talents was skiing; Bushell captained the Cambridge ski team and soon after was lauded as

---

* Unlike the cruel SS guards with a license to kill at Buchenwald, most of the eight hundred guards at Stalag Luft III had aged out of combat duty or were younger soldiers recovering from wounds. And because they were Luftwaffe, exterminating prisoners was not on their list of responsibilities or goals.
† The feature film released in 1963 starred the American actors James Garner and Steve McQueen. The English actor and later director Richard Attenborough (*Gandhi*) portrayed the character based on Roger Bushell.

the fastest downhill racer in England. Another talent was languages, which included being fluent in German and French.

What appealed to Bushell most, however, was flying. He joined the Royal Air Force in 1932, was promoted to flying officer two years later, and two years after that was elevated to flight lieutenant. Concurrently, Bushell managed to earn a law degree and he became a barrister, sometimes having RAF pilots as clients. Soon after the war broke out, he became a squadron leader and fought the Germans during the Battle of Britain.

It was during a fight in the skies over France in May 1940 that Bushell was shot down.* He had disabled two Messerschmitts and was going after a third when his plane was hit and he crash-landed. Though he survived uninjured, Bushell was found and captured by German soldiers. Perhaps if their commander had known Bushell's penchant for escaping, he would have let him go then and there.

His first escape was from Dulag Luft in June 1941, when eighteen British prisoners tunneled out. All were recaptured; in Bushell's case, he had made it to within a few hundred yards of the Swiss border when a German guard apprehended him. After being an inmate at Stalag Luft I for a short time, Bushell's next stop was a camp called Oflag X-C. There, another tunnel was begun, but the camp was closed down before completion. The inmates were put on a train to Oflag VI-B in Warburg, which provided Bushell with a different opportunity. He jumped off the train

---

* It was believed that the pilot who downed Bushell's Spitfire was Gunther Specht. The Luftwaffe officer had been blinded in one eye when his plane was shot down in December 1939, but several months later he returned to action. Specht was shot down again and returned again. He managed to stay in the air for most of the duration of the war, becoming a German ace with thirty-four victories and a recipient of the Knight's Cross of the Iron Cross. On New Year's Day 1945, during an attack on Allied bases, Specht was once more shot down, but this time he died, at age thirty.

while it was stopped at Hanover. Bushell was accompanied by Jaroslav Zafouk, a Czech officer. The two escapees made it all the way to Prague, where they were hidden in safe houses by the Czech underground. However, their timing was unfortunate.

In May 1942, Reinhard Heydrich was shot. By then, he had helped establish a new standard of Nazi evil. He had founded a branch of the Third Reich dedicated to using arrests and murder to reduce opposition to the Nazi Party. Heydrich had helped organize *Kristallnacht*, the November 1938 series of attacks against Jews in Germany and Austria, and he was one of the architects of the effort to kill Jews known as the Final Solution. His growing power and increasingly diseased mind allowed him to create the *Einsatzgruppen*, the special task forces that traveled in the wake of the German armies and murdered more than two million people by mass shooting and gassing, including 1.3 million Jews.

To stop Heydrich, who by the spring of 1942 was headquartered in Prague, Operation Anthropoid was concocted by the Czech government in exile. Czech and Slovak soldiers trained by British SOE agents launched an attack that wounded Heydrich, who died a week later. An apoplectic Hitler ordered reprisals, beginning with a roundup of Czech citizens who may have had any knowledge of or connection to the assassination. The action included assaults on the villages of Lezaky and Lidice, which were set ablaze after all males over the age of sixteen were shot and the women and children were shipped to concentration camps. Bushell was one of those arrested in the massive roundup. He survived a violent interrogation and, judged to have nothing to do with Heydrich's death, was sent to Sagan, where he joined other British and American prisoners at Stalag Luft III.

Bushell's skills and experience were so welcomed that he was made chairman of the camp's escape committee. He got busy. After a thorough study of the camp, the plan he conceived called for as many as two hundred to escape in one mass breakout. At a meeting of the camp committee he described how three tunnels—named Tom, Dick, and Harry—could be dug simultaneously. He reasoned that if one were discovered, it would never occur to the Germans that there might be two more underway.

Having been a barrister with courtroom experience, Bushell could be quite persuasive. He had to be, because at first members of the committee were gobsmacked by the plan's audacity, beginning with the number of men, all to be wearing civilian clothes, who would escape. Next: Three tunnels? And their construction would require the work of six hundred inmates. Time to get to work, said Bushell. He was dubbed Big X and became the project's overseer.

Oddly, while the tunnels were being dug, the restless Bushell organized an escape that took place in June 1943. Two prisoners disguised as Luftwaffe guards escorted twenty-four fellow prisoners out of the camp with the cover story that they were being taken to a delousing facility. They had not gotten very far when suspicious German soldiers stopped them. Two months later, the Tom tunnel was discovered and closed. But Bushell had been right that the Germans were inclined to believe they had thwarted the only escape attempt via tunnel, so work continued on the other two.

There was another attempt that seems not to have included Bushell but involved a separate tunnel. A group of prisoners constructed a gymnastic vaulting horse out of plywood left over from Red Cross parcels. Every day it was wheeled out to the same site near the perimeter, and as prisoners exercised on the contraption—as noisily as possible to neutralize the seismic microphones—other prisoners with tools lowered themselves out of it and dug a tunnel that went straight down, then under the fence, then up to the surface on the other side. At the end of each day's exertions, the hole was covered by wood and soil and the horse, containing the diggers and soil, was wheeled back into the barracks.

On the night of October 19, three British officers snuck out of the barracks, uncovered the hole, eased down into it, and squirmed through the tunnel. Once outside the camp, they took off. Two reached the port of Stettin and, stowing away in a Danish ship, escaped and would eventually get to England. The third officer took a train to Danzig, stowed away on a Swedish ship, and turned up in Stockholm; he too would return to England. Strangely, the success of this escape attempt coming two months after the Tom tunnel was revealed did not make the camp administration more vigilant.

Finally, in March 1944, the Harry tunnel, with its entrance hidden under a stove in one of the barracks, was completed. On the moonless night of the twenty-fourth, seventy-six prisoners—not the two hundred originally expected—led by Bushell crawled through the tunnel, emerged outside the camp, and took off. Alas, after all that effort, seventy-three of the prisoners who left Stalag Luft III that night were recaptured. Hitler ordered that they be shot along with the camp commandant and members of the Stalag Luft III administration. Hermann Göring managed to stop this extreme measure but could not prevent Heinrich Himmler and the Gestapo from executing fifty of the captured Allied officers.* Bushell had been discovered at a train station and turned over to the Gestapo and was murdered three days later.†

Joe Moser and the other new prisoners at Stalag Luft III could escape too. After all, it was considered their duty to at least attempt it. But for now, after the nightmare of Buchenwald, they were content to settle in and perhaps wait out the war, if it did

---

* Two men spared were Bob Nelson and Dick Churchill because the Germans mistakenly believed they were directly related to Admiral Horatio Nelson, hero of Trafalgar, and British Prime Minister Winston Churchill.
† Bushell's killers were tried for a war crime after the war ended and were convicted and executed. Bushell was buried in Poznan, Poland.

not last too much longer. And they were told by other prisoners that finally, in the aftermath of the Bushell-led escape and the Führer's fury, the camp administration was being more watchful. For now, the recent arrivals would focus on trying to restore their health and see if the right opportunity presented itself.

As his fellow flyers eased into a new existence that was almost luxurious by comparison, Joe Moser could not have imagined that an experience even worse than imprisonment in Buchenwald awaited him.

23

When the Allied airmen had arrived at Stalag Luft III, they had been given fresh clothes and identification photos had been taken. The latter, especially, was a sign that their new surroundings would be very different. Their early experiences at Buchenwald had told them they were not expected to live long nor to be transferred to another camp. But at Stalag Luft III, after Joe Moser's photo was taken—showing him wearing the winter coat he had just been issued—it was attached to a card. On it, neat script listed not just his name but his mother's name, his height and weight and hair color and a dozen other descriptive items, and that home was Bellingham, Washington. Also cited was that he had been transferred from K.L. (Konzentrationlager) Buchenwald.

Gazing at it, Joe ruefully observed that "the efficiency of the German system was amazing, even though it was getting to be late in a war that was quickly going very badly for the German regime."

A disappointment for the flyers was that at Stalag Luft III they would not be housed together. The Luftwaffe guards divided the men up and sent them to whatever barracks had beds available. The separations weakened the unity they had tried to preserve at Buchenwald, and many of the Allied airmen saw less of Colonel Lamason. However, the advantages of their new environment more than compensated for that.

As luck would have it, Joe was assigned to Block 104, and it was under the stove where he cooked meals that the Harry tunnel had begun. He would soon hear the story of the "great escape" from the longtime prisoners. Joe's six roommates were strangers to him but most reassuring was that "they looked like real human beings" and they "did not smell of the filth of diarrhea and dysentery. Most noticeably, they didn't have that empty, sunken, defeated stare that we had become accustomed to seeing on every face, including our own, at Buchenwald."

But meeting the other occupants of Block 104—four of them Polish flyers, the other two American—was unsettling too. Even though Joe, like the other Allied airmen, had showered and now wore clean clothes, there was still something inhuman about him. He was like a ghost returned from hell. Seeing their expression and understanding it, Joe wondered "if I would ever get the spark of real life back in my eyes."

Time at Stalag Luft III would tell. That first night when Joe stretched out to sleep, he noted that he "didn't have to share [his single bunk] with four other stinky fellows in a four-foot-wide wooden mattressless sleeping box in quarters so tight that if any turned we all had to turn at once." He was "the happiest and most content man in all of Germany." That first night he enjoyed his first deep and undisturbed sleep in months.

Even with the humane conditions at the new camp, the transition for the Buchenwald flyers was not a smooth one. Many found they could not tolerate the food, any food. It turned out the worst thing the existing prisoners at Stalag Luft III could do was be generous, offering portions of their rations as well as the contents of their Red Cross packages. Several of the newcomers became dangerously ill from wolfing down whatever was given to them.

There was another distressing aspect to their new life at the camp. The existing inmates were, of course, shocked by and curious about the emaciated conditions of the arrivals. The Allied flyers described their experiences at Buchenwald . . . and were either not believed or chided for embellishing their stories. In America and some other Allied countries, the death camps were a rumor, perhaps a baseless one. The mass extermination of millions of women and children as well as men was beyond comprehension and could not possibly be true. Nothing like that was filtering back from the prisoner of war camps to the general population. The other prisoners at Stalag Luft III were at the very least skeptical, and some thought the new prisoners had invented stories about their weakened condition, perhaps to cover for personal deficiencies or to take advantage of their generosity.

Another reason, Joe Moser surmised, for the skepticism was that "the POWs did really think that their experience of hunger and discomfort was about as bad as it could get and resisted the idea that their situation was pretty good compared to others." Joe and his fellow flyers found this "deeply frustrating."

What was not different about Stalag Luft III was that every morning the inmates were wakened with shouts of "Raus! Appell!" There was an anxious familiarity to having to hurry to the square where the roll call was done, and the same for the evening. As at Buchenwald, this was the method by which the German guards detected if there were men missing and would then look to see if an escape had occurred. What was quite different at Stalag Luft III, however, was that a missing *kriegie* had more likely slept through the shouting—not that he was too sick to rise or had died of disease or starvation during the night.

It was like the arrival of Santa Claus for the former Buchenwald inmates when they were handed their first shipment of Red Cross packages. Such shipments were delivered and distributed once a week. As per the Geneva convention, a Red Cross representative was allowed to chat with prisoners about their treatment. The distribution was supervised so that, at least while the Red Cross representative was there, the German guards did not hoard the packages. Occasionally, a package was withheld as punishment for some transgression, but for the most part the guards did not interfere.

The packages came from Canada, Great Britain, and the United States. The typical contents of an American package were a can of Spam, powdered or condensed milk, a small portion of canned meat, a can of cheese, margarine, biscuits, four ounces of coffee, eight ounces of sugar, prunes or raisins, two bars of soap, and five packs of cigarettes. The British package contained a can of sardines instead of Spam, and the British and Canadian packages had just one bar of soap and there were no cigarettes. The latter gave the Americans a great advantage because the coveted cigarettes could be exchanged for goods and favors, not just with other prisoners but with the Luftwaffe guards too.

The Buchenwald flyers settled into the established routine of Stalag Luft III. Days and then weeks passed, with the cold of winter infiltrating the camp. The newer arrivals could not help thinking about what life would have been like had they remained in Buchenwald, how many of them, if not all, would have died as they faced the harshness of winter while being riddled with diseases and barely clothed. Even after weeks had passed, Joe and the other men he had been with since that hot morning when they had left the Fresnes prison could not help comparing their present existence to the one that still haunted their dreams.

Life, however, was not easy for the prisoners. After all, they were in a camp under guard with still not enough to eat, and there were the tensions of living in close quarters and being watched and the absence of liberty. And death was also present, usually from disease, but sometimes more directly. Every so often the guards would be spooked by the sudden keening of the air-raid siren and would begin shooting at the barracks. Fortunately, their aim was poor, but one night a corporal named Miles was killed while sitting on his bed.

But for Joe and the others from Buchenwald "the drudgery and discomforts of camp life were always seen from the perspective of our days in the concentration camp. The difference was so great and so startling to us that as challenging as the circumstances in POW camp were, they always seemed so much more manageable, compared to the life in Buchenwald."

As far as all the Allied prisoners at Stalag Luft III knew, this would be their home until the war ended. That could be in a few weeks, the optimists said, or it could be in six months. Some news made its way to the camp that on both fronts the war was going badly for Germany, but in the absence of specifics, it was best to accept their incarceration as it was. As winter took hold, the POWs were glad for their sturdy barracks, stoves that provided heat and cooking, the passivity of the guards, and the reliability of the Red Cross.

Thanks to those American packages, there was enough soap to go around for all to wash clothes and take showers, even though the lack of hot water was harder to tolerate in December. Joe remarked that it was "amazing how in the deep of a Polish winter just how cold water can be without freezing." Thankfully, the barley soup doled out by the guards was usually hot. There was no prohibition against exercising and many of the men did so, running or walking around the camp perimeter. Aside from trying to be in somewhat fighting shape in case there was a camp uprising, exercise was a way to keep warm. In between the gatherings for the roll calls and food distribution, the men played cards, listened to or performed music, read books from the library, and even put on theater productions.

Joe was one of the prisoners who took advantage of the permission to write letters that would be sent on their way by the Red Cross. The contents had to be rather mundane because each letter was perused by Luftwaffe guards acting as censors, but Joe did not care about that. Absolutely vital was that he get word to his mother and siblings back home that he was alive. He wrote "standard stuff," but what he wrote did not matter, his family receiving a letter at all written in his hand sure did. Every time a Red Cross representative arrived at Stalag Luft III, Joe prayed he carried a letter from his mother, but he waited in vain. This was frustrating, but at least he had some hope.*

And Joe was given a job to do, which he performed faithfully. When it was his shift, he stood casually by his compound's gate to watch for any ferrets coming through. When Joe saw someone he did not recognize and he had any suspicions, he signaled a prisoner stationed farther inside the compound, who in turn passed the word on. If there was any activity going on that the prisoners did not want to be seen, it was covered up. Some of the "ferrets" turned out not to be spies, but to be on the safe side, they were left alone because the senior officers did not want the Germans to know the Allies had their own spies.

---

* What would have made Joe ecstatic was the knowledge that on Thanksgiving Day, of all days, a telegram had arrived at the Moser home. Fearing the worst, Mary Moser opened it to be informed by the War Department that her oldest son was alive and in a prisoner of war camp. Her prayers had been answered.

One day passed pretty much as the one before. After evening *Appell,* the prisoners returned to the warmth of their barracks and ate dinner, which often consisted of a thin slice of Spam, mashed potatoes, and diced kohlrabi, followed by coffee and maybe a small dessert if the cook had been in a good mood. Then the windows were covered by blackout shutters and lights were extinguished at 10:30. "Another day in Stalag Luft III was concluded," Joe recorded, "and one day soon melted into the next."

However, this relatively peaceful existence did not last until the end of the war. The Battle of the Bulge had not been the great breakout and reversal of fortune that Hitler had anticipated. The Russians and the Allies pushed relentlessly toward the eastern and western borders of Germany. One of the many contingencies to be considered by the Nazi government was what to do with its camps, both the concentration camps and its POW ones. They could have simply been abandoned, and some were, with their populations left to fend for themselves.

That was not the fate of Stalag Luft III. During the end-of-year holidays and into January the senior Allied officers speculated among themselves that the airmen were being kept imprisoned so they could be used as hostages, bargaining chips to finagle better surrender terms. Another possibility was that there would be a mass execution and then the camp bulldozed over. Maybe the German government was in such disarray that it was unable to settle on an option.

The inmates had decided that whatever was going on outside the walls of Stalag Luft III, inside them they were going to celebrate Christmas. In preparation for the day, for several weeks they had set aside whatever foods could be spared and would not spoil. And fortune smiled on them—a few days before Christmas, a new shipment of Red Cross packages arrived. The senders obviously had the holiday in mind because the cartons contained items like fruitcake and turkey and simple decorations.

For Joe Moser and the other prisoners, "celebrate" was not quite the right word since they were incarcerated far from home in a cold and isolated setting, but most were determined to make the most of it. There were religious services on Christmas Day, and "Holiday Harmonies" was the name of the Christmas production. Preparations of the holiday feast had begun the day before. Also on Christmas Eve, several of the *Kriegies* had adapted the wagon used to distribute mail, and "Santa's sleigh" moved through the camp with one of the flyers dressed as St. Nick in borrowed red-and-white attire and a pillow stuffed within his coat. On the holiday itself, the men fell on the Christmas feast ravenously. They all yearned to be home in Indiana, Arizona, New York, California, Utah, Texas, Georgia, and Washington, but at least they had this experience, and together they had done the best they could.

Once the holidays were past and the new year had begun, Colonel Lamason and the other senior Allied officers wondered if it might be time for an uprising to take over the camp. Allowing Berlin to determine what happened to the prisoners could be a dangerous strategy. Better to die fighting than be forced up against the barrack walls facing machine guns. The majority of the officers, though, could not imagine mass murders or even that the Germans would want to feed and guard prisoners at all if the country was coming close to collapsing.

These officers turned out to be tragically wrong.

24

In hindsight, the prisoners at Stalag Luft III wished they had staged an uprising. True, dozens if not more would have died in a hail of bullets, but that would have been a quicker death than what awaited them. And it was possible that guards, who were far from being elite German soldiers, would not have resisted and may instead have leaped into trucks and jeeps and escaped. They knew better than the prisoners did that the thousand-year Third Reich had only months if not weeks left to live.

Indeed, the Russians were rolling west and the exhausted and depleted German armies could not slow them down, let alone stop them. Burning to avenge their horrific losses of soldiers and civilians at the hands of the Germans since 1941, the Russians were smashing across Poland. The smart move for the Germans would be to just abandon all camps and allow soldiers and other personnel to retreat as swiftly as possible to bolster a new defensive perimeter. Instead, orders were issued to empty some camps and direct their inmates to camps farther west.

This meant facing the depth of winter. The Allied prisoners had heard reports claiming that it was the coldest one thus far in the twentieth century.* This did not deter the Nazi decision-makers. Fortunately, in Stalag Luft III at least, there were enough rumors circulating that the prisoners accepted that their stay at the camp was coming to an end and that they had better prepare for being exposed to the merciless winter conditions.

"Merciless" was actually an understatement for what much of Europe had been experiencing. It was especially brutal in the northern territories. In the Netherlands, for example, the early months of 1945 were known as *Hongerwinter*, or the "hunger winter," causing what was called the "Dutch famine." What that country experienced represented the cruelties the weather visited upon most of Europe's war-weary population December through March . . . though the other countries on the continent would be hard-pressed to outdo the suffering in the Netherlands.

What would become a widespread scenario had actually begun in the summer of 1944. In general, in the parts of Europe still occupied by the Nazis, food became even more scarce. As the Allies took more territory from the Germans, the liberated populations had access to food that was flown or trucked in. But because of its geographic position, the Netherlands was in a particularly vulnerable position. The Allies did manage to take control of the southern part of the country, but their advancing columns were halted at the Rhine when they were unable to take the bridge at Arnheim. In September, Dutch railway workers, at the urging of the government in exile, went on strike, hampering the German war effort. In a countermove, the Nazi regime ordered an embargo on food

---

* Prisoners had managed to smuggle in or construct a radio, which was hidden somewhere in the camp. It allowed the men to keep abreast of the latest reports on the progress of the Allies on one side and the Russians on the other. At regular intervals, runners would dash through Stalag Luft III to provide updates gleaned from the latest broadcasts.

transports to the occupied Netherlands. As autumn deepened, so did the hunger of the Dutch people.

The onslaught of an especially harsh winter made the situation worse. As bread, cheese, and other staples ran out, many of the 4.5 million people affected depended on sugar beets and tulip bulbs for food. It was estimated that in the Netherlands twenty-two thousand people died just from starvation alone. By the end of February, the average citizen in the occupied territory was existing on 580 kilocalories a day, roughly equivalent to what inmates at Buchenwald and other work camps were consuming to barely remain alive. Attempts to import food by water were stymied by the unusually low temperatures, which froze ports and canals. Residents had to tear apart abandoned houses and use their own furniture for fuel or risk freezing to death.*

The Allies did what they could. With even the Germans shocked by the widespread famine, they and the Allies forged an agreement that the Luftwaffe would not shoot down mercy flights in exchange for German positions not being bombed. This narrow humanitarian truce allowed for Operations Manna, Chowhound, and Faust, the names given to efforts by the U.S. Army Air Forces, Royal Air Force, and Royal Canadian Air Force to airlift supplies into occupied areas. This alleviated the worst of the shortages of food, but the famine would not truly conclude until the German occupation ended in May 1945.

Stalag Luft III was not in Holland, but by the third week of January below-freezing temperatures added the camp to the list of miserable areas of Europe remaining under German occupation.

---

* A child who barely endured the Dutch famine became internationally known as Audrey Hepburn. The life of the Oscar-winning actress would be affected in ways similar to other children of that place and time, as she suffered from edema, anemia, and respiratory illnesses. Much of her life was devoted to humanitarian causes through UNICEF, and she was just sixty-three when she died of cancer.

If the rumors were true, Joe Moser and the other flyers were about to be transported through the bleak, snow-covered landscape, and the prisoners tried to convince themselves that they were ready for it.

For weeks, they had lingered at morning and evening *Appell*, gradually acclimating themselves to the lowering temperatures. As cherished as the stoves were in their barracks, they had been fighting a losing battle against the frigid air, further aiding their acclimation. The former Buchenwald prisoners especially were thankful to have clothes and a winter coat instead of only a thin shirt and being barefoot, but what they had was still inadequate in January. And while those men had put a few pounds back on, had gotten through the dysentery and diphtheria, and had regained some strength, their condition still lagged behind those of the others at Stalag Luft III.

The unknown of the challenge ahead was unnerving. Sleepless nights became normal, and not just because of the frigid wind infiltrating the barracks. The prisoners' anxiety would have been much higher had they known the means of "transport" would be their feet.

Joe may have been less worried than some of the others. He had accepted by now that he had very little, if any, control over what would happen to him. "I felt that if I was to die in this seemingly endless war, why was it not in the plane crash? Or why wasn't I taken out and shot like the two who had tried to help me in France? Or like so many others held in Fresnes? Why did I survive Buchenwald? Many thousands didn't. Did they love their lives any less than I did? Did their families not count as much as mine? Was and is my life worth more than theirs? What would be would be." It was also a comfort that the devout Catholic continued the practice from Buchenwald of taking time every day to pray.

However, a fatalistic philosophy and prayers would probably

not be enough to save lives. Not knowing how many days they had left at Stalag Luft III, the prisoners hurried to prepare. They sewed blankets together to create thicker ones and stuffed newspapers inside the layers to better insulate them. With every meal, they put some food aside to bring with them wherever they were going. With whatever wood scraps could be gathered, sleds were built to haul the food, blankets, and extra clothes. Just keeping busy with such preparations provided some hope that they could meet the ordeal ahead. No matter what, though, the winter was so severe that they knew any prolonged exposure to it would be a test of survival.

On the twenty-fifth, Robert Buckham,* a lieutenant in the Royal Canadian Air Force, recorded in his diary:

The camp is tense tonight. The Russians are but forty-six miles distant at Steinau, west of the Oder River. This morning a long low rumble lasting for a half-minute was identified as gunfire. The Russian pace is fast. Tomorrow could be our day. We are prepared to pack immediately. Backsacks and packboards are in major production throughout the camp. Iron ration is being prepared as well. This is a "dry" cake, made with finely ground biscuits, chocolate powder, raisins, prunes (pitted), and black-bread crumbs. These ingredients are mixed with warm margarine which hardens as it cools. The finished product not only has the appearance of chewing tobacco but resembles it in other ways also. We ate potato peelings for lunch, once again, although the selection has narrowed considerably, after which we received a further bread ration. This is considered to be significant. Apart

---

* Buckham had been a prisoner at Stalag Luft III since being shot down in April 1943. A prolific sketch artist, he was of greater use to the Allied prisoners as a forger.

from the tension, our energies have been spent by trudging seven circuits. Twice around is considered to be about a mile. A near-panic was caused tonight by an unconfirmed rumour that the goons were actually pulling out and leaving us behind. There are an estimated 15,000 to 20,000 Allied Airforce POWs in the several compounds in this area and some conjecture has arisen that the Russians will arm us and order a common advance against the Germans.

Finally, on January 27, the camp inmates heard shouts of "Raus! Raus!" The guards told them to grab their few possessions and form lines. The immediate expectation of the prisoners on that freezing cold and already darkening afternoon was that they would soon be back at the train station, where they would once more be herded onto cattle cars for a barely tolerable journey. Emptying the camp would mean more men packed together, which, depending on the length of the trip, might not be too bad because they would be better able to keep warm.

As they stood in the stiff wind, the prisoners could hear a distant thudding sound. Several of the men immediately recognized it as artillery. How close the Russians must be!* In another day or two, they could be at the gates of the camp. To buy those couple of days, perhaps this was the time for an uprising. But everywhere they looked, machine guns, rifles, and pistols were trained

---

* Indeed, by the twenty-seventh, a Russian force led by Marshal Ivan Konev had fought to within sixteen miles of Sagan. That month he and Georgy Zhukov commanded the Soviet armies, which had launched a massive winter offensive in western Poland, driving the German forces from the Vistula to the Oder River. In southern Poland, Konev's armies seized Kraków. He was credited with preserving the city from Nazi-planned destruction by ordering a lightning attack on it. Konev's January 1945 offensive also prevented the planned destruction of the Silesian industry by the retreating Germans. Several months later, Zhukov would represent the Soviet Union when it received Germany's Instrument of Surrender in Berlin.

on them. True, sheer numbers would most likely mean that Stalag Luft III could be taken over, but having endured so much and gotten this far, not enough men were willing to die that day. So, they listened to the thunder from the east, shivering and waiting for orders.

One came from Colonel Lamason. The flyers had seen less of him and of each other because of being spread out through the camp. But this day, the New Zealander reasserted himself. "No escaping, no heroics," he told the men around him. "Forward, stay together and help each other."

It had been dark for several hours when the orders were finally issued to begin marching out of Stalag Luft III, compound by compound. It was not the turn of Joe and other residents of the North Camp until almost 4 A.M. "Stepping out into the strong northern wind, being hit in the face by a million stinging pellets of icy snow and sucking in my breath as the frozen air torched my lung tissue caused in me a sense of dread and fear that brought my Buchenwald days quickly to mind. Oh no, I thought, here we go again. I just hope I can make it."

25

When the march out of Stalag Luft III began, the temperature was nearing twenty below zero. It would dip to twenty-eight below by sunrise. Even robust, well-clothed men would have been in danger, and Joe Moser and the thousands of other prisoners, despite their preparations, were not clothed well enough to long endure such extreme conditions.

In a column that stretched for five miles, the prisoners marched hour after hour. There was some degree of hope that they would not be pummeled by the cruel wind too long. "We still thought it might not be too far to our destination," Joe noted, which could turn out to be a different train station or camp. "We were freezing, but such misery had to be temporary. It had to be, because if it was not we would die in it, and then, even then, the misery would be temporary."

They were not the only ones heading away from the Russian advance. Hundreds of residents of the Lower Silesia region, who expected vengeance would be visited upon them by the Red Army for the atrocities perpetrated by the German Army in Russia, were also on the move.* Families with everything they could pack into a cart struggled alongside the prisoners. Few sights would have been more pathetic.

The Allied prisoners were grateful that they had erred on the side of caution and now wore every piece of clothing they could wear and still move—two layers of pants, three layers of shirts, as many socks as would allow their feet to fit into shoes, and an extra pair of underwear stuck in a pocket. Still, the relentless cold wind managed to seep in, finding the tiniest openings.

Joe trudged alongside the six other men from Block 104. They took turns pulling the sled they had constructed. It was not heavy so much as clumsy and hauling it added to the weariness all the marchers were soon feeling. "We took turns, two of us at a time pulling it through the rough, frozen tracks in the snow. But the snow kept coming down, and now there was at least six inches on the ground. Deeper and deeper furrows were being cut with the edges becoming as sharp and unyielding as iron in the 28 degree below temperature. The sled sapped our energy and we had so little left to spare."

For a time, the men marched four or five abreast and tried to talk to each other to keep their spirits up. But some of the prisoners began to fall back, and the violence of the wind "sucked the air out of our lungs," Joe reported. Few noticed the subtle change in the sky to the east as dawn approached. "Step by step by crunching, slipping step" the Allied flyers pushed on, trying to

---

* Their fears were justified. As they fought toward the German homeland, General Zhukov had told his troops to "remember our brothers and sisters, our mothers and fathers, our wives and children tortured to death by the Germans. We shall exact a brutal revenge for everything." That revenge included a range of abuses visited upon German civilians, including the looting and burning of homes and raping of women.

keep some semblance of a formation, but "we soon slid slowly into an interminable line of single-file, hunched-over, dog-tired, frozen men. The line snaked for miles through the ice-encased countryside. Light came finally, creeping up slowly, but it brought no heat or comfort."

Dawn also brought a fresh snowstorm. The wind-driven flakes struck the faces of the marchers like shotgun pellets. When they could see their surroundings, there was little to see—a farmhouse, outhouse, abandoned structures. When allowed to rest the men simply dropped into the snow. There was nowhere to go for shelter anyway. Frozen fingers struggled to find within bundled clothing on sleds a small package of crackers or candy. For water, they dropped handfuls of snow in their mouths. The white lumps took painfully long to melt.

Colonel Lamason was at the head of a column that was eight men wide. To try to make the trek a little more manageable, he instructed each front rank to walk five minutes then peel off to join the rear of the column. This way, the same men would not be tramping down the thick snow. Unfortunately, Lamason may have been the only senior officer to think of this and the other columns continued to struggle.

The first of the marchers reached the town of Halbau at 9:15 A.M. that first day. However, there was to be no respite—the German guards told them they had to stagger on to the next town, Freiwaldau, which turned out to be over ten miles away. Yet when they arrived there, at noon, no adequate shelter could be found. The prisoners pushed on another six miles to the village of Leippe, where they were finally allowed to rest in barns. They had marched more than thirty-five miles.

The afternoon offered no respite from the horribly cold conditions and the all-consuming exhaustion. Joe came upon a body that had been dragged off and left on the side of the road. He expected to see more, and he was right. Joe could not tell if they had died as they marched or, faltering, were dispatched by the Germans. The guards were not faring much better: "Their rifles hung across their shoulders, no longer at the ready. The disparity between prisoner and guard disappeared in these inhuman conditions. Now we were all just men forced against our will to endure conditions that would test even the strongest to the limit."

Given the inattentiveness of the guards, escape might not have been that difficult. But escape to where? Clearly, the only chance of survival lay in keeping together, helping each other, goading each other ever onward. To a few men, the attempt to escape was appealing only because during it one of the guards might care enough to shoot.

Joe's fatalism turned gloomy as he shuffled past more bodies on the sides of the road. These prisoners had endured so much, only to become "a snow-covered mound. Would that be me soon? Would I just be a frozen lump to step over or around? Would someone bury me in this tiny field? Would a marker ever find its way over my rotting bones, or would a starving farm dog haul what was left of me into that dark woods over there?"

He tried to banish such thoughts, because certainly they were not helping him keep up with the ragged column. Where were they going? No one knew. Maybe the guards did, but it was too much effort to ask. And what did it matter? They would not get there anyway. To Joe and the thousands of other prisoners, the road they were on "meandered it seemed without purpose or design, sometimes passing through small villages of a few pitiful houses. Sometimes it would go uphill, making the effort to put one foot in front of the other an act of sheer willpower . . . each step was an act of courage and tenacity, each hour an eternity."

Darkness fell. Incredibly, the men, acting on sheer willpower, kept marching. No longer were there lone bodies on the sides of the road: They were being found in twos and threes and then as many as a half dozen. During the day, some of the bodies had been hauled up onto horse-drawn wagons driven by guards, but there was no longer any room. Then the bodies of prisoners that had been on the wagons had been tossed back into the snow to try to preserve the strength of the horses. However, they too were beginning to give out, dropping in their tracks.

At last they came to a village and the column was allowed to halt. Better yet, the guards informed them that they would spend the night there and to go find whatever accommodations they could. Joe and his six roommates from Stalag Luft III, who had continued to take turns dragging the sled, found an old movie theater. This would be their home for the night. The interior of the cinema with its empty seats and stage was almost luxurious: "It was out of the wind, out of the blowing snow and we were not marching, we were lying down, backs against the heavy wood covering the walls."

They pawed through the packages on the sled to find food that was not frozen and could be eaten. As they chewed they discussed the sled and determined it made no sense to keep dragging it along, wasting valuable energy that could not be recouped. Each of the men dug out a shirt and turned it into a small pack, filling it with a few tins of food and packages of biscuits. "We knew by now that we would die of cold and exhaustion before starvation could ever catch us," Joe reasoned. Soon afterward, pressed together for warmth, Joe and his companions fell asleep.

The familiar "Raus!" was heard at dawn. Joe, his body one seamless ache, wondered if, as at Buchenwald, some prisoners had died during the night and others, too weak to get up, would be shot. There was nothing he could do about that. Once up and moving around, he did feel better from having slept and managing to swallow the bits of food. Outside the theater, he and his companions were greeted by a dull gray sky and wind-blown sheets of snow. Those not being left behind, the dead or barely alive, once more formed into a long column that set off down the road.

After some time, all that kept Joe and most of the prisoners going was the routine of marching forward and the inability to think of anything else. "Keep one foot in front of the other," he thought. "What would be would be, keep it going, think of nothing, no plans, no hopes, just one foot in front of the other. Then one foot in front of the other."

One mile, two, the one after that, the frozen and exhausted men shuffled forward. Every so often, one dropped and a guard would drag the prisoner to the side of the road, out of the way. Sometimes a gunshot would follow; sometimes a bullet was not necessary. The hint of the sun through the clouds was directly overhead, and then it crawled through the cruel afternoon. Joe idly wondered which step would be his last, when he would finally find it impossible to put one foot in front of the other, when he would fall to his knees and then pitch forward onto his face. And then a guard, perhaps with an ounce of sympathy, but probably only a heavy weariness, would haul him off to the side of the road.

However, as though a miracle were occurring, later in the afternoon Joe began to feel better. It was like he had broken through to the other side of pain and exhaustion. He experienced "a growing warmth and with it a growing sense of well-being. Something deep inside me seemed to be saying that I was going to be OK, I was going home and it would feel so good."

That feeling expanded within him: "What started as a surprising sense of acceptance and peace slowly began turning to a kind of euphoria. The snow and cold and wind seemed to fill me with a kind of joy and anticipation. It was almost as if I was outside myself watching myself getting warmer, more peaceful and even joyful. It seemed the sky was lightening. It didn't seem so hard now. I could go on like this forever. Forever and ever."

Joe was not aware that the euphoria was the sensation experienced by those about to die from the combination of hypothermia and exhaustion. After a few more unsteady steps, darkness flooded his mind, and he collapsed. A final thought was that his fear of being left to die on a lonely road in a country thousands of miles from home was about to be realized.

26

By that evening, the column of prisoners who had managed to survive the incessant trudging through the icy snow had progressed to the medieval town of Bad Muskau on the Neisse River. There they were told to find shelter where they could. They fanned out only as far as their frozen feet could carry them. The men found some protection from the cold and wind in a variety of locations, including glass and tile factories (where, blessedly, furnaces were still stoked from the day's work), brickworks, a pottery shop, a local French POW camp, and even the main house and barns of an abandoned riding school.

Though a small village, Bad Muskau had been a resort destination before the war, and one carryover from better days was a small hospital. One of its patients that night was Joe Moser.

Unlike many of the other marchers who were left to die in the snow during the long and pitiless journey, when Joe had collapsed, two of his Stalag Luft III block mates had picked him

up . . . or did as best they could. Having very little strength remaining themselves, the men could not quite carry Joe. They
did not think he was dead, but he sure was dead weight. All
the two fellow flyers could do was drag Joe along as though he
had been the sled they had left behind. Fortunately, Bad Muskau
turned out to be only a quarter mile or so down the road. When
the two men and their burden arrived, they were directed to the
hospital.

Joe woke up in a large, clean room filled with beds, perhaps a
dozen of them. Once the shock of finding that he was alive wore
off, he felt a strange sensation: warmth. He could hear other men
in the beds groaning and even crying from frostbite and a variety of other painful ailments but overriding everything was the
warmth of the room. He knew this was not heaven, but right
then it was close enough.

Most likely, Joe was given food and water by the nurses, but
what meant most of all was sleep. He literally slept around the
clock and then kept sleeping until dawn. Mercifully, the German
officers supervising the march had realized that not dozens or
hundreds but thousands could die if the trek continued in such
inhumane conditions, so they waited out the latest snowfall and
allowed the prisoners to recuperate as best they could. Even so,
some died while in the village.

Joe heard, as though in a recurring nightmare, the shouts of
"Raus!" soon after he woke at dawn. "I would not stay back in
the hospital," he vowed. He eased out of the narrow bed feeling
"every bone and muscle complain as if I was 110 years old. But if
my group was marching, I would march too."

The Allied prisoners met in the middle of Bad Muskau and
re-formed into a long column. Again, there were German families
lining up beside them, an increasing number of people who feared
the Russians more than they loved their homes. The column set

off, cruelly pummeled by wind, but this time it hurled rain, not snow, at them. The air temperature must have risen to above freezing, but not by much.

On January 31, the lead marchers arrived at the rail hub of Spremberg. The column had marched about sixty-five miles from Sagan, and the Allied senior officers who survived estimated the death toll in the hundreds.* It was with some relief that the men were loaded into the familiar cattle cars waiting on the tracks. True, conditions inside were bleak, filthy, and severely overcrowded. But there was protection from the freezing rain and the prisoners could keep each other warm. Still, for Joe and the other airmen who had been in Buchenwald, there were unhappy reminders of the awful journey after leaving the Fresnes prison, one of them being the five-gallon buckets that soon filled with waste.

This string of cars contained about ten thousand prisoners. Two destinations awaited them, both in deepest Bavaria, either Stalag XIII-D at Nuremberg or Stalag VII-A at Moosburg. In the days that followed, many POWs from other Stalag Luft III compounds would, after they arrived, also be transported to one or the other of these camps.

In the case of Joe Moser and the others on the train, their next stop, after three days of weary and increasingly foul traveling, was the Nuremberg camp. Along the way, the prisoners, who were not given food and had to share the water in the five-gallon bucket, were "angry, overcrowded, desperately hungry and thirsty and completely uncertain about our fate." Though not immune to any of this, Joe was consoled by an epiphany: "Waking up in the hospital realizing that were it not for the love—I can call it

---

* Based on research done after the war, including interviews with survivors and German guards, a more reliable estimate of 1,300 dead was developed.

nothing else—of two men who themselves were suffering and near the end, gave me a perspective on life and living. When you truly understand you owe your existence and joys to others who had no real reason to sacrifice themselves for you, it is hard not to be affected or changed for the good."

Once again, they were at a train station, the cattle-car doors were dragged open, and the tired and sore and very hungry men gingerly disembarked. They once more formed into a column and trudged to their new home. "When we entered the camp, we knew we were no longer in Stalag Luft III."

Stalag XIII-D camp had been constructed on what had once been a Nazi Party rally area. It had become an internment camp in September 1939, housing prisoners from Poland in the weeks after Germany invaded that country and the war in Europe began. Other prisoners arrived as the Nazis took over more territory; then the camp began to burst at the seams when the Soviet Union was invaded and Russian prisoners flooded in. Crowded, unhealthy, and desperate conditions persisted through the war. Stalag XIII-D survived an Allied air raid in August 1943 with only a handful of prisoners killed. By the time Joe Moser and the thousands of others who had barely survived the long march arrived, food and other necessities were scarce.*

To the newcomers, having so recently been at a well-run prisoner of war camp, the interior of Stalag XIII-D seemed especially filthy. The Allied arrivals formed groups and set to work doing what they could. "It nauseated us to clean up the garbage, excrement, mud and broken items" left behind by the previous

---

* Ironically, immediately after the war Stalag XIII-D became home to fifteen thousand members of the SS imprisoned there. During this time, Nakam ("Revenge"), a Jewish organization of Holocaust survivors, placed a baker in the camp who made and served poisoned bread. While over two thousand German inmates were sickened, it is believed no more than a few died.

prisoners who had either died or been moved elsewhere. Joe continued: "I was asked if this was what Buchenwald was like. Yes, except Buchenwald was still worse I said, and I know I wasn't believed. It was indeed reminiscent of Buchenwald in toilet facilities, in cleanliness, in morale and in food. But here there was still hope."

That hope was that they might manage to stay alive long enough to see one of the onrushing armies, Allied or Russian, show up and liberate the camp. For some prisoners, the hope was rather faint because there was still plenty of winter to endure. At least, as Joe pointed out, however bad conditions were at the new camp, it was not Buchenwald.

Buchenwald was an especially nauseating discovery for the Allies. For months before that day in April 1945, stories of the Nazi concentration camps had been circulating, but it was not until Buchenwald, the first major concentration camp Allied troops entered with a full population of prisoners, that the entire scope of horror was understood.

It had not seemed possible, but conditions at Buchenwald had worsened in the months after the Allied flyers had been transferred to the Luftwaffe-run Stalag Luft III. The punishments delivered by the winter, the advances of the Allied and Russian armies, and the influx of prisoners from other camps made conditions at Buchenwald even more intolerable. The crematorium threatened to exceed its capacity to dispose of the mounting piles of inmates who had died from starvation, disease, the relentless brutality, or murder. It was something of a miracle that thousands of prisoners survived to see the spring.

Easter Sunday in 1945, which fell on April 1, "was a special day for the prisoners of Buchenwald concentration camp," according to *The Buchenwald Report*. "The news that U.S. tanks had penetrated the Fulda gap and were approaching the vicinity of Eisenach (about 40 miles west of Weimar) was an 'Easter present.' The prisoners vowed to stiffen their resistance to SS commands and to prepare for a possible armed showdown with the SS if they attempted to destroy the camp before withdrawing."

Two days later, Hermann Pister collected camp leaders in the theater and vowed to turn Buchenwald over to the prisoners rather than try to transfer them elsewhere or commit mass murder. He claimed he had refused an order from SS *Reichsführer* Heinrich Himmler to do the latter. No one believed him, and among the inmates preparations for an armed uprising continued.

Many of them were terrified and confused. "Our faces drawn, we stood about in little clusters, consoling each other with our theories," wrote Eugene Weinstock. "There was no more work. The SS soldiers themselves were growing more excitable by the minute, and therefore more dangerous, as they rushed about in a witless manner, waiting for orders. Then lightning struck from the clear sky."

That "lightning" was an announcement that every Jewish prisoner in the camp, even those on special details and in the hospital, was to report to the Appellplatz. The implication was clear—the time had come to exterminate all the remaining Jews. "We faced a desperate fight for time," Weinstock reported. "If we could stay alive another week, perhaps only a day, or even an hour, the liberation armies might arrive."

Most of the Jewish prisoners went into hiding. Some had identified good spots around the camp earlier, others went searching frantically under barracks and in mostly unused buildings, and some of those in mortal fear were housed in the barracks of non-Jewish inmates. Though not as motivated as they once might have been, the SS guards did the best they could. They eventually found and gathered together 1,500 of the 8,000 Jewish prisoners remaining at Buchenwald. They were marched out of the camp, purportedly to be delivered to another concentration camp. Along the way, however, most of the men were shot or died from exhaustion.

Four other men had gone into hiding, including Christopher Burney. They were the only ones left of the British SOE agents, with the intrepid "Tommy" Yeo-Thomas, the man of many aliases, having escaped several months earlier. Their survival ensured that the story of the torture and executions of the agents would be told.

Evacuations of non-Jewish prisoners were conducted until about twenty-one thousand prisoners remained at Buchenwald. It was those—at least, the ones who were able to from that population—who greeted the first American arrivals on April 11 and then the liberating forces the following day.

The first men to enter Buchenwald on the eleventh were twenty-four-year-old Lieutenant Edward Tenenbaum, the son of Polish Jews who had emigrated to the United States, and forty-three-year-old Egon Fleck, also Jewish. They later reported that when their jeep drove into the camp, they were greeted by thousands of cheering prisoners who limped, staggered, and crawled out of the buildings to shake their hands. The two Americans spent the night in Block 50, which previously had housed the experimental typhus laboratory, and at 5:30 the next morning, Tenenbaum and Fleck were awakened by a brass band. They appeared at the window and were again cheered by the prisoners, and they witnessed a parade of all the inmates who were able to participate. On that day, April 12, 1945, when Tenenbaum and Fleck were joined by American troops, Buchenwald was officially liberated.

"The Americans were appalled at the ghastly scene confronting them," writes Colin Burgess. "They had already driven past countless hundreds of bodies in the Weimar woods, where groups of evacuees had been massacred, but none of them was ready for the massive wave of hysterical living skeletons surging toward them. Shock followed shock for the Americans as they moved further into the camp. Beyond the filthy hordes of emaciated survivors were the corpses, piled haphazardly in mountains of putrefying flesh. It was a sight none of them would ever forget."

That would certainly be true for many who followed the soldiers into Buchenwald during the next several days. Word of unimaginable atrocities began to be broadcast around the world, with the foremost correspondent being the CBS reporter Edward R. Murrow. He had been speaking to the United States from Europe throughout the war, beginning with the London Blitz.

Murrow arrived on the scene three days after Buchenwald was liberated. One of his reports was about a visit to a barracks occupied by Czechoslovak prisoners: "When I entered, men crowded around, tried to lift me to their shoulders. They were too weak. Many of them could not get out of bed. I was told this building had once stabled 80 horses. There were 1200 men in it, five to a bunk. The stink was beyond all description."

Murrow and several companions roamed the camp. "As we walked out into the courtyard, a man fell dead. Two others, they must have been over 60, were crawling toward the latrine. I saw it but will not describe it."

He encountered hundreds of children, some as young as six. Dozens held out their arms to display the numbers tattooed on them. At the hospital, Murrow was informed that the day before, two hundred inmates had died. Most of those lying in the beds were too weak to move. He walked inside what had been a garage and found "two rows of bodies stacked up like cordwood. Some had been shot through the head, but they bled but little."

Murrow concluded his report: "Murder had been done at

Buchenwald. God alone knows how many men and boys have died there during the last 12 years. I pray you believe what I have said about Buchenwald. I reported what I saw and heard, but only part of it. For most of it, I have no words. If I have offended you by this rather mild account of Buchenwald, I'm not in the least sorry."

27

Joe Moser would not fully comprehend until later that the intervention of Hannes Trautloft was the reason that he and most of the other Allied flyers were not counted among the dead at Buchenwald.

As it was, Joe had arrived at Stalag XIII-D on February 5, and he remained there for exactly two months. The incarceration at the crowded camp was longer than many of the prisoners had anticipated given the rumors and reports making the rounds of Germany's crumbling defenses and the Allied forces on one side and the Russian forces on the other gobbling up large swaths of territory. Surely, as manpower and other resources became more precious, the Germans would simply abandon the POW camps. But that did not happen, at least not at Stalag XIII-D.

"We were ever closer to liberation and freedom," Joe reflected, "but with each step of the enclosing Allied armies, fears increased that ours would be one of those too common, too tragic stories in which the helpless soldier dies with freedom in sight." There was "a constant tension between rising hope and increasing fear."

A consolation could have been that the brutal winter finally began to give way to the overtures of spring: "But my memory of that is mostly of muck and rain with little sunshine or warmth."

However, conditions over time were improving somewhat thanks to the ongoing efforts of the new arrivals. The Allied flyers continued to "do our best to turn the stinking, filthy barracks into something livable without having any idea how long we might be there."

As with Stalag Luft III, week after week dragged by with no sign of a liberating army. Rumors swept the camp that to prevent further bloodshed, the Allies—though probably not the avenging Russians—would accept peace terms put forth by Germany. Either a much-weakened Hitler would be allowed to remain in power or he would turn the reins over to the military, which certainly did not want to continue fighting and sustain more losses. If there was a truce or perhaps a more definitive agreement, where would that leave Germany's prisoners? They could be kept behind barbed-wire and electrified fences indefinitely as pawns in ongoing negotiations or, ironically, as hostages to peace.

There was another fear among the men that Joe echoed: "Would [Hitler] order the Luftwaffe to bomb the camp? Would the guards in the towers encircling us be ordered to shoot and the readily available machine guns be set up to mow us down while we lined up for *Appell*?"

There was even a third cause for concern: air raids. Joe and the other Allied flyers from Buchenwald still clearly remembered the one the previous August that destroyed the factories adjacent to the camp and killed dozens. Nuremberg had become a frequent target. "Sometimes the bombers would come in huge waves—Lancasters or Sterlings—on massive night raids,"

Joe reported. "Other times, a single Mosquito would scream in before the air raid alert could be sounded and drop a single 4000-pound bomb with an ear-shattering, bone-shaking explosion."

As if that were not enough, "And sometimes the noon or afternoon sky would be filled with B-17s and B-24s unloading more destruction on the shattered city."

The various scenarios the airmen considered could play out only if the camp residents stayed alive, however. At Stalag XIII-D in February and March, the incredibly harsh winter refused to loosen its grip. The cold the prisoners endured was nearly unbearable. To keep stoves going, the men had to rip down the most decrepit of the wooden barracks, with their former inhabitants doubling and tripling up in other barracks.

Once more, as at Buchenwald, starvation became a possibility. All the German guards had left in the larder to distribute were potatoes and "teeth-cracking black bread and the thin gruel they called soup." During the two months of their imprisonment at Stalag XIII-D, Red Cross packages arrived just twice. Whatever health gains had been made at Stalag Luft III were quickly eroding at the Nuremberg camp. Old enemy scourges such as dysentery and diphtheria reappeared.

Every morning, the prisoners woke and stepped out of their barracks hoping to see the towers unmanned and not a guard in sight. But every morning was the same, shouts of "Raus!" calling them to *Appell*. Then one morning, April 5, the shouts were different. That morning was cold with a stinging rain, as usual, but the prisoners were ordered to gather their few possessions. All fifteen thousand of them formed a long column that marched out of Stalag XIII-D. They were directed south. It seemed astonishing that instead of giving up and going home, the German guards were taking them to yet another camp.

The weather was not dismal enough to keep local people indoors. As the men marched through the countryside, they saw farmers in their fields and villagers tending to gardens. Some of the prisoners, like Joe, had hoarded cigarettes, which they hurriedly traded to the German citizens in exchange for pieces of meat and anything else that could be shared to keep each other alive. Conditions were vastly different from the murderous march in January, but many of the men, weakened by malnutrition and disease, were just as likely to fall by the wayside, either dying there or being finished off by the guards.

The column could travel up to eight miles a day, and the men marched every day for over a week. During one break, Joe approached a farmer who offered a big smile and agreed to trade potatoes for cigarettes. Joe blamed his inadequate German language skills when the farmer told him that the war was over. The farmer elaborated, "Your president is dead. You have lost the war."

Seeing Joe's thunderstruck expression, other prisoners approached. The farmer addressed them: "President Roosevelt is dead. You cannot win now with your president dead."*

Shouts exhorted the prisoners to resume marching. News of President Roosevelt's demise rushed through the ranks. For some of them, this was a devastating blow, just more misery piling on—especially the younger men. In their adult lives they had known no other president than FDR, who had been in office for twelve years. Understandably, given the iron grip of the dictator Adolf Hitler for the same amount of time as Roosevelt's presidency, many Germans believed that the loss of the head of state also meant the loss of the war. How could Germany exist without the

---

* On April 12, only three months into his fourth term as president, Franklin Delano Roosevelt suffered a fatal stroke while at the "Little White House" in Warm Springs, Georgia.

Führer? But that was not the way things worked in the United States. Now it was Harry Truman teaming up with Winston Churchill and Josef Stalin to win the war against Germany and Japan.

On April 15, after ten days of marching, the prisoners who had survived the ordeal arrived at their destination. Stalag VII-A, north of the town of Moosburg in southern Bavaria, was, at eighty-six acres, one of the largest of Germany's prisoner of war camps. It was designed to house ten thousand prisoners, and immediately after it opened in September 1939 it filled up with Polish soldiers captured during the invasion. As German troops rolled through France in spring 1940, French captives were also crowded into Stalag VII-A. And as Nazi conquests continued, prisoners from England, Greece, Yugoslavia, and the Soviet Union were shoehorned in as well. The camp had the distinction of housing as many as twenty-seven Russian generals. And there were some Americans in the camp too, soldiers taken prisoner during the Battle of the Bulge. Of the thousand inmates who had died in captivity, most from diseases, eight hundred of them were Russians.

By the time Joe Moser and the fifteen thousand other prisoners had completed their seventy-mile trek from Stalag XIII-D to Stalag VII-A, the camp designed for ten thousand inhabitants held seventy-six thousand. Obviously, it was bursting at the seams. Food and water were scarcer than ever. There was no room in any of the dreadfully overstuffed barracks, so the new arrivals piled into tents. During the last two weeks of April 1945, the days were warmer but the nights could still be quite cold, and all the newer prisoners had with which to keep themselves warm in the Stalag VII-A tents were what they wore and any blanket or extra garments they had brought with them.

"The guards did their best to keep some form of order," Joe

reported, "but it was quite hopeless at this stage. It is remarkable given the overwhelming burdens that they actually tried to maintain bureaucratic standards." However, "Soon the effort of any sort of roll call was abandoned, and I was happy to put that part of my POW experience behind me."

Any food the men had brought or procured during the march was soon gone. All supplies at the camp dwindled to nothing. The arrival of Red Cross packages was only a daydream. The water was too foul to drink. Many of the inmates became too weak to move about, even to the latrines . . . though that mattered little, as they were overflowing, filling the air with an inescapable, sinus-curdling stench.

According to Joe, "Our hunger matched that experienced in Buchenwald. Now all of us felt it. It consumed us day and night with a desperation that makes you think that wood or cloth or a blade of grass might ease it. If cows could eat grass, why couldn't I?"

The most encouraging sounds to be heard—and they grew louder every day—was that of artillery. But each evening fell with no sign of Allied troops, the camp intact with its 240 guards still at their posts, and conditions becoming more desperate. Once again, Joe wondered if he would ever see his mother, brother, and sisters. How cruel it would be to die perhaps only days if not hours from freedom.

The army was doing its best to not only find and free prisoners but also to end the war in Germany. On April 28, the Fourteenth Armored Division crossed the Danube River at Ingolstadt. It passed through the Eighty-Sixth Infantry Division, which had established the bridgehead on the previous day with the mission of securing crossings of the Isar River at Moosburg and Landshut. Large numbers of German troops were falling back on Moosburg to cross the river. In the lead of the swift Allied advance were Brigadier General C. H. Karlstad and his American troops.

On the twenty-eighth, they advanced nearly fifty miles against sporadic resistance. That night, they were only four miles from Moosburg.

During the early morning hours of the twenty-ninth, a car approached a roadblock from the direction of Moosburg. The car was not fired on as it was seen to be flying a white flag. In the car were four men who asked to speak with a senior officer. The party included a representative of the Swiss Red Cross, a major in the SS, Colonel Paul S. Goode of the U.S. Army, and Group Captain Willets of the RAF, the latter two being prisoners at Stalag VII-A. The SS major carried a written proposal from the area commander, which he was to present to the commanding officer of the American force. The German surrender in that area would include the POW camp and its prisoners, many of whom were near death.

Joe Moser did not know about the negotiations. He was focused on how he would survive another day. He was one of the prisoners still able to walk, and he happened to be sitting on the ground near the camp's main gate. However, he did know, as did most of the prisoners, that the U.S. Army was very close. That morning, they could see troops and tanks massing atop a hill only a mile or so away. Apparently, Colonel Otto Berger, the Stalag VII-A commandant, was not giving up without a fight, because the guards positioned themselves at the front of the camp. As the Americans advanced, the Germans began firing rifles and machine guns.

Now the prisoners feared a quick and violent death instead of a slow, agonizing one.* "The gunfire was reaching a crescendo,"

---

* Because he would accept nothing short of total surrender, General Karlstad had rejected the truce the SS major had requested, seeing it as a delaying tactic while German officers tried to flee. However, thanks to the presence of the two Allied officers, Karlstad now knew of the existence and proximity of Stalag VII-A, and he ordered that artillery not be used in an attack on Moosburg.

Joe reported. "Bullets and an occasional tank shell were now entering the camp and I ducked into a trench, hoping and praying for the best. Everywhere I could see prisoners scattering, hiding, getting behind buildings or taking whatever shelter they could."

In Moosburg itself, the fighting raged in the streets. German troops surrendered in droves. At Stalag VII-A, seeing the inexorable advance of the Americans, some German guards tried to do the same. They slipped through the main gate and walked toward the army troops and tanks with their hands up. But SS officers with pistols drawn rushed to the front of the camp and shot the guards in the back. Then they too fell, struck by American gunfire.

An impatient General Karlstad, accompanied by two junior officers and three enlisted men, jumped into two jeeps and raced toward the POW camp. Thus, the entire advance unit was a total of only six men. They were met near the camp by still-armed German guards, over two hundred of them, who could have easily killed the Americans in a burst of gunfire.

Undeterred, the general and four of the men with him yanked out their firearms. The sixth, a lieutenant named Luby, stood up and manned one jeep's .30 caliber machine gun. Karlstad ordered the guards to surrender immediately. Without hesitation, they did. The Germans dropped their weapons in front of them and lined up. The two young officers and three enlisted men went rapidly down the line receiving the pistol belts from officers and making a quick search for arms in the pockets of the guards.

Inside the camp, a few minutes later, there was a loud crash. Joe struggled to his feet. What he saw was like a wild fantasy come true—a large vehicle had just burst into Stalag VII-A. "It tore the barbed wire gate apart and suddenly, right in front of me, not 20 yards away was a real American tank. There was a stunned moment. And then bedlam."

The liberators had arrived, and the prisoners were now, finally, safe. And overjoyed: "A roar went up from the camp that rolled through the acres, down through the narrow muddy corridors, in between the shabby tents, into the ramshackle barracks," according to Joe. It was "a roar of relief and joy and exhilaration that only the truly liberated can know."

He added: "The roar grew and grew—such a sound will lift your heart for the rest of your life once you hear it. Freedom. Just a word, but something good and brave men will give their lives for in a heartbeat."

As had occurred when the first Allied vehicle entered Buchenwald, inside Stalag VII-A the tank was surrounded by skeletal men laughing and weeping and pounding on the warm steel. In this crowd were Norwegians, Brazilians, French, Poles, Dutch, Greeks, Romanians, Bulgarians, Americans, Russians, Serbs, Italians, New Zealanders, South Africans, Australians, British, Canadians—men from every nation fighting the Nazis. They rushed to greet their liberators. So many flowed around and over the tank that for a time it disappeared.*

Then the ecstatic prisoners were joined by entering army soldiers, astonished by what they saw and feeling the outpouring of emotions like a series of waves. They too cried and yelled and hugged. Emotions ran even higher, if that was possible, as the Nazi swastika flag was lowered above the camp administration building and replaced by the flag of the United States of America.

As Joe recalled, "When we saw those stars and stripes rise into the blue sky of that late April day and replace the black and red slash of Nazi hatred, it carried with it the meaning of almost

---

* The senior member of the tank crew was even more overcome than his comrades: A few moments after entering the camp, he was greeted by a young American pilot. This was his son, who had been declared missing in action.

all that is precious in this life—family, security and most of all freedom."

Family: Joe Moser could finally think he would see his own after all. He did not know how or when, but the possibility had soared from just hours earlier. However, he realized, "Getting home would be the next and final adventure."

And not, as it turned out, an easy one.

28

As more American soldiers streamed into Stalag VII-A, inmates asked them the same question: "Do you have any food?" The soldiers were shocked at the appearance of the inmates and they were beginning to comprehend that the mass starvation of tens of thousands of men was only days if not hours away.

Immediately, the GIs began pulling out and offering their own rations. Everything edible they had on them, down to the tiniest piece of candy, was snatched out of their hands by quivering fingers and consumed. Joe Moser, being near the main gate, was able to wolf something down—whatever it was, it was food. The sight of more and more army soldiers and tanks in and around the camp was sustenance too. Many shared Joe's thought: "I was in American hands, and for the first time could start thinking about getting home. So I considered myself among the happiest and luckiest men alive."

The sheer number of prisoners at Stalag VII-A presented a logistics challenge to army brass. The war was not over yet, so General Karlstad and his men had to move on, chasing the disintegrating German forces deeper into the fatherland. And it was not enough to press Hitler to surrender—there was the race with the Russians. The Soviet Union had been an ally because defeating the Nazis was a shared goal, but the American and British governments had no illusions about Josef Stalin's other goal—take as much territory as possible to extend Communist rule westward, well into Europe. Beating the Russians to Berlin was the way to prevent one dictatorship from replacing another.

But the desperation of the starving inmates could not be put on hold. It was not known how many men may have perished in the previous few days, but no one doubted they would soon be joined by hundreds if not thousands more. Joe weighed close to what he did when he left Buchenwald, and his condition was far from rare. On that blessed day of liberation, he was surrounded by men whose ragged clothing hung on their bodies and whose gaunt faces expressed the pain and weariness of incessant hunger.

Former prisoners were prohibited from leaving Stalag VII-A that night. This was an easy command for army guards to carry out because truckloads of food were brought in. Plus, there was nowhere to go. The surrounding countryside had been chewed up by battle and emptied of almost all food and livestock—except for a windfall that enraged the inmates. As the soldiers had been going through the camp's buildings in search of hiding guards or residents who had been too weak to join the liberation festivities, they found Red Cross packages in the guards' quarters. Many had been opened. The remaining contents were quickly handed out.

This was just a mere drop in the bucket, but then the much bigger discovery was made: Word arrived from Moosburg that a warehouse filled with Red Cross packages had been found. These supplies were already on their way to the camp. The inmates' gratitude was mixed with loathing for the administrators of Stalag VII-A who had hoarded these provisions while tens of thousands were starving.

The next day, once more Joe was part of a column of men marching out of a German camp . . . but this time, it was to begin the long journey home. Several months ago, he had dreamed of being home for Christmas. He prayed nothing would prevent that from happening this year. As it was, "Walking through that main gate with my fellow prisoners and U.S. troops all around was like walking through a dream I had never quite dared to allow myself."

That first day, the former prisoners did not walk very far. Too few had the stamina to go anywhere, and the army bureaucrats were still organizing a system to process the prisoners and send them on to the next destination. Joe was one of the more comfortable prisoners that first night of freedom because he was among the men who slept in a barn on a farm just outside Moosburg.

Few things meant home more for the former Ferndale farmer than the feel and scent of hay. And the scent sure did not bother the city boys because "we stunk to high heaven, and it became much more obvious just how filthy and disgusting we were when we moved from the camp to the barn. The stench from myself and my fellow ex-prisoners overpowered any unpleasant odors from the animals that had been kept in the barn before us."

But after a week, feelings of comfort and complacency began to dissipate. True, living in a barn was infinitely better than conditions had been inside Stalag VII-A, and they had access to food. But still being confined like farm animals was not what Joe and the others had hoped for after liberation. They could not comprehend the huge bureaucratic and logistical challenges the army faced or the events that were transpiring that week while they slept in the barn.

Over ninety thousand men from the United States alone had been housed in German POW camps. As the war neared its end, they were being released as their camps were liberated in rapid succession. Caring for them and processing them were just two of the challenges. Another was that during that month of April 1945, the total number of German soldiers who surrendered on the Western Front was roughly 1.5 million. They too had to be processed and housed. And a massive effort was still underway to end the war.

The day after Stalag VII-A had been liberated, on April 30, Adolf Hitler committed suicide. With the Battle of Berlin raging above him and the Soviets surrounding the city, and his planned escape route cut off by the Americans, the Führer realized that all was lost. He died in the *Führerbunker* along with Eva Braun, his long-term partner whom he had married less than forty hours before their joint suicide. As part of putting his affairs in order, Hitler fired Hermann Göring and Heinrich Himmler after each of them had tried to seize control of the crumbling Third Reich. Hitler appointed Karl Dönitz as the new president of Germany and Joseph Goebbels as the new chancellor of Germany.*

Göring, who had effectively saved the lives of the Allied *Terrorfliegers* at Buchenwald, attempted to leave the country with his wife and daughter. He would not succeed; instead, fearful of being captured by the Soviets, he surrendered on May 6 to American officers at the border of Germany and Austria. He would be convicted of war crimes at the Nuremberg trials and sentenced to be hanged. His appeal of the sentence consisted of asking to be shot as a soldier rather than hanged as a common criminal.

---

* Goebbels's tenure as chancellor was quite short: He joined the ranks of high-level German suicides the next day.

The appeal was denied and the sentence was to be carried out on October 16, 1946. However, the night before, Göring somehow obtained and swallowed a potassium cyanide capsule.

After Hitler's death, there was sporadic fighting in and around Berlin. Finally, Germany officially surrendered on May 8. World War II was not over, of course, with Japan fighting on for another three months, but in Europe, more attention could now be paid to getting Allied prisoners back to their homes.*

Little of this was filtering down to Joe and the other former POWs in the barn outside Moosburg: "We sat there for a whole week without a clue as to what was really going on, not even knowing if anyone was taking our lives and needs into consideration." They could leave the barn to loosen their limbs and breathe in some fresh air but were told to stay close in case . . . in case of what, they did not know.

A few of Joe's barn mates wandered off, even hiking into Moosburg. One of them simply walked into offices that had been Gestapo headquarters there. He began rifling through file cabinets and discovered records of Allied POWs kept at Stalag VII-A. He grabbed a handful and would wind up bringing them all the way back to the United States.† Joe would have rather he returned to the barn with a cache of undelivered letters. He was desperate to have any contact with his mother. A letter from her would have been the next best thing to alerting her himself that her oldest son was alive.

---

* On May 5, Japan had managed to carry out its most deadly attack on the American homeland. On that day, one of the hundreds of balloons Japan had sent aloft, hoping the winds would carry them east, landed in a yard in Bly, Oregon, where a pregnant minister's wife and five adolescents sat picnicking after Sunday school. The bomb attached to the balloon exploded, killing all six of them.

† As will be relayed in the Epilogue, this spontaneous act of pilfering would have a profound impact on Joe Moser and the other *Terrorfliegers*.

On May 2, three days after Stalag VII-A had been liberated, the first American C-47s landed at the Moosburg airport. They began loading up groups of former prisoners, taking off, and returning for more. To Joe, there did not appear to be a system in place as to who got to leave when. Those in the barn "didn't know if our journey would start in an hour or a month."

Finally, several days later, "I happened to be in the right place at the right time."

A young private told him, "Load up." The young man did not know he was giving orders to an army lieutenant, but Joe did not care about that. And there was nothing to load anyway. With just the ragged clothes on his back, Joe jumped into a truck packed with other ex-prisoners and it trundled out to the airport. Joe was thrilled at the prospect of flying again, to be in a plane—though not his beloved Lightning P-38—for the first time in nine months, when previously he had flown almost every day for years. The C-47 "gooney bird" was a beautiful sight.

As luck would have it, soon after the packed plane took off, Joe began to feel pain in his mouth. It began to concentrate in one area of his gums. "I tried to ignore it, but it grew rapidly in intensity until it started to color all my senses. It was the worst toothache of my life." It was while he was in the middle of this increasing agony that an announcement was made on the plane of Germany's surrender. As Joe ruefully noted, "There was just something terribly unfair in this timing."

Two hours later, the C-47 landed in Rheims. As the plane unloaded, Joe saw men gazing at him—specifically, the swollen size of his jaw. He was told to board a bus that would take them to Le Havre on the French coast, and there they would clamber aboard a ship set to sail to the United States. But Joe could not go anywhere until the tooth was taken care of. He asked enough people that one finally told him about the base dentist.

"He took one look at the abscessed lower molar and said it was coming out." Joe was in complete agreement and continued to be when the dentist told him he had no more novocaine. "A moment and a jerk later, it was gone. Immediately I felt better."

However, it did not feel so good to discover that the bus to Le Havre had left. Joe wandered around Rheims and was fortunate to find a tent with an empty cot. The accommodations were not the most comfortable, but he fell into a deep and grateful sleep.

Joe was up early the next morning and found there was room on the next bus. Stepping off in Le Havre, he was directed to Camp Lucky Strike. Hundreds of rows of tents had been erected by army personnel and civilians to try to shelter the tens of thousands of soldiers who were just like Joe Moser—waiting to ship out for home. What appealed to him most about Camp Lucky Strike "was a kitchen tent with a long chow line and there was—unbelievably to me—plenty of food. Plenty of food!" Almost as appealing were the many latrines, and clean ones at that. And soon after came his first shower since leaving Stalag Luft III, and that had been in January, before the long march had begun. It was now the second week in May.

There was little for the mass of men at Camp Lucky Strike to do but wait to be told what to do next. Joe's patience was tested only for two days, and then he was informed that he was to leave Le Havre on May 19. He was struck by the coincidence of that being the birthday of his father, Joseph Sr., who had died nine years before. Joe took that as a good sign that he would indeed find his way home.

There was, thankfully, no delay. On the day his father would have turned sixty-two, a "beautiful May sunshiny day," Joe boarded the boat. It had once been a civilian passenger liner and each cabin had two bunks. He enjoyed the luxury of having his own bed all the way across the Atlantic Ocean. There was one glitch, though: The boat had to detour to Trinidad to deliver troops who were being redeployed. That would extend the trip to New York to three weeks. Joe tried to be stoic about it: What was another three weeks after not being home for years?

At least it was smooth sailing across the ocean. No storms rocked the boat, leaving Joe untroubled by seasickness. He bunked with only one other soldier. And there was no lack on board of something that had been very scarce for much of the past year: "Food. There was more than enough for everyone, and it was available night and day. I was very hungry. Very hungry. Suddenly, there it was. Food, endless food."

Joe could have no idea that what appeared to be a miracle would also be a curse. For now, though, on that voyage he wielded utensils with the best of them. And there was no guilt about eating. It wasn't like the more he ate, the less there was for the next guy. All across America, thousands of ranches and farms like the Moser one in Washington were producing millions of pounds of food, and no one would begrudge a second or third helping to soldiers returning from fighting for their country. The only reason to stop eating off one plate was to save room for what was on the next one. As a result, with every nautical mile, Joe was putting back on weight that had been missing for a long time.

Blinking back tears, Joe gazed at the Statue of Liberty as the boat entered New York Harbor. "It is a beautiful sight and especially meaningful to those who understand what liberty really means and the high price that must be paid for it." And of all days, this was his mother's birthday. What a gift it would be to know her son was alive and well. There was a room onboard that contained fifteen phones for contacting mainland households, but when Joe got down to it each one had a hundred or more soldiers on line to use it.

The passengers remained on the boat that night. Joe woke at

4 A.M. and found the phone room. There were only a few soldiers on each line, and he waited his turn. Finally, he grasped the receiver with shaking hands. Trying to keep his voice from breaking too much, Joe asked the operator to place a call to Mary Moser in Bellingham, Washington. After a few seconds, he heard the first ring. Then the second. Then every ring after that. It was between 1 and 2 A.M. on the West Coast; she had to be home. But there was no answer at the house. "I was almost in tears to not be able to talk to my mom."

He did not have an opportunity to try again, because all the passengers were herded off the boat. There was yet more processing to be done, and then the soldiers were separated by whatever the next step in their journey was. For Joe, it was getting on a train that left New York City on June 6. Once more, from a window on rails he watched America pass by, but he was now a much different man than the one who had been awed by the panorama a couple of years earlier. This time, the changing landscape could not pass by fast enough.

Finally back in his native state, Joe stepped off the train in a town outside of Seattle. He was still only twenty-three, but he felt years older. Without hesitation, he went to the first pay phone he saw and stuck several coins in. It rang, and this time there was a connection. "Hello?" said Mary Moser.

"Mom," Joe said.

"Joe? Joe, is that you?"

"Yes, it's me." Joe managed to choke out, "I'm in Auburn."

Mother and son burst into tears.

When they had composed themselves enough to have a conversation, Joe learned that his phone call out of the blue was not the revelation he'd thought it would be. His mother informed him that she had known he was alive and that at least some of his letters written in the first POW camp had found their way to

Washington. Joe was greatly relieved that his mother and siblings had not thought him dead for the entire time since he had taken off on his forty-fourth combat mission.

The next three hours were not the longest three hours of his life—every second at Buchenwald easily surpassed that—but they felt long enough. Finally, a familiar car pulled into the Auburn train station and "there she was, that dear, sweet lady who meant the world to me. She was crying and looked like she had cried all the way from Bellingham." And what about the Army Air Corps veteran who had survived everything thrown at him? "Her tough son who had been through hell cried in her arms like a baby."

Joe's return was more dramatic than he anticipated. Mother and son were just twenty miles from home, driving through the small town of Bow, when Mary Moser remembered that the wedding of a relative was taking place there and extended Moser family members were attending, "So we just popped in." The bride and groom were fine being upstaged when Joe, in a new Army uniform, entered the church basement and there were cries of joy and more tears.

However, Joe Moser's true homecoming began with being overjoyed to see his siblings again. Only one still lived at home, seven-year-old Rosalee. His other sister, Louise, had gotten married, though at least she and her husband remained in the Bellingham-Ferndale area. Frank Imhof now worked what used to be the Moser farm, and Joe's brother, Frank, lived in the old farmhouse and worked alongside his uncle.

Two weeks after returning home, Joe was invited by the Ferndale Lions Club to give a talk about his experiences as a pilot and a prisoner. He offered a straightforward presentation and was given polite applause. As he exited with everyone else, a man walking in front of him growled, "I didn't believe a damn word he said."

As Joe would discover from that night and a conversation weeks later with an Army Air Corps officer, no one believed he had been in what had come to be regarded as one of the more infamous concentration camps. As the officer said firmly, "No Americans were in Buchenwald." When Joe responded that of course Allied flyers, including Yanks, were there because he had been just one of dozens of them, the officer ended the conversation: "I don't know why you are insisting because it didn't happen."

Many Americans were still just learning about the existence of the Nazi camps like Auschwitz, Buchenwald, Bergen-Belsen, Treblinka, and the others, but specific information was almost nonexistent. On top of that, the U.S. government preferred that the imprisonment of the *Terrorfliegers* not be revealed because questions would be asked about what it knew about the Allied prisoners, when did it learn about them, and what, if any, attempts were made on their behalf. Like a lot of unpleasant realities in the war, best to forget and move on.

And with Joe and probably at least a few of the other Allied airmen, by the time they returned to their homes, they had put back on some of the weight they had lost. Joe, for example, had eaten his way across the Atlantic. When he claimed to have been a skeletal hundred-pounder, people scoffed or accused him of milking them for sympathy, or worse—he was out-and-out lying to make himself look like a hero.

Such reactions hurt: "I felt like someone had stuck a knife in me. That's it," Joe vowed, "I'm not talking about it again."

He focused on putting his life back together and on the future. Once he was officially discharged from active duty (he remained in the Army Air Corps Reserves), Joe went looking for a job . . . and a wife, "like most of us young men returning home."

He found the job first. With his brother having assumed responsibility for the farming, Joe instead went to work for the

Holland Furnace Company in Bellingham. He had always been mechanically inclined and "fixing furnaces fit me pretty well." It was not like toiling in the fields "but I did enjoy the people, and I could also keep to myself when I wanted to."

In November 1945, Joe attended the wedding of his Uncle Frank, who was only a few years older than him. His sister Louise and her husband were also at the wedding as was a friend of Louise named Jean Douglas. She caught Joe's eye. "I was as shy as I could be but, my goodness after all, this was a friend of my sister. What could one dance hurt."

Well, her toes, for one thing. Joe had not had much practice at dancing "but Jean seemed willing to help me out and tried to make me look less clumsy than I really was." He found that she enjoyed sports and, in fact, was "a darn good baseball player," having been a catcher on the Bellingham Bells semiprofessional baseball team during the war, when most of the players were women replacing the men who had gone into the service.

The night of Uncle Frank's wedding, Joe drove Jean home. It was at another wedding, on St. Patrick's Day in 1946, that he proposed. Jean accepted. That June, a year after Joe came home from the war, they became Mr. and Mrs. Joseph Moser. They would go on to have five children whose names all began with the letter J.

However devoted a husband Joe was, though, in a significant way he was leading a double life: "Jean and my children did not know of my time in Buchenwald," nor did others in his community. "After my painful experience of not being believed, plus the desire shared by so many of my fellow veterans just to get on with our lives, I kept the story inside." Incredibly, "They knew I had served in the military from the picture on a wall."

If that was the price to pay to have a normal life and allow the horrors of his wartime experiences to recede into the past, Joe paid it willingly. Inevitably, those experiences changed him, but he believed not in a bad way. "I have never looked at my country the same way," Joe reflected years later. "I paid a price, sure. But not like so many others. I do think the small price that I paid has made me much more appreciative than perhaps most for the cost of our freedom."

As the years passed, for Joe Moser this belief was as unshakable as his Catholic faith: "It is such a great privilege to live in the greatest country, the best country, the world has ever seen." And it was home.

Epilogue

It is love; love, the comfort of the human species, the preserver of the universe, the soul of all sentient beings, love, tender love.

—Voltaire, *Candide*

The incarceration of 168 Allied airmen in a Nazi concentration camp was not a story reported in the years following the end of World War II. One reason was that the United States government preferred that it not become a story at all. To be fair, there was little or nothing the administration of President Roosevelt could have done. Another reason that the story of survival did not see the light of day was the airmen themselves.

Many of the men and women who served in World War II returned home unwilling or unable to talk about their experiences. What we know now as post-traumatic stress disorder was then at best considered "shell shock" or "battle fatigue." Those who had experienced the worst of combat and who had been taken prisoner were more likely to suffer from it. Few military and even civilian systems were knowledgeable and equipped enough to help these veterans, and many veterans avoided experts, institutions, and even discussions anyway. Go home, get a job, get married, raise a family, get on with it.

A handful of those Allied airmen who had been imprisoned at Buchenwald tried to heal themselves, which included a visit to the camp during the decades after the war. For some there was closure but for others it was a heart-wrenching return to a place where they had experienced inhumane horror. For example, the RAF squadron leader Stanley Booker told the author Colin Burgess that when he was back at Buchenwald, "No birds sang and the ghosts of the past rose up to haunt me."

In 1979, the Konzentrationlager Buchenwald Club was revived when the Canadian flyer Art Kinnis invited several fellow Canadian airmen who had survived the camp to a meeting. Over the years, the KLB numbers would grow, and more meetings were held. During them, two flyers in particular were saluted for their actions. One of them, in absentia, was Hannes Trautloft, without whom the airmen would have been executed, and with their deaths their experiences may well have died with them.

Several months after intervening on the behalf of the flyers imprisoned in Buchenwald and helping to arrange their transfer to Stalag Luft III, Trautloft and other high-ranking Luftwaffe pilots staged a revolt against the Nazi government because of its inept and misguided military strategies that had cost the lives of German airmen. His punishment was to be fired from his position as inspector of the day fighters, and he was exiled to running a pilot school in Strassburg. Trautloft was still there when the war in Europe ended, his Luftwaffe record standing at 560 combat missions and 58 victories.

He became part of the new German air force, the Bundesluftwaffe, joining with a rank equivalent to a brigadier general in the

U.S. Air Force. He was a lieutenant general when he retired in 1970. He participated in and was honored by numerous veterans' organizations, including the KLB. Hannes Trautloft died in Bad Wiessee, Germany, in January 1995, two months before his eighty-third birthday.

The other flyer of distinction in this story is someone who did not gain immediate recognition; it took some time for the full tale to be told. When Phillip Lamason arrived in England in the late spring of 1945, Great Britain was still at war, doing its part against the Japanese in the Pacific Theater. He was offered command of a squadron based on Okinawa earmarked to participate in the intensifying raids on Japan. As he was considering the assignment, the Royal New Zealand Air Force declared that Colonel Lamason had done enough for his country and that he was to return home. And as it happened, the day after he set foot back in New Zealand, an atomic bomb was dropped on Hiroshima. On September 5, the train carrying the courageous officer pulled into Napier and Lamason was reunited with his wife, Joan, whom he had not seen in four years. They would spend the next sixty-four years catching up.

After the war and leaving active duty, Lamason, in search of a peaceful existence, became a farmer. He and Joan purchased over four hundred acres in Dannevirke, a town on New Zealand's North Island. In the 1980s and '90s, as farm responsibilities and his health allowed, Lamason attended the KLB reunions.* It was not until 1983, thirty-nine years after the order was issued, that he revealed he had known about the executions of the men scheduled for that October day in Buchenwald. This was done at

---

* Colonel Lamason was also an active member of the Caterpillar Club, a loosely structured but rather exclusive organization of pilots who used a parachute to bail out of a damaged plane.

a Canadian POW convention, and no one protested his decision to withhold that information.

During his quiet farmer years and subsequent retirement from agricultural labors, Colonel Lamason did not seek any attention for having been the senior officer of the Allied airmen at Buchenwald. "Apart from my family, people don't know of my involvement in these things." Even family members were mostly in the dark, with children recalling him saying only, "Whatever you heard about Buchenwald, it was worse."

Lamason remained in touch with the men formally under his command who "were from different countries, living together in one of the most horrific places on God's earth, but to a man they gave me their unquestioning loyalty, which meant a lot to me at the time. They were, and are, a tremendous group of men, and I feel deeply honored to have been their senior officer during that period."

However, over time he received attention anyway. In 1987, the government of New Zealand set up a fund to compensate members of the military who had been imprisoned in German concentration camps, and Lamason, for his time at Buchenwald, was given the equivalent of thirteen thousand dollars.

His role at the camp was only fully recognized seven years later, when he appeared in a Canadian documentary titled *The Lucky Ones: Allied Airmen and Buchenwald*. Then in 2004 another documentary, *Shot from the Sky*, much of it based on the book by Thomas Childers, was broadcast in the United States on the History Channel. And in 2011, the documentary *Lost Airmen of Buchenwald* was released, which included an interview with Lamason. By this point, his sacrifices and heroism had been well established.

The following year, in May 2012, Colonel Phillip Lamason died at age ninety-two on his farm in Dannevirke. Joan, the steadfast love of his life, had passed away three years earlier. The couple was survived by their two sons and two daughters.

Certainly two other officers important to Joe Moser were Burl Glass and Merle Larson. Glass served for more than twenty-six years and retired from the Air Force in 1968 with the rank of lieutenant colonel. He and his wife lived in Florida, where the Texan died at eighty-six in August 2005.

Larson and Joe Moser parted when the latter and other prisoners were forced to leave the Stalag VII-A camp at Nuremberg. Inadequate treatment of wounds the captain suffered when he was shot down had taken its toll and new infections were teaming up with older, lingering ones. He languished in the hospital, near death, his body covered with boils. "They gave me the last penicillin they had at the hospital," he later recalled. "That snapped me out and saved my life."

After the war, Larson remained in the military and retired as a U.S. Air Force colonel in 1972. He was also the recipient of two Distinguished Flying Crosses. Larson, who had defied death several times, passed away in 1998.

As the decades passed, Joe Moser was content to be a family man and, for forty years, a reliable "furnace repair guy," as he was known in the Ferndale and Bellingham area. Joe was also known as a good husband and father. Every day was blissfully normal: "We did our work, went to church and lived a grateful, if ordinary, life." They rooted for the Seattle and the Ferndale High football teams. Friends and neighbors knew he had been a pilot in the war and been a POW . . . but that was it.

Some nights could be harsh ones, though, because of nightmares. They took him back to Buchenwald. He would wake up screaming and sweating, hearing the crack of a kapo's stick on a man's head or back and the frothy snarling of the German shepherds, and he swore he could smell the smoke of the incinerator and feel ashes falling softly on his face.* There had been horrific details and deaths witnessed that would just not leave him be at night.

It was better in the daytime, because he had work and friends and activities and, of course, his wife, Jean, and their five growing children, and eventually grandchildren, to occupy him. Joe focused on what was positive in his life. "We went to ball games— endless ball games, by the time our kids and grandkids were playing." And when anyone asked him how he was doing, Joe had a standard yet heartfelt response: "Real good," with the emphasis on *real*.

Except for the nightmares. Talking to his family about his experiences may have helped, but he could not burden them with that. Plus, they were simply too awful. Why chance giving his loved ones nightmares too? How painful it would be for them to think of Joe the husband and father caged in a concentration camp like an animal—indeed, treated worse than the camp's animals—and each miserable day inching closer to death. And that seemingly endless march through the ice and snow of Germany in January 1945 when he had given himself up for dead.

No, he could not do that. Plus, what if, like that audience he had spoken to right after the war, they too did not believe him? Seeing that in his family's eyes would have been unbearable. And Joe might also have had to admit that he did not know who the two prisoners were who picked him up from that frozen road and dragged him to the next town, where he was revived. That was the reason he was here today and a husband and father and neighbor and trusted repairman, yet he would never be able to thank those two men for his life.

---

* For the rest of his life, Joe would have to leave a home or an event where bacon was being cooked.

There was another reason for the nightmares and hidden regrets—Joe had on his hands the blood of those two French farm boys. They had tried to help him escape after he landed in the field near Marchefroy in August 1944, and as a result that next morning they were put up against a wall and shot. For Joe, it was, year after year, very painful to acknowledge that those two young men would not be husbands and fathers and would not grow old playing with grandchildren. His incessant inner turmoil, suppressed during the day, was like a nocturnal animal that emerged and haunted his dreams at night.

And then two events occurred that changed the rest of Joe Moser's life.

The first took place in 1982, when he turned sixty-one and took the plunge, attending his first POW meeting. This one could not really be avoided because it was held in Bellingham. Members of the KLB were in attendance, including Jim Hastin, down from Canada, with whom Joe had become best friends during those early days of imprisonment. Joe was invited to give a talk at the meeting. This time, with KLBers present and in full support, Joe revealed that he had been one of the *Terrorfliegers* imprisoned in Buchenwald, one of those 168 Allied prisoners who had nearly died from starvation and disease. The audience was intrigued—by then, much more was known about the Third Reich's concentration camps and the inhumane conditions there. Many of those listening nodded with pained expressions on their faces . . . understanding, accepting, and finally believing.

Especially intrigued, though, was Bill Lewis, editor of a local newspaper, *The Lynden Tribune*. When his account of Joe's talk was published, it did the 1982 equivalent of going viral. It was picked up by national and international news services, and some of the other flyers who had served in Buchenwald contacted their local news outlets to corroborate what Joe had presented in Bellingham.

The other event occurred six years later. At that time, Art Kinnis was president of the KLB and Jim Hastin was the treasurer. One day, they were at Kinnis's home in Victoria, sorting through and organizing the group's archives. They came across a letter written to Kinnis in November 1945 from François Vermeulen, the farmer who had taken charge when Joe had landed in his field. It had been buried in the archives for forty-three years and never translated. The letter had been sent to Kinnis because, as Kinnis had told Joe on the train, this same village where Joe had crash-landed had also hidden Kinnis for several weeks after his RAF Lancaster bomber had crashed a half mile away.

Hastin and Kinnis had the letter translated, and then were very affected by what they read. In it, Vermeulen described the experiences of the local people for the rest of the war, including what had been done to help the French Resistance. He mentioned the day the plane of an American captain (giving Joe a promotion) had crashed and burned in a farm field and that the captain had survived. Léon Vermeulen, a younger brother, had been one of the two young farmers who had tried to help the pilot escape.

Realizing who François Vermeulen was referring to, Kinnis and Hastin called Joe and read him the letter over the phone. To an astonished Joe, what was most important about the letter was what was *not* in it—the older Vermeulen writing anything about his brother's death.

Subsequently, Joe tracked down Remco Immerzeel, a French schoolteacher who had taken it upon himself to collect information about Allied airmen who had been shot down over France and survived, particularly those who were sent to Buchenwald. Immerzeel, of course, knew of Joe Moser. He agreed to investigate further, though it was more than four decades after the events described in the letter.

The teacher learned that it was indeed Léon Vermeulen and

Henri Eustache, the two young farmers, who had been kept in the cellar with Joe the night of August 13. They were not executed the next morning . . . and there the story becomes even more remarkable. The driver of the local German commandant was a man named Paul Renaud, a Frenchman from Alsace who had been reluctantly inducted into the German army. When possible, Renaud committed subtle acts to help the French cause.

One of them occurred the morning of August 14, 1944. Renaud had been ordered to retrieve Léon Vermeulen and Henri Eustache from the cellar and bring them to be interrogated, and afterward they would be killed for having assisted a downed Allied pilot. The young "German" soldier did usher the two farmers out of the cellar, then took them behind the building. He took out his gun. No doubt, Léon and Henri thought they were about to be put up against the building's wall and executed. Instead, Renaud told them to run. Once the shocked young Frenchmen were at full speed, Renaud fired several shots in the air. He could at least report he had done what he could to stop the runaways.*

Knowing that the two young French farmers who had tried to help him escape had not died that day was the best news Joe could hear: "My life changed forever. I felt weak in the knees." Even better: "The nightmares that had plagued me all the years after the war finally stopped and did not return. It seemed like the last fetter the Germans had placed on me dropped away and I was free." For the first time in decades, Joe could sleep through the night.

As Joe neared ninety, he figured it was now or never to tell the

---

* After the war, Renaud, regarded as a hero for the many lives he had saved, was invited by the local people to stay and live in the area. He became the owner of a gas station, married a local girl, and passed away in the mid-1990s.

full story, or at least as much of it as he knew from his perspective. He and a Bellingham businessman, Gerald Baron, collaborated on *A Fighter Pilot in Buchenwald*, published locally in 2009. Joe experienced a new and profound sense of relief for having told his harrowing true tale first to his community, grandchildren, and extended family and now, finally, to whoever else might be interested.

As the foreword to the book begins, "For more than 40 years, homeowners in the small communities of Whatcom County, in the far northwest corner of the continental United States, welcomed a quiet, shy, dark-haired man into their homes. He was the furnace guy. For probably hundreds of people in Lynden, Ferndale, Blaine and Bellingham, Joe Moser is still the furnace guy. They had absolutely no idea that the short, smiling and quietly friendly man with the shining dark eyes and big hands was a true American hero."

The following year, Joe, fifty-five years after he had left, returned to Germany. Footage was being shot for the documentary, coproduced by Gerald Baron, that would be titled *Lost Airmen of Buchenwald*. The director and other producer, Michael Dorsey, interviewed Joe there and at the camp in Moosburg. Accompanying the former POW were two of his daughters and a nephew. Dorsey had begun the project to document the wartime experience of his grandfather, Elmer Freeman, who had also been shot down over France, incarcerated in Buchenwald, marched to the other camps, and liberated at Moosburg.

For Joe Moser, seeing the camps again was both a painful experience and a life-affirming one. He told Dorsey that he harbored no hatred toward the Germans. Instead, he said he was a changed man, one filled with gratitude and perspective. "Life is worth living," Joe said. "I'm glad I went through all this, but I wouldn't wish it on anyone else."

After the 2011 premier of *Lost Airmen of Buchenwald* that filled

Mount Baker Theatre in Bellingham, Moser, Baron, and Dorsey went onstage to talk to the cheering viewers. "We believe you now!" an audience member shouted.

Joe's final years were, predictably and as he preferred, quiet ones. In 2015, he had another moment in the spotlight when, at a ceremony in Seattle, Joe was presented with the French Legion of Honor, recognizing his forty-four Lightning P-38 combat missions and his survival in Buchenwald. Also that year, he was the first person profiled for the Washington Remembers series of interviews of World War II veterans conducted by the Washington secretary of state's office. "I've had a wonderful life," Joe said. "I would go through it again to keep our freedom. I know I could be angry for what I had to go through, but it made life worth living."

That Memorial Day, he served as the grand marshal of the Honoring Our Heroes parade in Bellingham. What Joe told the local paper, *The Herald,* was no surprise to the people who knew him: "I went through an awful lot, but I don't feel I'm a hero. I thought they could find somebody better."

By that September, when Joe turned ninety-four, he was battling cancer. Unlike against the enemy he had fought seventy years earlier, he lost this battle. On Wednesday, December 2, 2015, Joseph Moser, a humble American hero, died at home, surrounded by family, and at peace.

ACKNOWLEDGMENTS

Even with all the information in *Lightning Down* gleaned from other sources, the book could not have been written without the heartfelt efforts of Joseph Moser and Gerald Baron to tell Joe's astonishing story. I am grateful to them and for the generous cooperation of the Moser family. A tip of the cap also to the documentary filmmaker Michael Dorsey.

Once again I have the privilege of an acknowledgments section to thank the kind people at libraries and other research centers who were also very generous to me. They include Gilly Carr and the Frank Falla Archive, Kirstin Fawcett, Kenneth Fields, Mike Harold and the Phil Lamason Heritage Trust, Dolores Ho and the National Army Museum, Kate Igoe and the National Air and Space Museum, Stewart Kampel, Vicki Killian, Library of Congress, Sue Mullin and the John Jermain Library, Matthew O'Sullivan and the Air Force Museum of New England, Chantal Salerno, Brian Sherwood and The British Library, Ansgar Snethlage and the Military History Museum, Amy South and the New Zealand Defence Force, James VunKannon, and Elliott Wrenn and the U.S. Holocaust Memorial Museum.

A writer benefits from the support of his publisher and I have certainly had that from St. Martin's Press. I am especially grateful to Marc Resnick, Sally Richardson, Rebecca Lang, Danielle Prielipp, Laura Clark, Andy Martin, Lily Cronig, and others who have helped this book stick the landing. More thanks go to Scott Gould, RLR Associates, and Nat Sobel and the team at Sobel-Weber Associates. Special thanks to Lisa Cowley for her above and beyond attention to detail.

It has been "once more unto the breach, dear friends, once more." Though not as dashing as King Henry, I am equally grateful for the support and encouragement of friends and family.

BIBLIOGRAPHY

I would like to highlight four of the books listed below for their especially important contributions to this story. *Lightning Down* could not have been written without access to *A Fighter Pilot in Buchenwald*, and I am grateful to Gerald Baron for the creation of that memoir with Joe Moser. Also of great benefit were the books researched and written by Colin Burgess and by Thomas Childers. And the astonishing work by Eugen Kogon is indispensable to anyone who begins to feel complacent about the presence of fascism and evil in the world.

BOOKS

Abzug, Robert. *Inside the Vicious Heart: Americans and the Liberation of the Nazi Concentration Camps*. New York: Oxford University Press, 1985.

Beck, L. C. *Fighter Pilot*. Los Angeles: Wetzel Publishing, 1946.

Burgess, Colin. *Destination: Buchenwald*. Kenthurst, Australia: Kangaroo Press, 1995.

Burney, Christopher. *The Dungeon Democracy.* New York: Duell, Sloan and Pearce, 1946.

Caidin, Martin. *Fork-Tailed Devil: The P-38.* New York: iBooks, 2001.

Carroll, Tim. *The Great Escape from Stalag Luft III.* New York: Pocket Books, 2004.

Childers, Thomas. *In the Shadows of War: An American Pilot's Odyssey Through Occupied France and the Camps of Nazi Germany.* New York: Henry Holt, 2002.

Collins, Larry, and Dominique Lapierre. *Is Paris Burning?* New York: Grand Central Publishing, 1991.

Crane, Conrad C. *American Airpower Strategy in World War II: Bombs, Cities, Civilians, and Oil.* Lawrence: University Press of Kansas, 2016.

Christy, Joe, and Jeff Ethell. *P-38 Lightning at War.* New York: Charles Scribner's and Sons, 1992.

Grehan, John, and Martin Mace. *Unearthing Churchill's Secret Army.* South Yorkshire, England: Pen and Sword Military, 2012.

Hackett, David A., ed. *The Buchenwald Report.* Boulder, CO: Westview Press, 1995.

Hammel, Eric. *Air War Europa: Chronology, 1942–1945.* Pacifica, CA: Pacifica Press, 1994.

Halmos Jr., Eugene E. *The Wrong Side of the Fence: A United States Army Air Corps POW in World War II.* Shippensburg, PA: White Mane, 1996.

Jackson, Sophie. *Churchill's White Rabbit: The True Story of a Real-Life James Bond.* Gloucestershire, England: History Press, 2012.

Julitte, Pierre. *Block 26: Sabotage at Buchenwald.* New York: Doubleday, 1971.

Kinnis, Art, and Stanley Booker. *168 Jump Into Hell: A True Story of Betrayed Allied Airmen.* Self-published, Victoria, Canada, 1999.

Kogon, Eugen. *The Theory and Practice of Hell: The German Concentration Camps and the System Behind Them.* New York: Farrar, Strauss and Giroux, 1950.

Maher, William P. *Fated to Survive: Memoirs of a B-17 Flying Fortress Pilot/ Prisoner of War.* Spartanburg, SC: Honoribus Press, 1992.

Marshall, Bruce. *The White Rabbit.* London: Evans Brothers, 1952.

Makos, Adam, with Larry Alexander. *A Higher Call*. New York: Berkley Caliber, 2013.

Moser, Joe, and Gerald R. Baron. *A Fighter Pilot in Buchenwald*. Bellingham, WA: All Clear Publishing, 2009.

Pederson, Hilary, and Associated Writers. *"I Would Not Step Back . . .": Squadron Leader Phil Lamason*. Merthyr Tydfil, Wales: Mention the War, 2018.

Poller, Walter. *Butchers of Buchenwald*. London: Souvenir Press, 1961.

Seaman, Mark. *Bravest of the Brave: The True Story of Wing Commander "Tommy" Yeo-Thomas—SOE Secret Agent*. London: Michael O'Mara Books, 1997.

Speight, James G. *Fork-Tail Devil*. Bloomington, IN: Author House, 2015.

Stanaway, John, and Bob Rocker. *The Eightballers: Eyes of the Fifth Air Force*. Atglen, PA: Schiffer Military History, 1999.

Swindt, Karl. *429th Fighter Squadron: The Retail Gang*. Sacramento: Heritage Publications, 1978.

Weinstock, Eugene. *Beyond the Last Path: A Buchenwald Survivor's Story*. New York: Boni and Gaer, 1947.

INDEX

A-20 planes (U.S.), 38, 56
African Front, 17, 22–24, 36
Aichach prison, Germany,
    129
Air Medal, 46, 60, 66
air-to-air refueling, 25
Air War Europa (Hammel), 55
Albrecht, Betty, 95
Allen, Roy, 103, 188, 197
*American Airpower Strategy in World
    War II* (Crain), 143
Appell ("roll call"), 145, 149, 159–60, 169,
    184, 193, 196, 200–201, 216, 236,
    241, 263
Army Air Corps, U.S., 11, 101n.
    See also 429th Fighter Squadron,
    aka "Retail Gang"
    basic training in, 13, 14–21, 29–30
    humanitarian truces by, 240
    Moser's enlistment in, 12–13
    Operation Chattanooga Choo-Choo
    by, 46
    salaries, 41n
Auschwitz concentration camp, Poland,
    124, 135, 281
    death toll at, 121
    liberation of, 122

B-17 Flying Fortress planes (U.S.), 31,
    32, 38, 41–46, 65, 263
    Buchenwald factory bombing by,
    161–64, 167–68
B-26 bombers (U.S.), 38–39, 56
Baker Street Irregulars, 176
Balachowsky, Alfred, 191–92, 192n,
    197–98
Banks, Bill, 50, 60–61, 64–68
Bar, Heinz, 36
Baron, Gerald, 293
Bastable, Harry, 115
Battle of Berlin, 274
Battle of Britain, 22, 142, 176, 208, 212,
    225
Battle of the Bulge, 236, 265
Beck, Levitt Clinton, 18, 39, 47, 54, 56,
    174–75, 175n, 218n
Beer Hall Putsch, Germany, 212
Bellingham Bells (baseball team), 282
Benoist, Robert, 181–82, 182n
Bergen-Belsen concentration camp,
    Germany, 124, 281
    liberation of, 122
Berger, Otto, 267
Birmingham Belle (C-47), 55
"Bitch of Buchenwald," 128

Block 46, Buchenwald, 131
Block 50, Buchenwald, 258
Block 51, Buchenwald, 146–47
Block 58, Buchenwald, 186–87, 192–94
Booker, Stanley, 285
Boulle, Pierre, 153
Bradley, Omar, 62, 73
Braun, Eva, 274
Breitscheid, Rudi, 164, 166
Brereton, Lewis H., 24
The Bridge on the River Kwai (Boulle),
    153
brothels, concentration camp, 145–46
Bryson, Robert H., 5
Buchenwald concentration camp,
    Germany. *See also* concentration
    camps; POWs/prisoners
    airmen/Moser as POWs at, 117–18,
        136–219, 218n, 280–91, 293–94
    airmen's execution threat at,
        200–201, 205–18, 286–87
    bombing of factories at, 161–64,
        167–68, 263
    brothel at, 145–46
    characteristics of, 117, 121–22, 125,
        136–48, 259
    children prisoners at, 186–87, 192–94
    commandants of, 125–35
    death toll at, 121, 121n, 135
    Edward Murrow's broadcast from,
        259–60
    executions/murders at, 124, 126–28,
        133–34, 145, 147–48, 180–82,
        193–94, 196–201, 205–18, 257–60,
        286–87
    Goethe Oak at, 125, 145, 166
    International Camp Committee at,
        191–92
    kapos at, 150–52, 198–99, 199n
    KLB Club at, 190, 285–86, 290–91
    liberation of, 122, 256–60, 269
    living conditions at, 118, 121–22,
        125–58, 170–71, 184–96, 216, 256
    Luftwaffe's visit to, 207–13
    meals at, 150, 153, 153n
    medical experimentation on
        prisoners of, 127, 131, 146–47,
        197
    origins of, 122–24, 125
    prisoner hierarchy at, 150–52
    processing of prisoners at, 136–42
    SOE agents imprisoned at, 175–82,
        197–99, 207

The Buchenwald Report, 123–25, 127,
    151–52, 256
"The Buchenwald Song/Hymn," 119,
    119n
Buckham, Robert, 242
Burgess, Colin, 96, 107, 118, 161, 171,
    195, 200, 258, 285
Burney, Christopher, 179–80, 180n, 191,
    199, 258
    airmen execution plans and, 200, 209,
        209n
Bushell, Roger, 224–29

C-47 "gooney bird" planes (U.S.), 55–57,
    276
Caidin, Martin, 45
Camp Lucky Strike, Le Havre, France,
    277
Candide (Voltaire), 284
Carter-Edwards, Ed, 196
Cerveny, Don, 27
Chapman, Ken, 154, 171–73
Childers, Thomas, 103, 138, 170, 188,
    193, 287
Choltitz, Dietrich von, 98–99
Christy, Joe, 31–32
Churchill, Winston, 142, 176–77,
    265
Circuit newspaper, 223
Combat Network, French Resistance,
    95
Comet Line (escape route), 172, 175
Communist Party/communism, 166,
    272
concentration camps. *See also specific*
    camps
    Auschwitz, 121–22, 124, 135, 281
    Bergen-Belsen, 122, 124, 281
    brothels at, 145–46
    Buchenwald, 117–219, 153n, 199n,
        218n, 256–60, 263, 269, 280–91,
        293–94
    categories of, 124
    Dachau, 124, 126, 130
    death totals, 121, 121n, 124–25, 124n,
        135
    kapos at, 150–52
    liberation of, 122, 256–60
    Majdanek, 122, 128
    medical experiments on prisoners of,
        127, 131, 146–47, 197
    Nordhausen-Dora, 122
    Ohrdruf, 122

origins of, 122–24
prisoner hierarchy at, 150–52
Ravensbrück, 124, 145
Riga, 124
Sachsenhausen, 132
Treblinka, 121, 281
Crain, Conrad C., 143

Dachau concentration camp, Germany, 124, 126, 130
Death's Head unit, SS, 132
"Death Train," 130
de Gaulle, Charles, 67
Desitter, Prosper, 175, 192
Desoubrie, Jacques, 171–75
Destination: Buchenwald (Burgess), 161
Deutsche Ausrüstungswerke factory, Weimar, Germany, 156–58
  bombing of, 161–64, 167–68
Dietzsch, Arthur, 198–99, 199n
Ding-Schuler, Erwin, 131–32, 197–99, 199n
Distinguished Flying Cross, 25, 53, 154, 288
Dodkin, Kenneth, 178–80
Dönitz, Karl, 274
Doolittle, James, 34
Dorsey, Michael, 293–94
Dulag Luft POW camp, Germany, 225

Edwards, Laurence Hugh, 60
Eicke, Theodor, 132
Eighth Air Force, 34, 55, 159
Eighty-Sixth Infantry Division, 266
Einsatzgruppen forces, 226
Eisenhower, Dwight, 54
Ethell, Jeff, 31–32
Eustache, Henri, 82–84, 89–91, 290–92
Excelsior (freighter), 26–27
Experimental Station Block 46, Buchenwald, 131

Faber, Armin, 36
famine, 239–40
Ferndale Lions Club, 280
Ferndale, Washington, 7–13, 105, 221, 280–83, 288–89, 293
Fighter Pilot (Beck), 18, 174–75
A Fighter Pilot in Buchenwald (Moser/Baron), 293
Final Solution, 226
flak (anti-aircraft fire), types of, 51
Fleck, Egon, 258

Florstedt, Hermann, 127
Focke-Wulf Fw 190 planes (German), 36, 39–40, 44–45, 58, 64
Fork-Tail Devil (Speight), 40
Fork-Tailed Devil (Caidin), 45
474th Fighter Group, Ninth Air Force, 15
438th Troop Carrier Group, 55
429th Fighter Squadron, aka "Retail Gang." *See also* Moser, Joseph Frank; Ninth Air Force
  basic training of, 16–21
  Electronic Combat Squadron of, 25
  escort missions by, 32–35, 38–46, 49, 54–55, 58, 72
  Moser's assignment to, 15–16
  offensive missions by, 34, 36–37, 40, 49–53, 58–79
IV Fighter Command, 15
Fourteenth Armored Division, 266
Fourth Infantry Division, 99
France, 294
  French Resistance forces in, 59–60, 80–84, 89–91, 94–97, 99–118, 99n, 101n, 143–44, 171–75, 198–99, 290–92
  Vichy government in, 143
  warfront in, 23, 25, 36, 38–39, 45, 49–116, 290–92
Franco, Francisco, 208
Frederick III, Emperor of Germany, 164
Free France forces, 99, 206
Freeman, Elmer, 293
French Legion of Honor, 294
French Resistance, 99, 99n
  Allied airmen rescues by, 59–60, 80–84, 89–91, 290–92
  Combat Network in, 95
  as German prisoners, 60, 94–97, 100–118, 101n, 143–44, 198–99
  Nazi collaborators within, 171–75
  women of, 95–97, 116–17
Fresnes prison, Paris, 144, 154, 175, 179–80, 206
  executions at, 101–2
  Moser's stay at, 1, 93–102

Gable, Clark, 154
Gannon, Kim, 203
General Military Government Court for the Trial of War Criminals, Dachau, 128–29

Geneva Convention, 105, 118, 139, 155, 224, 233
  POW vs. "terrorist" designations and, 112, 142–44, 218
Gestapo (national police), 131, 178–79
  founding/function of, 123, 212
  POW treatment by, 85–97, 98–102, 144, 175
Gestapo Laws of 1936 (Germany), 123
Giller, Edward, 45
Glass, Burl, Jr., 21, 36, 38–39, 56, 71–73, 93
  background of, 16
  post-war life of, 288
Goebbels, Joseph, 274, 274n
Goode, Paul S., 267
Goodrich, Glenn, 64–65, 65n
Göring, Hermann, 208, 212n
  capture/death of, 274–75
  Gestapo's founding by, 123, 212
  Hitler's relationship with, 212–13
  POW treatment and, 144, 206, 211–13, 215, 219, 228
Grand Prix, 181
Grehan, John, 176–77
Grunherz-Geschwader unit, Luftwaffe, 208
Guinness, Alec, 153
Gustloff Armament Works, Weimar, Germany, 156–58
  bombing of, 161–64, 167–68

Hague Convention, 130
Hamburg Uprising, 1923, 166
Hammel, Eric, 55
Harker, Ronald, 33
Hartmann, Erich, 35
Hastin, Jim, 105, 148, 171, 290–91
Hayes, Graham, 94
Heinkel 111 bombers (Germany), 70
Hemmens, Philip D., (POW), 112, 218n
The Herald (Bellingham), 294
Hessel, Franz, 198–99
Hessel, Helen, 198–99
Hessel, Stéphane, 198–99, 199n
Heuerman, Paul, 61
Heydrich, Reinhard, 226
Hibbard, Hall, 31
High, Dave, 113–14
A Higher Call (Makos), 206
Himmler, Heinrich, 145, 257, 274
  as Gestapo head, 123, 212

POWs and, 177, 191, 200, 215, 219, 228
Hindenburg, Paul von, 166
Hitler, Adolf, 22–23, 41, 164, 166, 208, 226, 236, 262, 264, 272. See also Nazi Germany
  concentration camp origins by, 124
  Göring's relationship with, 212–13
  Paris's liberation and, 98–99
  POW execution orders and, 177, 181, 215, 228–29
  suicide of, 274–75
Hodges, Courtney, 73
Holcomb, "Pappy," 69
Holland Furnace Company, Bellingham, Washington, 282
Hongerwinter ("hunger winter"), 239
Hoven, Waldemar, 127

"I'll Be Home for Christmas," 203
Imhof, Frank, 8–9, 12, 280, 282
Immerzeel, Remco, 291–92
International Camp Committee (Buchenwald), 191–92
In the Shadows of War (Childers), 103
Italy, defeat of, 23

Japan, 30, 275
  balloon offensive by, 275n
  Pearl Harbor attack by, 12, 16, 21, 24, 32
Jews, 146
  concentration camp deaths of, 121, 121n, 124–25, 132, 226, 257–58
  the Final Solution ideology and, 226
  Kristallnacht attacks against, 132, 226
Johnson, Clarence, 31
Jones, Mrs. J. Wilson, 21

kapos (prisoner administrators), 150–52
Karlstad, C. H., 266–68, 267n
Kartveli, Alexander, 33
Kent, Walter, 203
Kinnis, Art, 105, 190, 285, 291
KLB Club (Konzentrationlager Buchenwald)
  formation of, 190
  post-war gatherings of, 285–86, 290–91
Knochenmühlen ("bone mills"), 124
Knox, George, 93
Koch, Karl-Otto, 125–29, 134

Koch, Margaret Ilse Kohler ("Bitch of
    Buchenwald"), 126–29, 129n, 134
Kogon, Eugen, 130–33, 149, 197–99
Kohler, Uwe, 129
Konzentrationlager Buchenwald.
    See KLB Club
Kriegie newspaper, 223
Kristallnacht, 132, 226

Lamason, Joan, 286–88
Lamason, Phillip
    airmen execution plans and, 200–201,
        209–11, 209n, 214, 216–18
    background of, 154
    death of, 287–88
    German capture of, 171–73
    post-war life of, 286–87
    as POW leader, 103, 103n, 106, 112,
        139, 153–58, 160, 167–68, 175,
        179–80, 182, 186, 190–92, 200–201,
        209–11, 209n, 214, 216–18, 231,
        237, 244, 247
Landing Craft, Infantry (LCIs), 66
Larson, Merle, 39n, 50–53, 60–62, 66,
    68, 93
    background of, 16–17
    German capture of, 173–74
    post-war life of, 288
    as POW, 100–103, 155, 210
Lean, David, 153
Lefaucheux, Mme., 106, 110–11
Lefaucheux, Pierre, 106, 106n, 111
Lend-Lease Bill, 1941 (U.S.), 32
Lenin, Vladimir, 166
Leopoldi, Hermann, 119, 119n
Levey, Roland, 68
Lewis, Bill, 290
Link Trainer, 14–15
Lockheed, 11, 16, 31–32. See also P-38
    Lightning planes
Lohner-Beda, Fritz, 119, 119n
Los Angeles Times, 20
Lost Airmen of Buchenwald
    (documentary), 287, 293–94
Luby, Lieutenant, 268
The Lucky Ones (documentary), 287
Luftwaffe (German air force)
    Bf 109 planes of, 35–36, 66
    civilians bombed by, 142
    Focke-Wulf Fw 190 planes of, 36,
        39–40, 44–45, 58, 64
    JG 54 unit of, 208
    losses by, 212–13

POW administration by, 101, 205–19,
    220–68
The Lynden Tribune, 290

Mace, Martin, 176–77
Mafalda of Savoy, Princess, 164–65,
    165n
Majdanek concentration camp, Poland,
    122, 128
Makos, Adam, 206
Marshall, Bruce, 180
Merkle, Milton, 40
Messerschmitt Bf 109 planes (German),
    35–36, 66
Milner, Leon, 54
Moosburg, Germany, 274–76
    Stalag VII-A at, 254, 265–73, 269n,
        272–73, 293
Moser, Frank, 9, 12, 280, 281
Moser, Jean Douglas, 282, 289
Moser, Joseph Frank
    Army Air Corps enlistment by, 12–13
    assignment to 429th Fighter
        Squadron by, 15–21, 25, 32–46,
        49–53, 58–79
    assignment to Neuilly-la-Forêt air
        base by, 66–73, 93
    assignment to Warmwell air base by,
        27–46, 49–66
    athletic pursuits of, 10–11, 82
    background of, 7–8
    basic training of, 13, 14–21, 29–30
    birth of, 7, 8
    book by, 293
    childhood of, 9–13
    commendations of, 46, 53, 66, 294
    death of, 294
    education of, 10–11
    German capture of, 80–93
    homecoming of, 276–81
    plane crash/bailout by, 74–80
    post-war life of, 281–83, 288–94
    as POW at Buchenwald
        concentration camp, 117–18,
        136–219, 280–83, 289, 293–94
    as POW at Fresnes prison, 93–102
    as POW at Stalag Luft III, 220–44,
        252
    as POW at Stalag VII-A, 265–73, 293
    as POW at Stalag XIII-D, 254, 255–56,
        261–63
    POW transports of, 1–4, 102–17, 218,
        220–22, 243–55, 263–65, 289–90

Moser, Joseph Frank (*cont'd*)
    promotions of, 53, 68
    PTSD of, 288–93
    return to Buchenwald, 2010, by,
        293–94
Moser, Josephine, 9
Moser, Joseph Melchior, 7–10, 277
Moser, Louise, 9, 280, 282
Moser, Mary Imhof, 8–13, 93
    son's POW status and, 235n, 278–80
Moser, Rosalee, 9, 280
Murrow, Edward R., 259–60
Mussolini, Benito, 23

NAAFI (Navy, Army, and Air Force
    Institutes), 27, 27n
Nazi Germany. *See also* concentration
    camps; Hitler, Adolf;
    POWs/prisoners; World War II;
    specific defense forces
    Beer Hall Putsch in, 212
    Einsatzgruppen forces of, 226
    Gestapo forces of, 85–102, 123, 131,
        144, 175, 178–79, 212
    Hitler's death and, 274
    Kristallnacht attacks by, 132, 226
    Luftwaffe forces of, 35–36, 39–40,
        44–45, 58, 64, 66, 101, 142,
        205–68
    manufacturing pipeline of, 23–24, 35,
        156–58, 159–63, 167–68, 209
    Poland's invasion by, 22
    political suppression in, 122–24,
        164–66
    POW *vs.* "terrorist" designations by,
        112, 142–44, 218
    SS forces of, 102–219
    surrender of, 275
    war loss contingency plans by,
        236–44, 256–58, 262
Netherlands, 239–40
Neuilly-la-Forêt air base, France,
    66–73, 93
Newton, Alfred, 199
Newton, Henry, 199
New Zealand
    Phillip Lamason of, 103, 103n, 106,
        112, 139, 153–58, 160, 167–68,
        171–73, 175, 179–80, 182, 186,
        190–92, 200–201, 209–11, 209n,
        214, 216–18, 231, 237, 244, 247,
        286–88
    POW compensation fund in, 287

Royal Air Force of, 60, 101n, 221,
    269, 287
Ninth Air Force, 55
    429 Fighter Squadron of, 15–21, 25,
        32–46, 49–53, 58–79
    origins/evolution of, 24–25
    strategies of, 34, 45–46, 49–50
Nordhausen-Dora concentration camp,
    Germany, 122
Normandy invasion, France
    execution of, 55–57, 213
    planning of, 50, 53–54
Nuremberg, Germany
    Stalag XIII-D at, 254–56, 255n, 261–65
    war criminal trials at, 274
Nute, Major, 54

Oflag VI-B POW camp, Germany, 225
Oflag X-C POW camp, Germany, 225
Ogden, Merle, 20–21
Ohrdruf concentration camp, Germany,
    122
101st Airborne Division, 55
Operation Anthropoid (Czech), 226
Operation Chattanooga Choo-Choo
    (Allies), 46
Operation Chowhound (U.K.), 240
Operation Faust (Canada), 240
Operation Manna (U.S.), 240
Orsini, Madame, 172–75

P-38 Lightning at War (Christy/Ethell),
    31
P-38 Lightning planes (U.S.), 5, 7, 11–12,
    25, 81, 89, 105, 173, 276, 294
    bailing out of, 45, 77–80, 79n
    characteristics of, 30–31, 31n
    enemy nicknames for, 30
    escort missions by, 32–35, 38–46, 49,
        54–55, 58, 72
    offensive missions by, 34, 36–37, 40,
        49–53, 58–79
    training on, 13, 15–21, 29–30
P-47 Thunderbolt planes (U.S.), 33–35,
    38, 46
P-51 Mustang planes (U.S.), 32–35, 38,
    46, 105
Paris, France
    Fresnes prison in, 1, 93–102, 144, 154,
        175, 179–80, 206
    liberation of, 98–104, 174
    Nazi collaborators in, 171–75
Pearl Harbor attack, 12, 16, 21, 24, 32

Peleuvé, Harry, 198–99
Perry, Ray, 101
Pertschuk, Maurice, 179
Philipp of Hesse, Prince, 164–65, 165n
Pister, Hermann, 128–30, 164, 190–91,
    200, 206, 210, 214–15, 257
Poland, invasion of, 22
Portugal, 24
POWs/prisoners, 60, 83–84
    concealment efforts regarding, 281,
        284
    disbelief regarding, 232, 256, 260,
        280–82, 289–91, 294
    documentaries on, 287, 293–94
    executions/murders of, 90–91,
        114–15, 124, 126–28, 133–34, 145,
        147–48, 180–82, 193–94, 196–201,
        205–18, 257–60, 286–87
    Geneva Convention protections on,
        105, 112, 118, 139, 142–44, 155,
        218, 224, 233
    interrogation of, 85–86, 88, 92–93,
        96–97
    liberation of, 122, 256–73, 269n
    living conditions of, 118, 121–22,
        125–58, 170–71, 184–96, 216,
        222–24, 230–37, 241, 255–56,
        262–63, 265–66, 272–73
    Nazi collaborators and, 171–75
    Red Cross packages/support for, 3,
        100, 102, 105, 117, 192, 218, 221,
        223–24, 232–36, 263, 266, 272–73
    torture of, 95–97, 100, 104–16,
        126–28, 131, 133–34, 139–40,
        145–48, 147n, 178, 178n, 196
    transport of, 1–4, 102–17, 218,
        220–22, 243–55, 263–65, 289–90
    uniform designations of, 146
Prevost, Geneviève, 172, 172n
Prevost, George, 171–72, 172n
Pyle, Ernie, 65

Quesada, Elwood "Pete," 25, 25n, 43,
    49, 62, 65

RAF. See Royal Air Force
Ravensbrück concentration camp,
    Germany, 124, 145
Red Cross, 18, 26, 267
    POW packages/support from, 3,
        100, 102, 105, 117, 192, 218, 221,
        223–24, 232–36, 263, 266, 272–73
Renaud, Paul, 292, 292n

Richthofen, Manfred Von, 212
Riga concentration camp, Latvia, 124
Robert, Jan, 191–92, 192n
Rommel, Erwin, 24
Roosevelt, Franklin D., 31n, 264, 284
Royal Air Force (RAF) (U.K.), 17, 28, 29,
    56, 63, 101n, 102, 105, 114, 178,
    191, 225, 267, 285
    civilians bombed by, 142
    humanitarian truces by, 240
Royal Canadian Air Force, 3, 101n, 105,
    113, 169, 233, 242, 269, 285
    humanitarian truces by, 240

Sachsenhausen concentration camp,
    Germany, 132
Scharf, Bernard, 210–11
Schneider, Paul, 131
Schönere Zukunft journal, 131
Second French Armored Division, 99
Seversky, Alexander de, 33
Shot from the Sky (documentary),
    287
Small Scale Raiding Force, 94
SOE. See Special Operations Executive
Sommer, Walter Gerhard Martin,
    132–35
Southgate, Maurice, 199
Soviet Union
    concentration camp liberation by,
        122
    Eastern Front fighting by, 23–24,
        35–36, 35n, 205, 213, 236, 238,
        242–43, 243n, 245–46, 246n, 256,
        261, 265, 272, 274
    POWs/captives from, 146, 191, 197,
        205–6, 209–10, 255, 265
Spaak, Suzanne, 95
Spanish Civil War, 35, 137, 208
Special Operations Executive (SOE),
    226
    agents at Buchenwald, 175–82,
        197–99, 207
    executions of, 180–81, 197–99
    founding of, 176
Speight, James G., 40, 45
Spierenburg, Splinter, 191
Spitfire planes (U.K.), 33, 36
SS (Schutzstaffel) (Nazi army), 102–16
    concentration camp management by,
        117–219
    Death's Head unit of, 132
    founding of, 123

Stalag Luft III POW camp, Poland
  airmen/Moser at, 220–44, 252
  characteristics of, 222–24
  escape attempts at, 224–29
  evacuation of, 238–55, 254n
  living conditions at, 222–24, 230–37,
    241
Stalag Luft I POW camp, Germany, 225
Stalag VII-A, Moosburg, Germany, 254
  airmen/Moser at, 265–73, 293
  liberation of, 266–73, 269n
  living conditions at, 265–66, 272–73
Stalag XIII-D POW camp, Nuremberg,
    Germany
  airmen/Moser at, 254, 255–56,
    261–63
  evacuation of, 263–65
  living conditions at, 255–56, 262–63
  SS imprisonment at, 255n
Stalin, Josef, 166, 265, 272
Stars and Stripes, 5, 64
Sweden, 24
Swindt, Karl, 18, 26

Tenenbaum, Edward, 258
Terrorfliegers designation, 112, 142–44,
    218
Thacker, Buford, 40, 59
Thälmann, Ernst, 165–66
Thomas, Earl, 43
Trautloft, Johannes "Hannes," 207–11,
    213, 214–15, 261, 285–86
Treblinka concentration camp, Poland,
    121, 281
Truman, Harry, 265
Turkey, 24

United Kingdom (U.K.), 23
  Battle of Britain in, 22, 142, 176, 208,
    212, 225
  RAF of, 17, 28, 29, 56, 63, 101n, 102,
    105, 114, 142, 178, 191, 225, 240,
    267, 285
  SOE agents of, 175–82, 197–99, 207,
    226
United States (U.S.). See also Army Air
    Corps, U.S.
  Pearl Harbor's bombing in, 12, 16,
    21, 24, 32
  POW concealment by, 281, 284
  POW repatriation by, 271–78

Roosevelt's death in, 284
  war production in, 23, 31–32, 31n
United States Air Forces Central
    Command, 214

Vermeulen, François, 81–82, 291
Vermeulen, Léon, 82–84, 89–91, 290–92
Vichy government, France, 143
Victor Emmanuel III of Italy, King, 164
Voltaire, 284
von Lindeiner-Wildau, Friedrich
    Wilhelm, 223–24

Warmwell air base, U.K., 27–46, 49–66
Wasem, Clinton, 40, 62, 72–73
Washington Remembers series, 294
Weinstock, Eugene, 122, 140, 146, 184,
    257
Willets, Captain, 267
World War I (WW I), 106, 125, 166,
    177, 212
World War II (WW II). See also
    concentration camps; POWs/
    prisoners; specific countries
  African Front of, 17, 22–24, 36
  Allied strategies in, 34, 45–46, 49–50,
    55–56, 65–66, 73–74
  Battle of Berlin in, 274
  Battle of Britain in, 22, 142, 176, 208,
    212, 225
  Battle of the Bulge in, 236, 265
  Eastern Front of, 23–24, 35–36,
    35n, 205, 213, 236, 242–43, 243n,
    245–46, 246n, 256, 272, 274
  famine during, 239–40
  French Front of, 23, 25, 36, 38–39, 45,
    49–116
  Germany's surrender in, 275
  humanitarian truces in, 240
  neutral countries in, 23–24
  Normandy invasion in, 50, 53–57,
    213
  Pearl Harbor attack in, 12, 16, 21,
    24, 32
  Poland's invasion in, 22

Yeo-Thomas, Forest Frederick Edward
    "Tommy," 177–79n, 177–80, 191,
    197–200, 258

Zafouk, Jaroslav, 226

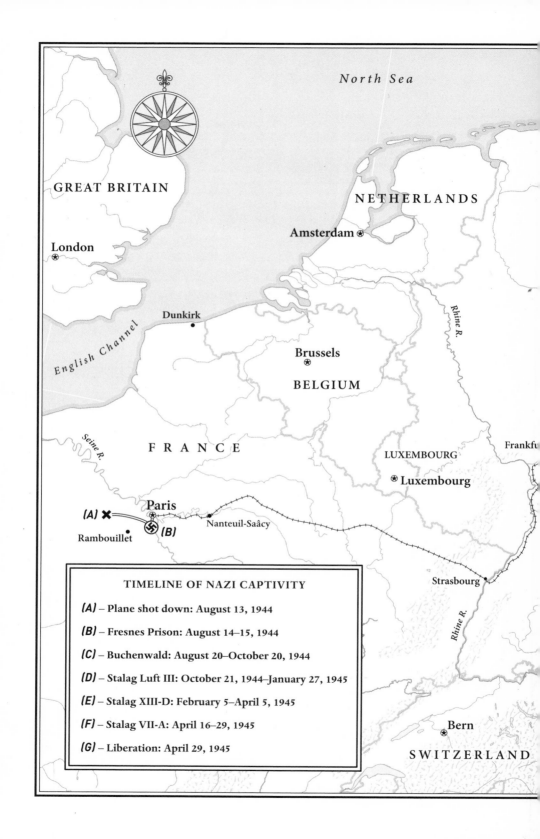

North Sea

GREAT BRITAIN

NETHERLANDS

Amsterdam ✣

London ✣

Dunkirk •

English Channel

Rhine R.

Brussels ✣

BELGIUM

Seine R.

FRANCE

LUXEMBOURG

Frankfu

✣ Luxembourg

(A) ✖ Paris ✣
Rambouillet • ☰ (B)
Nanteuil-Saâcy •

Strasbourg •

Rhine R.

TIMELINE OF NAZI CAPTIVITY

(A) – Plane shot down: August 13, 1944

(B) – Fresnes Prison: August 14–15, 1944

(C) – Buchenwald: August 20–October 20, 1944

(D) – Stalag Luft III: October 21, 1944–January 27, 1945

(E) – Stalag XIII-D: February 5–April 5, 1945

(F) – Stalag VII-A: April 16–29, 1945

(G) – Liberation: April 29, 1945

✣ Bern

SWITZERLAND